CAMPBELLISM EXAMINED

AND

RE-EXAMINED.

BY

REV. JEREMIAH B. JETER, D.D.

OF RICHMOND, VIRGINIA.

NEW YORK:

SHELDON AND COMPANY.

RICHMOND: T. J. STARKE.

1860.

TO THE

ESTEEMED BRETHREN,

AT WHOSE REQUEST, THIS WORK HAS BEEN PREPARED,

IT IS RESPECTFULLY INSCRIBED BY

THE AUTHOR,

WITH HIS EARNEST PRAYER TO THE

"FATHER OF LIGHTS,"

THAT IT MAY PROMOTE THE CAUSE OF TRUTH AND PIETY.

CONTENTS.

"REV DR. J. B. JETER,

DEAR SIR:—

THE undersigned ministers and members of Baptist churches, have been deeply impressed with the importance to our churches of a succinct and popular treatise upon the rise, progress, character, and influence of the sect of Christians called Disciples, or Campbellites. The knowledge which your position has given you of this subject, and the clearness of thought, justness of view, candor of spirit, which have marked the passage on this subject contained in your memoir of the late Rev. Andrew Broaddus, have induced us respectfully to request that you will at your earliest convenience prepare a work of the character above described.

The undersigned believe that by complying with this request, you will do an essential service to the cause of truth, and advance the glory of our Holy Redeemer.

ELISHA TUCKER,*	EDWARD LATHROP,
M. B. ANDERSON,	GEO. W. SAMSON,
HEMAN LINCOLN,	J. M. LINNARD,
C. W. HOUGHTON,	A. D. GILLETTE,
S. S. CUTTING,	J. C. STOCKBRIDGE,
W. B. JACOBS,	S. F. SMITH."

* Since the above request was signed, in May, 1852, Doctor Tucker, of Chicago, Illinois, has been called from his labors to his reward. I know, loved, and venerated him. He was a noble specimen of a Christian minis-

ter. With enlarged views, ripe experience, sound judgment, and a conservative spirit, he was eminently fitted to be, as he was, a leader in "the sacramental host of God's elect." By his expansive and generous sympathies, he was allied to men of all parties, and all sections; but by his devotion to truth, he was identified with the advocates of evangelic Christianity. His life was a beautiful commentary on the doctrine which he embraced, and his death a happy termination of a life of toil and usefulness. I need not say more of this excellent servant of Christ, and less in justice to my feelings, I could not say.

J. B J.

INTRODUCTION

THE term *Campbellism* is used in this treatise, not as a term of reproach, but of distinction. No other word denotes the system which it is proposed to examine. Mr. Alexander Campbell, of Bethany, Virginia, and the party embracing his views, have assumed several appellations. They have styled themselves "*Reformers*," "*Christians*," and "*Disciples*." Without discussing their exclusive claim to these titles, it is clear that from neither of them can any term be derived which will fairly distinguish their system of doctrine. The word *Reformation* has been appropriated, by common consent, to denote that great moral revolution, of which Luther and Calvin were the prime agents. The term *Christianity* can never be wrested from its universally established import, to express the views of any sect or party, however good, wise or great. From the word *Disciple,* indefinite as an appellative, no term can be derived to signify the views of those who adopt the name. Mr. Campbell claims to have discovered the "*Ancient Gospel.*" Without at this time conceding or denying the equity of his claim, it may be observed that the inquiries now to be made have reference not to the *Ancient Gospel,* recorded in the writings of the evangelists and apostles, but to the speculations of Mr. Campbell, contained in his voluminous works, concerning this gospel, and which have been received as true by the friends of the "*Current Reformation.*" To call these speculations the *Ancient Gospel,* would be a manifest misnomer. I am then under the necessity of employing some indefinite term, a tedious circumlocution, or the word *Campbellism* to denote the system under discussion, and the last course seems preferable.

This system is with great propriety termed *Campbellism.* Systems of philosophy, science, and religion, have usually been designated after their discoverers, first promulgators, or most distinguished advocates. Mr. Campbell is the author, and most eminent proclaimer of the peculiar doctrines, which, within the last thirty years, have spread in the Southern and Western states, under the title of "*The Reformation.*" No other man has added an article to the system, subtracted one from it, or materially modified it. Many truths are taught by Mr. Campbell in common with other Christians; very few of the principles for which he pleads are strictly new; but having revived, modified, and placed in new combinations some antiquated sentiments, and added to them a few original speculations, he is fairly entitled to all the honor, and obnoxious to all the censure which his system merits.

It is not my purpose to write a *history* of Campbellism. I have neither the inclination, time, nor means to do it. Nor do I design to confine myself to a polemic discussion. Campbellism, like other things earthly, has passed through various and important changes. To arrive at just views of it, we must carefully notice its rise, progress, modifications, and influence, as well as its distinctive principles. It must be viewed from different standpoints, and under different phases, that its true character may be understood. My purpose is to furnish a faithful delineation of the system—its principles, spirit and influence—to censure the evil, and commend the good.

Various considerations have prevailed with me to undertake this work. The subject to be examined is important. It were vain to deny that Campbellism has exercised an extensive influence on the religious sentiment of the country. We are interested not less as philosophers than as Christians to inquire into the causes of this success. The proposed treatise is demanded by public curiosity. What is Campbellism? This question, asked by many, is not easily answered. Some perceive no distinction between it and the views generally entertained by the Baptists; and others consider it a dangerous system of error. A calm, discriminating and faithful examination of it, cannot fail to profit both those who embrace, and those who reject it. All these considerations would probably have failed to induce me to undertake the work, had not brethren, whose judgment is worthy of respect, and with whose request it is a pleasure to comply, urged me to engage in it.

Of my fitness for the task the reader will judge by the manner of its execution. I have enjoyed very fair opportunities of forming correct opinions of Mr. Campbell's system. I first saw him in the year 1825. Since that time I have been a careful observer of his course. I have watched the gradual development of his principles, and marked their influence on the churches. I have read most that has been published by him and his opponents on the various points in debate. I have conversed much with persons embracing and zealously supporting the *Reformation.*

It is my purpose to conduct this investigation in the spirit of candor and fairness, knowing that nothing can be gained to the cause of truth and righteousness by sophistry, misrepresentation and detraction. No sentence incompatible with the claims of justice, and christian courtesy shall intentionally escape my pen ; nor shall I withhold a frank and faithful expression of my opinions on all points which I deem important.

I do not hope to be able to meet the expectation, and satisfy the wishes of all my readers. Some will think me too lenient, and others too severe—some will think that I concede too much, and others too little. Truth generally lies between extremes. I am more anxious, I trust, to please God than men —to promote the cause of truth than to gain a victory. Writing for no sect or party, but for all who desire to know the truth, I ask nothing of my readers, except an unprejudiced consideration of the facts and arguments presented in the work. The interests of the writer and reader are identical ; and the same law which requires him to publish, requires them to receive, the truth.

CAMPBELLISM EXAMINED.

CAMPBELLISM IN ITS INCEPTION.

CIRCUMSTANCES, it has been frequently affirmed, make men. The remark is not true in an unqualified sense; but it cannot be questioned that circumstances exert a mighty influence in forming the tastes, opinions, and characters, and guiding the lives of most men. Mr. Campbell, much as he has boasted of his independence of thought and conduct, has not risen above this common law of humanity. He is, to a great extent, what his peculiar circumstances—his early training and associations, and his subsequent relations, avocations, and conflicts—have made him. He bears, most clearly, the impress of the mould in which he was cast. He was educated in the University of Glasgow, in Scotland. If he was not brought up among the Seceders—as he probably was—he was early connected with that most rigid of all the Presbyterian sects, adopted their views, and fully imbibed their spirit. "I have," said he, "tried the pharisaic plan, and the monastic. I was once so straight, that, like the Indian's tree, I leaned a little the other way. And however much I may be slandered now as seeking 'popularity,' or a popular course, I have to rejoice to my own satisfaction, as well as to others, I proved that truth, and not popularity was my object; for I was once so strict a Separatist that I would neither pray nor sing praises with any one who was not as perfect as I supposed myself." Chn. Bap., p. 238. Had Mr. C. not passed his early years in Scotland, his religious views and career would have differed widely from what they have been. Many of his speculations have been Scottish importations. To which of the Seceder sects he was attached, does not appear, but it is presumed from his early phariseeism, to the straitest. It would be strange, if his education in the school of bigotry and intolerance, had not given complexion to his spirit, character to his opinions, and direction to his labors, in after life.

In August, 1809, this young Seceder, with a certificate of church membership in his pocket, set sail from the city of Greenock, in Scotland, for the United States, and, after a narrow escape from shipwreck, landed safely in the city of New York, in the ensuing September. He brought with him the Reformation in embryo. Before he left the fatherland, his faith "in creeds and confessions of human device" was considerably shaken. Whether the iron rigor of his creed, by which he had been fettered, had any influence in unsettling his faith does not appear. From New York, he immediately repaired to Washington, Penn., and commenced his American career, with what he proclaimed as an important discovery, "that nothing not as old as the New Testament should be made an article of faith, a rule of practice, or a term of communion among Christians." This truth was the "pole-star" to guide him in all subsequent researches and labors. We cannot but congratulate him on his discovery, while we confess our surprise that he should have been so long in making it. It was *the* doctrine—the main pillar of the great reformation led on by Luther, Calvin, and other worthies, in the sixteenth century. It had never been called in question by any respectable Protestant sect, or even writer. The most zealous advocates of human creeds ascribed to them no authority, except what they derived from the Scriptures. They might, by a misinterpretation of the Scriptures, put unscriptural articles into their creeds, or they might pervert the Scriptures to make them harmonize with their inherited creeds ; but not a creed-monger could be found who maintained, or even dreamed, that any thing "not as old as the New Testament should be made an article of faith."

Guided by this "pole-star," Mr. C. soon began

to make progress in religious knowledge. His "pole-star" proved to be "the morning star of the reformation." In July, 1810, he publicly avowed his "convictions of the independency of the church of Christ, and the excellency and authority of the Scriptures." He now commenced a series of desultory, itinerating labor—"pronouncing," to use his own style, "orations on the primary topics of the Christian religion," in Western Pennsylvania, and the contiguous parts of Virginia and Ohio. In 1811, he married, and became a resident, and, as soon as the laws would permit, a citizen of Virginia. About this time, he was led to question the divine authority of infant sprinkling; and, after a long, serious, and prayerful examination of all the sources of information within his reach, to reject it, and to solicit immersion on a profession of faith. He was baptized by Elder Matthias Luse, in the presence of Elder Henry Spears, in June, 1812, and soon after was ordained one of the Elders of the church at Brush Run. He did not, at first, design to connect himself with the Baptist denomination, but forming a better acquaintance with some of the members of the Redstone Baptist Association, composed of churches partly in Pennsylvania, and partly in Virginia, he induced the church with which he was connected, to sue for admission into that body, and presenting a written declaration of their faith, they were received in the fall of 1813. From this period, until 1823, Mr. C. continued his labors as a Christian teacher, in North-Western Virginia, without any very important results. But his mind was far from being stationary. Light dawned on it apace. He was preparing, either with or without design, to become the advocate of what he deemed a great reformation, and the Corypheus of a large party. Chn. Bap., p. 92.

Mr. Campbell, having burst the bonds imposed on him by his early creed, pursued his religious investigations, without restraint, except such as was laid on him by natural temperament, early impressions, and mental capacity. He had now ceased to be a pharisee. He could sing and pray with his fellow-Christians. But mingling with them, he soon began to speculate on their manifold errors. His penetrating eye perceived, or he thought that it perceived, and he did not lack moral courage to proclaim, that "the present popular exhibition of the Christian religion is a compound of Judaism, heathen philosophy, and Christianity." Chn. Bap., p. 9. The phrase "popular exhibition of the Christian religion" is somewhat equivocal; and yet there can be no reasonable doubt as to the sense in which he uses it. It could be nothing to his purpose to affirm that the exhibitions of Christianity made by Romanists, German Rationalists, or the advocates of baptismal regeneration, are such a compound. Among these classes of religionists he was not laboring. He, doubtless, referred to the exhibition of Christianity usually made by the prevailing religious denominations of the country. These different Christian persuasions, mostly maintaining, along with some errors, almost inseparable from human imperfection, the vital, soul-saving truths of the Gospel, were in his estimation, exhibitors of a compound of "Judaism, heathen philosophy and Christianity."

That there may be no mistake on this subject, another quotation from the pen of Mr. C. will be furnished.

"If Christians were, and may be the happiest people that ever lived, it is because they live under the most gracious institution ever bestowed on men. The meaning of this institution has been buried under the rubbish of human traditions for hundreds of years. It was lost in the dark ages, and has never been, till recently, disinterred. Various efforts have been made, and considerable progress attended them; but since the Grand Apostacy was completed, till the present generation, the Gospel of Jesus Christ has not been laid open to mankind in its original plainness, simplicity and majesty. A veil in reading the New Institution has been on the hearts of Christians," &c. Chn. Sys., p. 180.

With the truth or falsehood of these opinions, we have, at present, no concern. It is, however, desirable to take an accurate observation of Mr. Campbell's position. The above language defines, quite unambiguously, his own conceptions of the ground which he occupied. The Christian institution—the Gospel of salvation—had been buried, under a mass of traditions, for ages. Various efforts had been made, at different times, by men of great reputation for learning, piety, zeal, and fidelity, to remove the superincumbent mass, with small success. Then the Reformer of Bethany arose, dug away the rubbish, and exposed, in the light of day, the long lost Gospel, in all its beauty, simplicity and majesty. These are, certainly, high pretensions. They may be just, and if so, we should know it, that we may render homage to our benefactor. We propose in the progress of this work, to make strict inquiries concerning the justice of these claims.

Mr. C. was now prepared to enter earnestly on the prosecution of his mission. Having analyzed the "popular exhibition of the Christian religion," and pointed out its primary elements, and having made considerable progress in disinterring the "ancient Gospel" from the deep grave in which for centuries it had lain, he was naturally desirous that the benefits of his discoveries and labors should not be confined to an obscure corner of Virginia. The candle was not lighted to be put under a bushel. The morning star of the new Reformation must shed its effulgence in a wider sphere. That he might have a channel for disseminating his newly formed opinions, Mr. C. commenced publishing a small monthly pamphlet, entitled the *Christian Baptist.* The first No. was issued from Buffalo, afterwards called Bethany, Brooke County, Va., July 4th, 1823. The day was aptly chosen for the commencement of the enterprise. Consecrated to the celebration of American Independence, it was thenceforth to be distinguished as the commencement of a struggle for the liberation of the churches from priestly domination. The publication of the Christian Baptist marks an era in the history of Campbellism. For seven years it was the repository of the lucubrations of Mr. C. and of his numerous correspondents, who rapidly sprang up through the country. It was edited with ability. As it will hereafter be necessary to examine many articles in this work, it is sufficient now merely to express the opinion that it contains some things worthy of commendation, more that are entitled to no particular notice, and a great mass of rubbish. Mr. C. has boasted much of the independent, generous, and fearless manner in which his periodicals have been conducted. He has professed to publish both sides of every controversy. It may be remarked, that policy frequently assumes the garb of liberality. He was a skillful and popular debater—handled a ready pen—was desirous to gain notoriety, and promote the circulation of his paper—and controversy was the pabulum on which he lived and thrived. It is easy to perceive that under such circumstances, sound policy as well as liberality, would court discussion. Liberality is envinced, not by an eagerness for disputation, but by a candid, fair, and considerate treatment of our opponent. Few theologians were qualified to enter the lists with a disputant so ready, adroit and sarcastic as he was, and most of that small number, feeling but little interest in his labors or speculations, deemed it sound policy, if not liberality, to decline gratifying his penchant for debate.

It does not appear to have been the purpose of Mr. C., at least in the commencement of his Reformation, to organize a new sect. That his labors tended to that result was clear to every discerning, attentive, and impartial observer. Sectarianism was the object of the most intense aversion—an aversion probably heightened by the remembrance of his previous Seceder intolerance. His favorite project was to fuse the various Christian sects, not, it would seem, by the fire of love, but of criticism and ridicule, and from the melted mass mould, in what he termed, the "ancient Gospel," a new and glorious body. Let us hear him on this point.

"I have no idea of adding to the catalogue of new sects. This game has been played too long. I labor to see sectarianism abolished, and all Christians of every name united upon the one foundation on which the Apostolic Church was founded. To bring Baptists and Pædo-baptists to this, is my supreme end." Chn. Bap., p. 217.

No intelligent Christian can object to the end which Mr. C. proposed to accomplish. The union of all true Christians on the Apostolic foundation, is an object most devoutly to be wished. All good men pray for it. But we must carefully inquire, whether the means by which he proposes to attain this object, are Scriptural and efficacious. We are now prepared to contemplate Campbellism under another phase.

CAMPBELLISM IN ITS CHAOS.

THE period of Campbellism which it is now proposed to examine, extends from the first appearance of the Christian Baptist to the time when Mr. Campbell, and those persons who adopted his peculiar views, and entered into his spirit and aims, were excluded from the Baptist denomination. This period may with equal propriety be termed its *chaotic* or its *belligerent* state. *Belligerent* it certainly was. The publication of the Christian Baptist was an open, formal declaration of war against all the religious sects and parties in the country; and most fearlessly, skillfully and furiously was it waged. Criticism, logic, eloquence, sarcasm, ridicule, and especially caricature and sophistry were the missiles employed in this warfare. Revelation, history, and fiction were laid under contribution in the conflict. At first, Mr. C. stood alone, battling single handed, as he fancied, against the disciplined hosts of sectarianism; but soon he was joined by a band of volunteers, less learned strategic, and cautious, but by no means less valorous, confident and aggressive, than himself. Almost all who came over to his side were from the first warriors, of dauntless spirit, panoplied from head to foot. So great was their ardor, and so fierce their onslaught, that, for a time, it seemed as if one could "chase a thousand, and two put ten thousand to flight."

This was no less the *chaotic* than the belligerent period of Campbellism. It would have puzzled the most careful, discriminating and candid reader of the Christian Baptist to form any clear conceptions of Mr. Campbell's principles or aims. He eschewed all the common and well defined terms of theology. His teaching was almost entirely negative. He was neither a Unitarian nor a Trinitarian, neither a Calvinist nor an Arminian ; but what he really was, or desired to be, none could certainly affirm. It was clear that he rejected "the popular exhibition of the Christian religion ;" but not clear what he would substitute for it. Many opinions and practices held sacred and dear by most Christians, were by him openly and sarcastically denounced ; but his own views were concealed, or cautiously and obscurely revealed. The title of his monthly periodical—"The Christian Baptist"—might seem to identify him with the Baptist denomination ; but the appearance was illusory. Agreeing with the Baptists on the action and subjects of baptism, he differed widely from them on the design of the ordinance, and on many other doctrinal, experimental and practical subjects; and in the sequel they received a full share of his censure and opposition. True, he constantly and earnestly insisted that the Scriptures are the only and sufficient rule of faith and practice, but in this opinion there was nothing distinctive. He held it in common, not only with the evangelical Protestant sects, but with Unitarians, Universalists, and almost every class of religious fanatics and errorists.

Mr. Campbell aspired to the honor of being a *Reformer*. The changes which he wrought in some of the churches are styled by him and his admirers the *Reformation*. That a reformation was needed by the Christian sects of that time none, who possess a tolerable acquaintance with their condition, and the claims of the Gospel, will deny. Indeed, what church, or member of a church, does not, in some respects, and in some degree, need reformation? There was needed then, as at all times, an increase of religious knowledge in the churches, but, more than this, an increase of piety. The reformation demanded by the times was in spirit and practice, rather than doctrine. They were then, as now, far too worldly, formal and inefficient. Among the Baptist churches there were some sad evils. In parts of the country, the churches were infected with an antinomian spirit, and blighted by a heartless, speculative, hair-splitting orthodoxy. These churches were mostly penurious, opposed to Christian missions, and all enlarged plans and self-denying efforts, for promoting the cause of Christ. In general, the careful study of the Scriptures, the religious education of children, the proper observance of the Lord's day, a wholesome, scriptural discipline, the reasonable support of pastors, and, in fine, devotion to the Redeemer's cause, were too much neglected. The pious and intelligent fathers, before Mr. C. was heard of, saw, confessed and lamented these evils ; and sought, in a kind and faithful manner, to correct them. But they are not of easy correction. Having their root in habit, or established opinions, or, worse still, in depravity, they can be eradicated only by the divine blessing on judicious and faithful efforts. Had he labored, with discrimination, fairness and fidelity for the correction of these, and similar evils, even if his zeal had not always been tempered with discretion, nor his courage with moderation, he would not have incurred the displeasure, or provoked the opposition of the intelligent and candid in the Baptist denomination. He attacked some of these evils with ability, but in a spirit and manner far better adapted to irritate than to convince ; and even those who were reformed by his arguments, lost as much in spirit as they gained in knowledge, and became fiery disputants rather than meek and lowly Christians. But his plans of Reformation were, by no means, limited to the evils which have been specified. His views on the subject were radical. He seemed to be commissioned to "pluck up, to pull down, and to destroy." Scarcely anything believed or practiced among Christians met his approbation. He gave himself up to the comparatively easy, and not very profitable task, of fault-finding. But to indulge no longer in general remarks, it is proper to descend to particulars.

The object of Mr. Campbell's first and most virulent attack was, what he styled, the "*Kingdom of the Clergy.*" The term *clergy* is not found in our English version of the Scriptures. It was at the beginning of this Reformation, as at present, used, and well understood, to mean ministers of the gospel—men whose office it is to give religious instruction and conduct religious worship. It was rarely found in the reports of ecclesiastical bodies, but was commonly employed by secular writers to denote the pastors and teachers in every Christian communion. The clergy of this country were a numerous class, invested in different Christian communions with very different degrees of authority; but in all exercising only such as was cheerfully accorded to them by the people among whom they labored. Entirely destitute of civil power, they had no means of maintaining their spiritual authority but the sanctity of their lives, the usefulness of their labors, the weight of their arguments, and the consent of their flocks. They were an important class; and they derived their importance from their official station, their various toils, and their extended religious influence. They were by no means faultless. Some of them were ignorant, conceited and vain ; others were proud, haughty and imperious ; others still, were hypocritical, mercenary and base ; and not a few were worldly, selfish, and sycophantic. Against these evils, no vigilance or fidelity on the part of the churches, or their rulers, could perfectly provide. Among the twelve apostles, one was a devil. But as a body, the clergy of the evangelical denominations were intelligent, pious, self-denying, diligent, and faithful in their vocation. Among them were many men of shining abilities, and most exemplary devotion to the cause of Christ—the excellent of the earth. Considering their talents, and their position in society, no class of the community was so meagerly rewarded for their toils and sacrifices. Many labored for nothing, but the pleasure of doing good—a larger number, perhaps, for a bare support—and very few were able, after maintaining themselves and their families, to lay by a surplus from their salaries for a season of affliction or infirmity. These statements will scarcely be called in question by any person having information on this subject, and possessing common candor. To discriminating and just censures of the clergy, no reasonable objection can be offered. Their official rank should not shield them from merited reproach, but, rather, subject their conduct to a more rigid scrutiny, and their sins to a severer condemnation. But every friend of religion, morality and good order, must revolt at seeing them rudely attacked, ridiculed, traduced, and held up to the scorn of the infidel and blasphemer. In all time, they have been subject to the reproach and scoffing of sceptics and opposers of the Gospel; but it was surely strange that a Christian minister should vie with these, or even exceed them, in their congenial work.

Mr. Campbell's first aim was to overthrow the power and influence of the popular clergy.

"To see Christians," he wrote, "enjoy their privileges, and to see sinners brought from darkness to light, are the two great objects for which we desire to live, to labor, and to suffer reproach." This was very well. But by what means did he propose to secure these important objects? He shall answer. "In endeavoring to use our feeble efforts for these glorious objects, we have found it necessary, among other things, to attempt to dethrone the reigning popular clergy from their high and lofty seats, which they have for ages been building for themselves. . . . . In opposing and exposing them, and their kingdom, it is not to join the infidel cry against priest or priestcraft;" (certainly not!) "it is not to gratify the avaricious or the licentious; but it is to pull down their Babel, and to emancipate those whom they have enslaved, to free the people from their unrighteous dominion and unmerciful spoliation." Chn. Bap., 32.

The clergy were informed, no little to their surprise, that their order had its origin, not merely in the perversion of Christianity, but in the speculations of the most ancient pagan philosophers. Listen to his words.

"Little do many think, and indeed little do they know, that the modern clergy are indebted to Pythagoras, Socrates, Plato, Aristotle, Zeno, Epicurus, and a thousand pagan philosophers, Jewish and Christian theorists, for the order of things which they found ready to their hand, as soon as they put on the sacerdotal robes." Chn. Bap., 54.

It would be easy to fill a volume with quotations resembling the above, but it is unnecessary—these may serve as specimens. Mr. C. employed all the resources of his various learning and fertile genius to subvert the influence of the clergy, and bring them into popular contempt. They were stigmatized as "textuaries," "scrap-doctors," "theoretic doctors," "populars," "priests," "hirelings," and "goat-milkers." The *Third Epistle of Peter* is an ingeniously written burlesque of the clergy, with just truth enough to make it plausible and biting, and divert attention from its gross exaggeration, and merciless injustice. Chn. Bap. 166. They were, in Mr. Campbell's estimation, a set of mercenary hirelings, actuated in their labors by no better motive than the love of lucre.

"They have," said he, "shut up every body's mouth but their own; and theirs they will not open unless they are paid for it." "A hireling is one who prepares himself for the office of a 'preacher,' or 'minister,' as a mechanic learns a trade, and who obtains a license from a congregation, convention, presbytery, pope, or diocesan bishop, as a preacher or minister, and agrees by the day or sermon, month or year, for a stipulated reward."

According to this definition, the man who from love to Christ and souls, prepares himself, by the most earnest, attentive and prayerful study of the Scriptures, for the Christian ministry, and receives for his ministerial toils a stipulated reward, even though that reward may be far less than he could receive in some respectable, secular avocation, is a hireling. Lest, however, a suspicion should arise that Mr. Campbell's teaching on this subject has been misunderstood, we must have another quotation from his pen.

"Upon the whole, I do not think we will err very much in making it a general rule, that every man who receives money for preaching the Gospel, or for sermons, by the day, month, or year, is a hireling in the language of truth and soberness."—Chn. Bap., 71, 233.

It is due to Mr. C. to remark, that he admitted

that there were some good men among the clergy—a few, who differing from their class, were pure in spite of the corrupting influence of their office. It is proper, also, to state that in the commencement of his editorial labors, he specially excepted the "Elders or Deacons of a Christian Assembly," from all his censures of the "Christian Clergy." Chn. Bap., 8. Who these "Elders and Deacons" were, it is not easy to determine. At that time Mr. C. was connected with the Baptist denomination, and very few, if any congregations, had embraced his peculiar views. It probably had reference to the officers of Baptist churches bearing these titles ; it was not long, however, before he discovered that there were clergy in these churches as well as in others. He writes—

"There is one spirit in all the clergy, whether they be Romanist or Protestant, *Baptist* or Pædobaptist, learned or unlearned, their own workmanship, or the workmanship of others." Chn. Bap., 94.

It is fair to permit Mr. C. to define what he means by a Baptist clergyman. "I have known, he writes, "a young Baptist priest made and finished in Philadelphia, go to the State of New York, preach a few times to a rich congregation, give in his letter, and in two or three weeks be called out from among the brethren to become their bishop ; and that, too, before he has got a wife, or a house, or a family to rule well. Such teachers I must rank among the clergy, and, indeed, they soon prove themselves to have a full portion, and sometimes a double portion of the spirit of the priesthood." Chn. Bap., 94.

It is not quite clear what constituted the claim of this "young priest" to rank among the clergy. Was it the fact that he was educated in Philadelphia—that he became the bishop of a wealthy congregation—or that he had not "got a wife"—or was it all these circumstances combined, that made him one of the clergy? The Baptists, neither in Philadelphia, nor elsewhere, deemed any man, either young or old, fit to take upon himself the sacred office of bishop, without furnishing evidence of sincere piety, and a desire to enter on the episcopal work, and possessing suitable qualifications for the service. They might entertain, as doubtless in many cases they did, defective views of episcopal qualifications, and they might be deceived in the motives of candidates for the office, but in no instance did they knowingly induct any man into the office without judging him to be holy, of good report, and possessed of gifts for performing its functions. The truth is, the term "*clergy*," in Mr. Campbell's vocabulary, denoted all ministers of every Christian denomination, who did not adopt his peculiar views, enter into the spirit of his Reformation, and co-operate with him in the accomplishment of his plans.

Simultaneously with Mr. Campbell's attack on the

clergy, he denounced all *Creeds* or *Confessions of Faith*, as the fruitful source of discord, schism, and mischief. The term "*Creed*," in its ecclesiastic sense, denotes a summary of Christian doctrine. There is in Christendom a great variety of creeds, from the so-called Apostle's Creed down to the Christian System, composed by Mr. Campbell, as an exhibition of the principles of his Reformation. Some are in the main sound, and some are unsound; some are evangelical, and some are anti-evangelical; the worst contain some truth, and the best, perhaps, some error. Of the lawfulness of writing a creed there can be no reasonable doubt. Every intelligent Christian has a creed, written or unwritten. There are certain facts, truths and principles, which he believes and maintains, and the belief of which he deems essential to the existence of true holiness. He may, or may not write these articles of his belief, but they are equally his creed; and equally efficacious in controlling his conduct, whether they be written or unwritten. The writing of them is merely placing in a visible form what previously existed in his mind; and doing so contravenes no law of Christ, and violates no moral obligation. But what is here affirmed of an individual, may, with equal clearness and propriety, be affirmed of a church of Christ. They have, and of necessity must have, a creed—it may be latitudinous or rigid, may comprehend many articles or few, may be written or traditional—and this creed is their bond of union. This remark is as true of the churches organized by Mr. Campbell, as of any churches in Christendom. They profess, indeed, to make the Bible their creed —but to say nothing of the fact that they make this profession in common with all Christian denominations, and with Mormons—there is a grand fallacy in it. It is not the Scriptures objectively, but subjectively considered—in other words, not the Scriptures as they exist in the original languages, but the Scriptures as they are understood, interpreted, and maintained by themselves—that form the basis of their union. There are certain points of Scripture doctrine in which they agree, and by which they are identified. These may be few, and may seem to them to be unequivocally contained in the Bible—but the belief of these is indispensable to admission into their fellowship. They do, it is true, insist that their members shall speak of Bible things in Bible terms. To restore a pure, or Scriptural speech, is one of the main objects of the Reformation for which Mr. C. pleads. But in their boasted purity of speech, there lurks another great fallacy. They do not use Bible terms. The Bible, with a few slight exceptions, was written in the Hebrew and Greek tongues; and they derive their theological terms from a translation of the Bible made by fallible men. Besides, Bible terms are of no significance or value but as they are understood; and they may serve the purposes of ignorance, error, or hypocrisy, as well as of knowledge. In fine, if men are united by the adoption of certain terms, or phrases, even though these may be Scriptural, apart from the meaning attached to them, they are influenced by sound rather than sense—by form rather than substance—by appearance rather than truth.

Creeds, like everything else, human and divine, that comes within mortal reach, may be used for good or evil purposes. To prevent or correct misrepresentations, to promote unity of faith, and to secure the instruction of church members, and their children, in the most important principles and duties of the Christian system, are considerations which, in the view of the intelligent and candid, justify the drawing up and printing of a creed. There are certain principles—such as the existence of God—the inspiration of the Scriptures—the resurrection of Christ, &c.—the belief and admission of which are deemed by every church, indispensable to fellowship ; and it may be wise and necessary for a church in some cases, to avow and proclaim them. When the Brush Run church, of which Mr. Campbell was a member, sought to gain fellowship with the Redstone Association, they presented "a written declaration of their belief," drawn up, no doubt, by the Reformer himself. Chn. Bap., p. 92. And why was this creed presented but for the purpose of satisfying the Redstone Association that the Brush Run church was worthy of Christian fellowship? And if it was lawful for this church to publish her "declaration of belief," to prove her title to fellowship, it must have been equally lawful for the Redstone Association, or any Christian church, to publish her "declaration of belief," to show whom she thought worthy of fellowship. Indeed, the Redstone Association in receiving the Brush Run church into her fellowship, on her "written declaration of belief," did, in the most solemn and authoritative manner, adopt and avow that declaration as her creed. That creeds have sometimes been employed for unlawful and mischievous purposes, no one acquainted with ecclesiastical history can question. They have too frequently been used as a substitute for the Scriptures, to embalm error, and to bind the consciences of men, and have, in many instances, engendered a spirit of speculation, strife, and persecution, and led to the most painful schisms.

Whether it is *expedient* for all churches, under all circumstances, to publish a creed, is a question which it is not proposed to discuss. My opinion is that it is not. Churches have flourished without a written creed—and by this is meant, that they have adhered to divine truth, abounded in the fruits of righteousness, and have, in a good degree, secured the ends of their organization. On the other hand, churches, having sound, evangelical creeds, have, in many instances, sunk into formality, error and corruption.

Mr. C. was not alone in his opposition to creeds. Many good and wise men doubted their expediency, and others were convinced that, on the whole, they were of mischievous tendency. A majority of the Baptist churches in the United States, had no written creed at all, and the few that did have, had only a very brief summary of doctrine, practically of no moment. But Mr. C. was from temperament or habit essentially an ultraist. His onslaught on creeds was fierce, and indiscriminate. It was the boasted peculiarity of his Reformation that it was hostile to all creeds, heterodox or orthodox, bad or good. "So far as this controversy resembles them," (he says, referring to other controversies concerning creeds,) "in its opposition to creeds, it is to be distinguished from them in this all-essential attribute, viz. :—*that our opposition to creeds arose from a conviction that whether the opinions in them were true or false, they were hostile to the union, peace, harmony, purity, and joy of Christians ; and adverse to the conversion of the world to Jesus Christ.*" Chn. Sys., 9. How opinions in harmony with the Bible, embracing fundamental, soul-saving truths, lucidly, concisely, and systematically expressed—should produce such direful effects, it would puzzle an ordinary man to conceive ; but so Mr. C. believed and maintained.

And I must, too, do him the justice to state, that his course was in perfect harmony with this conviction. All creeds, Romanist and Protestant, Calvinistic and Arminian, rationalistic and evangelical, voluminous confessions of faith, and concise summaries of doctrine, came in for an equal share of his denunciations. If there was any difference, the Westminster Confession of Faith, (Presbyterian,) and the Philadelphia Confession of Faith, (Baptist,) received the largest measure of his censure. All churches having creeds were, according to his views, involved in the same condemnation and corruption. The purity, the wisdom, the intrinsic excellence of their creed, could not preserve them from a blight. That I may do no injustice, and save myself from the suspicion of exaggeration, I will quote his own language. "The worshipping establishments now in operation throughout Christendom, increased and cemented by their respective voluminous confessions of faith, and their ecclesiastical constitutions, *are not churches of Jesus Christ, but the legitimate daughters of that mother of harlots, the Church of Rome.*" Mill. Har., vol. 3, 362. "What of the apostacy—do you place all the sects in the apostacy? Yes; all religious sects who have any human bond of union; all who rally under any articles of confederation"—that is, summary of doctrine, however Scriptural, clear, and important—"other than the Apostle's doctrine"—that is, according to the Bethany vocabulary, the whole volume of revelation—" and who refuse to yield all homage to the ancient order of things"—that is, the long-lost Gospel, disinterred by Mr. Campbell. Mill. Har., vol. 3, 362. From these quotations, it appears, that according to the "ancient Gospel," as understood at Bethany, any body claiming to be Christian, adopting a summary of doctrine, as fundamental articles of belief, though the articles be true, and the belief of them indispensable to salvation, is no church of Christ—but a sect—a harlot—and the daughter of a harlot.

The writer is reminded of a discourse, which, not long since, he heard Mr. C. deliver—a discourse whose doctrine was in striking harmony with the above extracts. His text was, Eph. iv. 4–6. His theme was chiefly the unity of the body of Christ. The church, he insisted, was a *body*—not a mass, but an organized, symmetrical, and beautiful body. But Christ has only one body—a head with seven bodies would be a monster. But if Christ has only one body, what body is it? Not the Roman Catholic body—not the Episcopalian—not the Presbyterian—not the Lutheran—not the Methodist—not the Baptist. He did not inform us, however, what body is the body of Christ. He trusted in the intelligence and candor of his hearers to infer that the body of Christ is the body that embraces the "ancient Gospel," and that has restored the "ancient order of things." The sermon was eloquent, plausible, and sophistical. If a head with seven bodies is a monster, a head without a body is useless. It is natural to inquire, If the party adopting the peculiar views of Mr. C., is really the body of Christ, where was his body before the light shone from Bethany, and while all the sects were in the smoke and bondage of Babylon ?

All this sophistry vanishes before Scriptural definitions of the term *church*. It is used in two distinct senses in the New Testament. In some places it means an organized, visible body of believers, assembling in one place for the worship of Christ. In this sense of the term, we read of the "church of God which is at Corinth," "the churches of Galatia," "the churches of Judea," &c. The Apostolic *churches* were all built on the same foundation, governed by the same laws, animated by the same spirit, and all co-operated in the same good cause ; but they did not constitute *one great, organized hierarchy*. If "*the church*," in this sense of the term, was the body of Christ, then he had more than one body—he had *seven* bodies in Asia, and we know not how many in Judea, Galatia, and other regions. In a few places the word *church* signifies the whole body of believers in Christ. This is the church for which he gave himself, Eph. v. 25. This is the body of which he is the head, Eph. i. 22, 23. To this body belong all in whom dwells the *Paraclete*, whatever their name, or visible connections, may be. Of this body, the true Christians, admitted by Mr. C. to be found among the sects, are living members. The churches of the Reformation do not constitute this body, but the pious among them are components of it. Now, the sophism of Mr. C. consisted in substituting the former for the latter sense of the term church in his text—a sense which it does not fairly admit.

When Mr. Campbell commenced his Reformation, he found various *benevolent or religious associations* in existence, having for their object the diffusion of Divine truth, and the extension of the kingdom of the Messiah. Among these institutions we may mention Mission, Bible, Tract, and Education Societies, and Sunday Schools, whose titles indicate, with sufficient precision, to the common reader, their respective spheres of operation. The objects contemplated by these associations were of the highest importance, and appealed most powerfully to the sympathies and liberality of the pious. It were uncandid to deny that they originated with wise and good men, in the love of truth, and in an earnest desire to promote the salvation of sinners, and the glory of the Redeemer, that they were sustained by the generous sacrifices, fervent prayers, and self-denying, and, in some cases, heroic labors of their friends; and that they had been successful in a measure corresponding with these toils and sacrifices, and adapted to inspire gratitude for the past, and confidence in regard to the future. Whether the best plans had been adopted to carry forward the work of evangelization was certainly a debatable question; and none were more solicitous for its proper solution than those who were most prominently and actively engaged in the prosecution of these various plans. To affirm that vanity, selfishness, and sectarian zeal had no part in the maintenance of these schemes, would be to affirm what no person, the least acquainted with the imperfections of human nature, would believe. But it may be safely affirmed, that since the days of primitive Christianity, no systematic efforts for the diffusion of truth and piety have involved so large an amount of self-denial, privation, toil, sacrifice and suffering, as modern missions to the heathen, with their various kindred enterprises. The friends and supporters of the different benevolent institutions were entitled to the most candid and liberal treatment from those who, differing from them as to the expediency of their plans, sympathized with them in the sublime and glorious objects at which they aimed.

Mr. Campbell commenced his editorial career with pretty strong opposition to these religious enterprises. Finding them identified with what he called the popular Christianity of the day, he deemed it necessary to subvert their influence that his reformation might triumph. In his preface to the Christian Baptist, he thus wrote:

"There is another difficulty of which we are aware, that, as some objects are manifestly good, and the means attempted for their accomplishment manifestly evil, speaking against the means employed we may be sometimes understood as opposing the object abstractly, especially by those who do not wish to understand, but rather to misrepresent. For instance—that the conversion of the heathen to the Christian religion is an object manifestly good all Christians will acknowledge; yet every one acquainted with the means employed, and of the success attendant on the means, must know that these means have not been blessed; and every intelligent Christian must know that many of the means employed have been manifestly evil. Besides, to convert the heathen to the popular Christianity of these times would be an object of no great consequence, as the popular Christians themselves, for the most part, require to be converted to the Christianity of the New Testament." Chn. Bap., 4.

It is not surprising that the Reformer, convinced that the sects did not preach the "ancient Gospel," and needed themselves to be converted to the Christianity of the New Testament, should have been without sympathy for their missionary schemes. They were, in his judgment, unauthorized by Christ, and subversive of his throne and government. His plan for the conversion of the world, or what he supposed the Divine plan, was first to convert all Christian sects to the Christianity of the New Testament. Till this desirable object could be attained, not an effort was to be put forth for the conversion of the heathen. "An attempt," said he, "to convert Pagans and Mahometans to believe that Jesus is the Son of God, and the sent of the Father, is also an attempt to frustrate the prayer of the Messiah, and to subvert his throne and government." Chn. Bap., 135. But even after the conversion of the Christian sects, and their union in one church, no missionaries are to be sent forth for the conversion of the heathen. "The Bible," he says, "gives us no idea of a missionary without the power of working miracles. Miracles and missionaries," and, he might add, preaching the Gospel, "are inseparably connected in the New Testament." Chn. Bap., 15. Christians must "form themselves into societies independent of hireling priests and ecclesiastical courts, modelled after the forum, the parliament, or national conventions," and "cast to the moles and to the bats the Platonic speculations, the Pythagorean dreams, and Jewish fables they have written in their creeds;" "return to the ancient model delineated in the New Testament;" "and keep the ordinances as delivered to them by the apostles." Then suppose a Christian church were to be placed on the confines of a heathen land, as some of them must inevitably be, the darkness of paganism will serve, as a shade in a picture, to exhibit the lustre of Christianity. Then the heathen around them will see their humility; their heavenly-mindedness, their hatred of garments spotted with the flesh, their purity, their chastity, their temperance, their sobriety, their brotherly love; they will observe the order of their worship, and will fall down in their assemblies, as Paul affirms, and declare that God is in them of a truth." Such was the Bethany plan for evangelizing the world. But if the work of evangelization on the "confines of heathen lands" should progress slowly, and it should seem desirable to adopt more active and aggressive measures for its prosecution—then to avoid the necessity of sending missionaries, for which there is no scripture authority, if there can "be found such a society," as that above described, though it be "composed of but twenty, willing to emigrate to some heathen land, where they can support themselves like the natives, wear the same garb, adopt the country as their own, and profess nothing like a missionary project; should such a society sit down and hold forth in word and deed the saving truth, not deriding the gods nor the religion of the natives, but allowing their own works and example to speak for their religion, and practicing as above hinted; we are persuaded that, in process of time, a more solid foundation for the conversion of the natives would be laid, and more actual success resulting, than from all the missionaries employed for twenty-five years. Such a course would have some warrant from Scripture, but the present has proved itself to be all human." Chn. Bap., 16–17.

It is not my purpose to discuss at large this scheme for evangelizing the world, but I must make a few remarks in passing. That churches should be pure and conformed to the New Testament model; and that such churches, situated on the borders of heathen lands, or elsewhere, would exert a good influence, must be conceded. That they would have full authority to emigrate to a heathen country, and hold forth the word of life; and that doing so, they might be useful, must also be admitted. But what reason there is for claiming for this scheme of propagating the Gospel peculiarly the Divine sanction, I know not. As a plan for converting the heathen it is sustained neither by apostolic precept nor example. Aggressions on the domain of heathenism have always been made by missionaries—who have gone forth, singly or in small bands, with or without the power of working miracles, with the truth of Christ on their lips, and the love of Christ in their hearts, to instruct, persuade and convert men, and to found churches amid the surrounding darkness. This is God's plan—enforced by the command of Christ, and the example of the apostles—and sanctioned by the experience of the Christian world. The substitute proposed by Mr. C. is untried, impracticable, chimerical.

Had the Reformer confined himself to the advocacy of his new scheme of converting the world to Christ, or to candid, generous and faithful criticisms on the missionary, and other benevolent schemes of the time, his labors would probably have attracted but little attention, or, at most, would have produced no serious strife. But such a course did not accord with the genius and spirit of the man. At first, and for a short time, he wrote rather cautiously and hesitatingly concerning Christian missions. "It may be worthy," said he, "of the serious consideration of many of the zealous advocates of the various sectarian missions in our day, whether, in a few years, the same things may not be said of their various projects which they themselves affirm of the Catholic missions, and missionaries." Chn. Bap., 14. But this inquiring tone soon gave place to that of dogmatism and denunciation. Upon the benevolent associations, the vials of his unmitigated wrath were soon poured out. All the resources of his learning, wit, and ridicule, were employed to undermine their influence, and bring them into contempt. Whatever was published in infidel, or semi-infidel papers in disparagement of missionaries, was promptly transferred to the columns of the Christian Baptist, without comment, or with approbation; while allusions to the self-denials, toils, sufferings, and successes of missionaries, were studiously omitted. Mr. Campbell's chief instrument in opposing Christian missions, and promoting his Reformation, was caricaturing—an art for which his genius peculiarly fitted him. But, as his opposition to missions, and cognate enterprises, had much influence in severing the Reformers from the Baptists, I will quote copiously from the columns of his monthly pamphlet, pretty much at random on these topics.

"The *order* of their assemblies (the primitive churches,) was uniformly the same. It did not vary with moons and seasons. It did not change as dress nor fluctuate as the manners of the times. Their devotion did not diversify itself into the endless forms of modern times. They had no monthly concerts for prayer; no solemn convocations, no great fasts, nor preparation, nor thanksgiving days. Their churches were not fractured into missionary societies, Bible societies, education societies; nor did they dream of organizing such in the world. The head of a believing household was not in those days a president or manager of a board of foreign missions; his wife the president of some female education society; his eldest son, the recording secretary of some domestic Bible society; his eldest daughter, the corresponding secretary of a mite society; his servant-maid, the vice-president of a rag society; and his little daughter, a tutoress of a Sunday-school. They knew nothing of the hobbies of modern times. In their church capacity alone they moved. They neither transformed themselves into any other kind of association, nor did they fracture and sever themselves into divers societies. They viewed the church of Jesus Christ as the scheme of Heaven to ameliorate the world ; as members of it, they considered themselves bound to do all they could for the glory of God and the good of men. They dare not transfer to a missionary society, or Bible society, or education society, a cent or a prayer, lest in so doing they should rob the church of its glory, and exalt the inventions of men above the wisdom of God. In their church capacity alone they moved." Chn. Bap., 6.

" 'MISSIONARIES TO BURMAH.—On Wednesday, the 11th of June, at Utica, New York, the Rev. Jonathan Wade and his consort were set apart as missionaries to the Burman empire, by a committee of the board of managers of the Baptist General Convention. An interesting sermon was delivered on the occasion by the Rev. Nathaniel Kendrick, from 2 Tim. ii. 10. 'Therefore I endure all things for the elects' sake, that they also may obtain the salvation which is in Christ Jesus with eternal glory.' Rev. Alfred Bennet led in offering up the consecrating prayer. Rev. Daniel Hascall gave Mr. Wade an appropriate charge, and the Rev. Joel W. Clark gave him the right hand of fellowship, 'that he should go to the heathen ;' Rev. John Peck addressed Mrs. Wade, and Rev. Elon Galusha gave her the right hand of fellowship. Rev. Elijah F. Willey offered the concluding prayer. The services were performed in Rev. Mr. Atkins' meeting-house. The day was fine, and the assemblage was very large, and proved, by their fixed and silent attention to the services, how much they felt for the world that lieth in wickedness ; and by a collection of $86.23 taken on the spot, they showed a willingness to share in the pleasure and expense of spreading the Gospel in all the earth.

" 'Mr. Wade is a young man, and a native of the state of New York. He received his classical and theological education in the theological seminary at Hamilton. He appeared before the committee a man of good sense, of ardent piety, and understandingly led by the Spirit of God to the work in which he has now engaged. Mrs. Wade is from a respectable family in Hamilton, Madison County, daughter of deacon Lapham. Her early piety and active zeal in the cause of her Redeemer, has encouraged the hope that she will be eminently useful in the cause of missions with her husband.—*Latter Day Luminary.*'

" *Note by the Editor.*—How accordant is the language and spirit of the above to the following passage from the 13th chapter of the Acts of the Apostles :—'On Wednesday, the 11th of June, A. D. 44, the Rev. Saulus Paulus and the Rev. Joses

Barnabas were set apart as missionaries to the Gentiles dispersed throughout the world, by a committee of the board of managers of the Baptist General Convention, met in the city of Antioch. An interesting sermon was delivered on the occasion by the Rev. Simon Niger, from Isaiah xlii. 4 : 'The isles shall wait for his law.' Rev. Lucius, of Cyrene, led in offering up the consecrating prayer. Rev. Manaen gave Mr. Paulus and his companion (Mr. Barnabas) an appropriate charge ; and the Rev. John Mark gave them the right hand of fellowship, 'that they should go to the heathen.' The Rev. Lucius, of Cyrene, offered up the concluding prayer. The services were performed in the Rev. Mr. Simon Niger's meeting-house. The day was fine, and the assemblage was very large, and proved, by their fixed and silent attention to the services, how much they felt for the world that lieth in wickedness ; and by a collection of $86.25, they showed a willingness to aid the Rev. Mr. Paulus, and the Rev. Mr. Barnabas in carrying the Gospel to the heathen.

"Mr. Paulus is a young man, and a native of the city of Tarsus ; he received his classical and theological education in the theological seminary in Jerusalem. He appeared before the committee a man of good sense, of ardent piety, and understandingly led by the spirit of God to the work in which he has now engaged.

"I is, then, plain that the above notification is

just in the spirit and style of this passage from the 13th chapter of the Acts. But in the common translation, the original loses much of its aptitude and beauty; for lo! it reads thus: 'Now there was in the church that was at Antioch, certain prophets and teachers; as, Barnabas, and Simon that was called Niger, and Lucius of Cyrene, and Manaen, which had been brought up with Herod the tetrarch, and Saul. As they ministered to the Lord, and fasted, the Holy Ghost said, Separate me Barnabas and Saul for the work whereunto I have called them. And when they had fasted and prayed, and laid their hands on them, they sent them away.'" Chn. Bap., 17.

"Our objections to the missionary plan originated from the conviction that it is unauthorized in the New Testament; and that, in many instances, it is a system of iniquitous peculation and speculation, I feel perfectly able to maintain both the one and the other of these positions. . . . . Not questioning the piety and philanthropy of many of the originators, and present abettors of the missionary plan, we must say that the present scheme is not authorized by our King. This, I think, we proved some time ago; and no man that we have heard of, has come forward to oppose our views. Indeed, I think, we have few men of any information, who would come forward openly to defend the plan of saving the world by means of money and science; of converting pagans by funds raised indirectly from spinning-wheels, fruit stalls, corn-fields, melon patches, potato lots, rags, children's playthings, and religious newspapers, consecrated to missionary purposes; and from funds raised directly by begging from every body, of every creed, and of no creed whatever. By sending out men to preach begging sermons, and to tell the people of A.'s missionary patch of potatoes producing twice as much per acre, as those destined for himself and children; of B.'s uncommon crop of missionary wheat, a part of which he covetously alienated from the missionary to himself, and, as a judgment upon him, his cow broke into his barn and ate of it until she killed herself; of E.'s missionary sheep having each yeaned two lambs a-piece, while his own only yeaned him one a-piece, and a variety of other miracles wrought in favor of the missionary fund. I say, what man of good common sense and of a reasonable mind would come forward to defend a scheme of converting the world by such means, and by the means of that very 'vain philosophy' and 'science falsely so called,' condemned by the apostles." Chn. Bap., 53, 54.

"*Mr. Robert Cautious* . . . You think that it was rather going to an extreme to rank Bible societies with other popular schemes. Perhaps a more intimate acquaintance with our views of Christianity would induce you to think as we do upon this subject. We are convinced, fully convinced, that the whole head is sick, and the whole heart faint of modern fashionable Christianity—that many of the schemes of the populars resemble the delirium, the wild fancies of a subject of fever, in its highest paroxysms—and that these most fashionable projects deserve no more regard from sober Christians, Christians intelligent in the New Testament, than the vagaries, the febrile flights of patients in an inflammatory fever. We admit that it is quite as difficult to convince the populars of the folly of their projects, as it generally is to convince one in a febrile reverie, that he is not in the possession of his reason." Chn. Bap., 33.

"I honestly confess that the popular clergy and their schemes appear to me fraught with mischief to the temporal and eternal interests of men, and would anxiously wish to see them converted into useful members, or bishops, or deacons of the Christian church. How has their influence spoiled the best gifts of heaven to men! Civil liberty has always fallen beneath their sway—the inalienable rights of men have been wrested from their hands—and even the very margin of the Bible polluted with their inventions, their rabbinical dreams and whimsical nonsense. The Bible cannot be disseminated without their appendages, and if children are taught to read in a Sunday school, their pockets must be filled with religious tracts, the object of which is either directly or indirectly to bring them under the domination of some creed or sect. Even the distribution of the Bible to the poor, must be followed up with those tracts, as if the Bible dare not be trusted in the hands of a layman, without a priest or his representative at his elbow. It is on this account that I have, for some time, viewed both 'Bible societies,' and 'Sunday schools,' as a sort of recruiting establishments, to fill up the ranks of those sects which take the lead in them. It is true that we rejoice to see the Bible spread, and the poor taught to read by those means; but notwithstanding this, we ought not, as we conceive, to suffer the policy of many engaged therein to pass unnoticed, or to refrain from putting those on their guard who are likely to be caught by 'the sleight of men and cunning craftiness.'" Chn. Bap., 80.

The foregoing extracts pretty clearly indicate the spirit and manner of Mr. Campbell's warfare against Christian missions, and similar enterprizes. Some points in them, however, are entitled to special attention.

Notice, in the first place, a manifest fallacy in argument. The argument is implied, not distinctly expressed, by Mr. C. It is this—all religious institutions not existing in the days of the apostles are unauthorized. There were no mission and Bible societies in the days of the apostles. Therefore these societies are unauthorized. The fallacy in the argument lies in not distinguishing between what is essential and what is circumstantial in Christianity —a difference fully admitted by Mr. C. Chn. Sys., p. 74. Christianity has its doctrine, facts, laws, and promises ; and these are settled and immutable ; but many things relating to the progress and establishment of Christianity were, of necessity, left to be decided by time and circumstances—in short, by expediency. In the days of the apostles, there were no translations of the Scriptures, no houses, so far as we are informed, erected for religious worship, no religious periodicals, no Christian editors, and no alms-houses ; but are all these unauthorized ? May not Christian churches, and individual Christians, combine for any, and every good purpose, in such manner as they may deem expedient, provided that in so doing they violate no law of Christ ? But what law—what moral obligation, is violated by missionary societies ? They propose to convert the world to Christ—is this right ? They propose to accomplish the work by the promulgation of the Gospel of Christ—is this authorized ? They propose to diffuse the light of the Gospel by sustaining and encouraging men who believe and love the Gospel, and exemplify its excellence in their lives, to proclaim it among the heathen—is this unauthorized ? The truth is, if Christians are authorized to do any thing, they are authorized, as churches or individuals, to enter into any combinations, or employ any means, not interdicted by divine authority, to spread the knowledge of salvation. "*Let him that heareth say, Come.*"

In the next place, direct your attention to Mr. Campbell's usual art of caricaturing, and aiming to bring into derision, sacred and solemn things. One among many instances of its exercise may be selected for illustration. The account furnished by the Latter Day Luminary of the setting apart of Mr. and Mrs. Wade as missionaries to Burmah is plain, unostentatious, solemn, and in good taste. Mr. and Mrs. Wade have proved themselves, by a long life, to be eminently humble, self-denying, and devoted servants of Christ. The ministers who participated in the services of the occasion were among the best men living—venerable for their age, their piety, their wisdom, and their labors. The services were most appropriate—consisting of prayer, preaching the word, suitable addresses, and giving the right hand of fellowship. The assembly was large, attentive, and deeply interested; and the scene was one on which, no doubt, angels looked with delight, and God with approbation. Had such men, in such a service, and under such circumstances, erred, their error would have deserved to be treated with the greatest candor and forbearance. Yet this very scene is, in a note by the Editor of the Christian Baptist, caricatured, with heartless and revolting levity; and that too at a period when the writer could not plead in extenuation of his course the indiscretion of youth.

The Christian Baptist, having attained a wide circulation, exerted a potent influence against the cause of Christian missions, and Christian benevolence generally. The sentiments which it inculcated, and the spirit which it infused, on these subjects, were too congenial to the indolence and selfishness of human nature, not to meet a cordial reception from many. Wherever the Christian Baptist spread, the cause of missions declined. "Your paper," wrote a Kentucky correspondent, "has well nigh stopped missionary operations in this State." Chn. Bap., 144. And what was true of its blighting influence in Kentucky, was equally true of its influence in Virginia, Ohio, and every place, where its visits were welcomed.

"*Christian Experience*" is a phrase, not found in the Scriptures, and not, perhaps, wisely chosen, but it was, at the commencement of Mr. Campbell's reformation, as it is now, in very common use, and of well defined, and well understood meaning. It related to a subject of great importance—one held in the highest estimation by all evangelical Christians. It denotes that series of conflicts, exercises and emotions, springing from a gradual knowledge of Divine truth, and the influence of the Holy Spirit, which results in the conversion of the soul to Christ, and accompanies this event Much has improperly passed under the name of Christian experience; and great mischief has arisen from ignorance or misconception on the subject. Many persons have mistaken excitements, fancies, dreams, and other extravagances, for genuine conversion, and not unfrequently amid much ignorance and superstition have been found the marks of sincere piety. Christian experience is greatly modified by temperament, education, religious instruction, and the circumstances under which conversion occurs. Men of a phlegmatic temperament may embrace the Gospel with comparatively little feeling. Men of ardent temperament and vivid imaginations, like John Bunyan, and Colonel Gardiner, are likely to receive the Gospel with intense and overwhelming emotions, and these emotions are sometimes accompanied by fancied "visions and revelations." We should carefully distinguish between what is circumstantial and what is essential in Christian experience. We should separate the chaff from the wheat. All that is superstitious, visionary, extravagant—in fine, all that will not bear the test of Scripture, should be rejected; but we should beware of condemning the precious with the vile—the genuine with the spurious. Conviction of sin, godly sorrow, faith in Christ, an obedient spirit, love, peace, joy and hope, are elements of genuine Christian experience. No intelligent, evangelical Christian has ever placed saving experience in any thing short of those impressions, exercises and feelings which are essential to a passage "from death unto life." Every godly man clings with unyielding tenacity to the reality of his Christian experience. He would no sooner renounce it than his salvation. There may, indeed, be religion—its name—its form—its pomp—its sacrifices—without it; but it is spiritless, heartless and worthless.

Mr. Campbell's early writings on the subject of experimental religion gave great pain to the friends of spiritual Christianity. Some things which he published on this subject were worthy of grave consideration. He exposed with clearness and severity the illusions and extravagances which, among the uncultivated and ignorant, especially the negroes, was current as Christian experience. These evils were seen, deplored, and opposed by all well informed Christians, long before he commenced his Reformation. They are evils inseparable, perhaps, from the progress of earnest piety among an illiterate and excitable people; but from which a speculative, heartless formalism is a certain preservative. He condemned the practice common among Baptists and some other evangelical Christians of requiring from candidates for church membership a relation of their experience. The practice he considered to be, not only unauthorized, but injurious. That it has sometimes been abused by the ignorant, or misjudging, none will deny; but that churches should avail themselves of the best means in their power—imperfect, at best—to judge correctly of the sincerity, knowledge and piety of persons wishing to enter into their fellowship, seems evident from the nature of the connexion. And a brief, clear narrative of their religious exercises, or direct answers to a few plain, pertinent questions adapted to elicit information on this subject, will greatly facilitate this object. Philip did not baptize the Ethiopian eunuch, who requested baptism, until he had catechised him. Acts 8 : 37. True, the evangelist propounded but one question to the candidate—or, at least, in the concise narrative furnished by Luke, only one is recorded—that, under the circumstances, being deemed sufficient. It should be borne in mind that the Ethiopian was an intelligent man—a reader of the Scriptures—had been to Jerusalem to worship—and had been receiving personal instruction from Philip. The evangelist asked the candidate the question which was most likely to elicit the true state of his heart, and the answer was satisfactory. This example, so far from restricting pastors or churches, in the examination of candidates for baptism, to this brief and single question—a question never, so far as we are informed, proposed to any other applicant for the ordinance, in apostolic times—fairly authorizes them to make such inquiries as the intelligence, known characters, and circumstances, of the candidates may appear to require. But whether the necessary information shall be obtained by asking questions, or by the connected narrative of the candidates for church fellowship, is a point about which none but hair-splitting speculatists would stickle. Though Mr. Campbell differed from the Baptists generally on this subject, the difference would have caused no serious strife between them. His views on this point were not peculiar. Several evangelical denominations, held in high and deserved estimation by the Baptists, received members into full communion without requiring a recital of their Christian experience. What the Baptists maintained was, that persons were not entitled to church membership, without the various exercises, comprehended in conversion, or regeneration, which they termed "Christian experience," and which are particularly pointed out in the commencement of this article. On this point they have never wavered, and, God grant, they never may. The propriety of relating an experience before a church is one thing—the indispensable necessity of an experience —a "*Christian* experience"—in order to legitimate church communion is another, and far more important matter.

Now, it was in regard to the latter, and not the former point, that the remarks of Mr. Campbell caused so much pain among considerate and earnest Christians. He treated the subject with a levity, sarcasm, and disregard of the feelings of holy men, which can be fairly characterized by no term less offensive than shocking. Good men stood aghast at the freedom and severity with which he treated a subject that they had been accustomed to regard with feelings of awe, not, perhaps, unmingled with superstition. It is just to him to say that, so far as I can perceive, he did not deny the reality or the necessity of what others termed "Christian experience," but he wrote equivocally on the subject. He knew that he was accused of rejecting Christian experience—spiritual religion—and that his peculiar views of faith and repentance were supposed to lead to this result—and yet the frank and full avowal on these points, requisite to quiet the fears, not of the captious, but of the intelligent, pious and candid, who looked with favor on some portions of his Reformation, was studiously withheld. Some paragraphs, considered alone, would appear to establish the soundness of his views on experimental religion; but others would throw a doubt over his meaning. To satisfy those who called in question the correctness of his opinions on this subject, he wrote—"It is said that we have taught that there is no necessity of being born again by the Spirit of God; and that we have denied that Christians are new creatures, and that we have confined all divine grace to the apostolic age. Now we must confess that we did not intend to communicate such ideas; nor do we think that such can be fairly gathered from our words." But soon he added—"We have discovered that something under the name of "experimental religion" is the very soul of the popular system"—and the reader has seen the estimate in which he held that system. Chn. Bap., 64. See also pp. 48-49.

A few quotations must suffice to exhibit the views of Mr. Campbell on the subject of experimental religion, and his spirit and manner in discussing it.

"It is, perhaps, chiefly owing to the religious theories imbibed in early life from creeds, catechisms, and priests, that so few comparatively enjoy the grace of God which brings salvation. The grace of God, exhibited in the record concerning Jesus of Nazareth, affords no consolation. The hopes and joys of many spring from a good conceit of themselves. If this good conceit vanishes, which sometimes happens, despondency and distress are the consequences. While they can, as they conceit, thank God that they are not like other men, they are very happy; but when this fancied excellency disappears, the glad tidings afford no consolation: anguish and distress have come upon them. This, with some of the spiritual doctors, is a good symptom too: for, say they, '*if you do not doubt we will doubt for you.*' When they have worked then into despondency, they minister a few opiates, and assure them that they are now in a safe and happy state. Now they are to rejoice, because they are sorrowful; now they are to feel very good, because they feel so very bad. This is the orthodox 'Christian experience.' This is the genuine work of the Holy Spirit!" Chn. Bap., 138.

Did Mr. Campbell really believe that this caricature, which he drew, was "*the orthodox Christian experience*"—"*the genuine work of the Holy Spirit*"—for which the evangelical Christians of that time pleaded? It is charitable to think so. But how a man of Mr. Campbell's intelligence, erudition, general information, and accurate observation, could have reached such a conclusión, it is not easy to comprehend. It will not be denied that the evil which Mr. Campbell portrayed was real, and deserved correction. In all religious denominations there may be ignorant, enthusiastic and misguided teachers. He will concede that there are such in the churches enrolled under the banner of his own Reformation—or if he should not, the means of his conviction are at hand. But is it fair to charge the crudities and errors of such teachers to orthodoxy? No evangelical Christian denomination, has ever endorsed such an experience as Mr. Campbell has delineated in this paragraph, either from his prolific imagination, or the teachings and doings of ignorant enthusiasts. He may be safely challenged to furnish from any creed, document, accredited writer, or respectable journal, of any Christian persuasion, the outline of an approved experience, so defective and unscriptural as this "orthodox Christian experience." I have been in the Christian ministry more than thirty years, and I have no recollection of having read in any book, or heard from the lips of any teacher, approved by any orthodox Christian denomination, the description of a saving experience, which did not include Godly sorrow, the renunciation of sins, and trust in Christ for salvation. To represent an experience, having no allusion to conviction of sin, sorrow for it, hatred of it, the abandonment of it, faith in Christ, love to him, and an obedient disposition—in short, a change of heart—not as the experience of a few ignorant and excited enthusiasts—but as "the orthodox Christian experience"—"the genuine work of the Holy Spirit," is to *misrepresent*—it may be, ignorantly, or carelessly, or in the heat of party zeal—but nevertheless to misrepresent, most grossly, the class of men among whom is to be found most of the intelligent piety which the world contains.

It is proper to furnish another extract on this subject, of later date, but of similar spirit. Chn. Sys., p. 244, 245.

"EFFECTS OF MODERN CHRISTIANITY.—Our greatest objection to the systems which we oppose, is their impotency on the heart. Alas! what multitudes of prayerless, saintless, Christless, joyless hearts, have crowded Christianity out of the congregations by their experiences before baptism! They seem to have had all their religion before they professed it. They can relate no experience since baptism, comparable to that professed before the "mutual pledge" was tendered and received. It was the indubitable proofs of the superabundance of this fruit, which caused me to suspect the far-famed tree of evangelical orthodoxy. That cold-heartedness—that stiff and mercenary formality—that tithing of mint, anise, and dill—that negligence of mercy, justice, truth, and the love of God, which stalked through the communions of sectarian altars—that apathy and indifference about '*thus saith the Lord*'—that zeal for human prescriptions, and above all, that willing ignorance of the sayings and doings of Jesus Christ and his apostles, which so generally appeared, first of all created, fostered, and matured my distrust in the reformed systems of evangelical sectaries."

When Mr. Campbell commenced his labors, the state of Protestant Christendom was not such as the pious heart might desire. In all communions there were obvious, acknowledged, and grievous evils. The comparative inefficacy of all the means employed for the moral renovation of men was but too manifest. All good men united with the devout Psalmist in the desire, "Oh, let the wickedness of the wicked come to an end!" But did these evils in the churches spring from "*experiences before baptism ?*" Did the requiring of experiences preparatory to baptism and church fellowship crowd Christianity out of the churches, by introducing "multitudes of prayerless, saintless, Christless, joyless hearts ?" Or did these evils originate in the moral corruption of human nature, and the deteriorating tendencies of a world enslaved by sin ? A large majority of the evangelical churches did not require "experiences before baptism ;" what "crowded Christianity" out of them ? There were great and deplorable evils in the churches gathered and instructed by the apostles—and that too before they closed their ministry—did "experiences before baptism" produce them ? The truth is, nothing could be more unfair, unphilosophical, and deceptive, than to reason as Mr. Campbell did. He had, in some respects, an easy task before him. It demanded but little research or labor to detect, publish, and magnify the evils in the various Christian communions. All these evils Mr. Campbell boldly and confidently ascribed, without discrimination, fairness, or qualification, to "sectarian bigotry," "popular Christianity," "evangelical orthodoxy," or "*experiences before baptism.*" With equal zeal and assurance, he proclaimed that the sovereign remedy for all these evils, was a return to the "Ancient Gospel,"—not as it had been received and practised by the wise and good of every land, but as it was understood and interpreted at Bethany. Many saw and deplored these evils, earnestly desired their correction, and embraced the Bethany exposition of the Gospel that their wishes might be realized. Churches were organized according to the "ancient order of things," from which there is no danger that Christianity will be crowded out by "experiences before baptism." The public have had an opportunity of comparing the fruits of the Reformation with the fruits of "the far-famed tree of evangelical orthodoxy." It is not proper to anticipate what it is proposed to state in another part of this work; but I will mention a single fact. A few years ago, one of the earliest, most intelligent, and devoted of the friends of the "ancient order of things," said candidly, that *the Reformation had not proved as perfect in practise as it was in theory.*

Some extracts having been given from the writings of Mr. Campbell, as specimens of his manner of treating experimental religion, it is proper that he should have the benefit of his apology for the severity of his style.

"The reader," he says, "may perhaps think that we speak too irreverently of the practice and of the experience of many Christians. We have no such intention. But there are many things when told or represented just as they are, which appear so strange, and, indeed, fanciful, that the mere relation of them assumes an air of irony." Chn. Bap., 141., Note.

Whether the defense mends the matter, the reader must judge for himself. Another, if not a better, apology for Mr. Campbell's course may be suggested. If he was really convinced that "orthodox Christian experiences" were, as he represented them, Christless, graceless and senseless—an artificial despondency cured by noxious opiates—then, perhaps, no apology was necessary. We can only lament that a man of his conceded abilities should have had his judgment so sadly perverted—by no matter what baleful influence.

As it is proposed, in another part of this volume, to examine particularly the principles of Campbellism, I shall in this chapter merely glance at *those which distinguished this period of the Reformation.* It has been already observed, that the teaching of Mr. Campbell, through the columns of the Christian Baptist, was negative rather than positive—was intended to overthrow, and bring into disrepute the popular theology, rather than to develope any peculiar religious principles. The current teachings of all the prevailing Christian sects, whether oral, or written, whether in creeds, sermons, expositions of the Scriptures, or any other form, were deemed by him, and his admirers, vain speculations, philosophical subtleties, or orthodox nonsense. Gradually, and slowly, however, his doctrinal peculiarities began to be evolved. Having referred to the periodicals and other works, which advocated his peculiar principles, he wrote—

"The CHRISTIAN BAPTIST in *seven* annual volumes, being the first of these publications, and affording such a *gradual* development of these principles as the state of the public mind and the opposition would permit, is, in the judgment of many of our brethren, who have expressed themselves on the subject, better adapted to the whole community as it now exists, than our other writings." Chn. Sys., p. 10.

Whether Mr. Campbell did not express his doctrinal views clearly, or with uniformity; or whether his opponents were unable, or unwilling to comprehend his meaning, need not now to be decided. I certainly have never known a religious teacher whose views were involved in so much mist and uncertainty. From his writings might be culled passages, which would satisfy the most strenuous advocates of orthodoxy in respect to his soundness in the faith; and from the same pages, other passages which seemed to threaten the very foundation of evangelical Christianity. By some he was charged with holding the most pestilential errors; and by others he was considered the ablest uninspired expounder of the Christian faith. It began to be apparent, however, that there were serious discordances between his doctrinal views and those entertained by evangelical Christians, and especially the

Baptists, with whom he was particularly connected. These differences had reference to faith, repentance, regeneration, the remission of sins, the influence of the Holy Spirit, and other points of minor importance. He was understood to teach and maintain that faith is a simple persuasion that Jesus is the Messiah, which demands no influence of the Holy Spirit to incline the mind to its exercise—that repentance is a reformation of life—that regeneration is identical with baptism—that the remission of sins is enjoyed only through baptism—and that the Holy Spirit is bestowed only on the baptized. On no point, perhaps, did his teaching give such general dissatisfaction as in regard to the influence of the Holy Spirit in the moral renovation of man. The Baptists, in common with other orthodox Christians, held this doctrine to be of vital importance. His teaching on the subject was, or to many it seemed to be evasive, contradictory, unsound, and of pernicious tendency. The reader will perceive in the following quotation the spirit and influence of his writings on this solemn and important subject.

"I read, some time since, of a revival in the state of New York, in which the Spirit of God was represented as being abundantly poured out on Presbyterians, Methodists, and Baptists. I think the converts in the order of the names were about three hundred Presbyterians, three hundred Methodists, and two hundred and eighty Baptists. On the principles of Bellamy, Hopkins, and Fuller, these being all regenerated without any knowledge of the Gospel, there is no difficulty in accounting for their joining different sects. The spirit did not teach the Presbyterians to believe that 'God had foreordained whatsoever comes to pass;' nor the Methodists to deny it. He did not teach the Presbyterians and the Methodists that infants were members of the church, and to be baptized; nor the Baptists to deny it. But on the hypothesis of the Apostle James, viz: 'Of his own will begat he us by the word of truth.' I think it would be difficult to prove that the Spirit of God had any thing to do with the aforesaid revival." Chn. Bap., 50.

By some persons Mr. Campbell was suspected, and charged with leaning toward *Unitarianism*. For this impression I have never found any good ground. In his zeal to introduce what he termed "a pure speech," he rejected the words "Trinity," and "Trinitarianism," and also some notions, more or less prevalent, concerning the Trinity; but so far as I can discover, he clearly and uniformly maintained the doctrine of Christ's Godhead, and the vicarious and expiatory nature of his sufferings.

It is unnecessary to pursue this subject much farther. It is not my purpose to point out all the sentiments and practices among evangelical Christians which incurred his displeasure, and provoked his animadversions. The war was as general as it was fierce and relentless. Nothing was so venerable, so sacred, and so important, in the estimation of others, or so strongly entrenched in popular favor, as to shield it from his attacks. Objects, in themselves confessedly good, were denounced because they were pursued with sectarian zeal, and for sectarian purposes. In all the pages of the Christian Baptist it will be difficult to find a sentence commendatory of any institution, plan, custom, labor or interest of Christendom, apart from his own cherished Reformation.

CAMPBELLISM IN ITS FORMATION.

Various causes contributed to augment the influence of Mr. Campbell, to diffuse his peculiar notions, and to facilitate the progress of his Reformation. His information, self-command, boldness, and indomitable ardor, eminently fitted him to lead a party. His temperament, intellectual habits, and aspirations were all adapted to impel him to abandon the beaten track of thought and labor, and to impart to his writings and preaching the charm of novelty. His views might not be scriptural, or wise, or important; but they were, at least, uncommon—and this was sufficient to render them acceptable to a certain class of minds. By his fearless and forcible defense of the distinctive sentiments of the Baptists, in his debates with Messrs. Walker and McCalla, he secured extensively the confidence and esteem of the denomination. They were proud to acknowledge him as the bold and puissant champion of their cause—and they made the acknowledgment with more pleasure, because he had risen up suddenly, and in a quarter least ex-

2

pected. They were, therefore, ready to pay not only a candid but a confiding regard to anything he might publish. His ability and prowess as a public extempore debater, had given him a prestige most favorable to his influence and success. His opponents too, with few exceptions, unwittingly promoted the Reformation. Instead of an open, manly and resolute discussion of the objectionable points in his scheme; they carried on a petty warfare, censuring frequently without discrimination, wasting their resources in the discussion of trifles, and always ready to retreat at the first appearance of serious danger. I do not intend to reflect on the motives, or abilities, of the excellent fathers who early participated in the discussion of Campbellism—they pursued the course to which their judgment or their circumstances led them—but Mr. Campbell was too adroit an opponent not to interpret their guerrilla warfare as a proof of his invincibility, and the soundness of the cause which he had espoused.

His opposition to sectarianism has been already mentioned; and from this opposition, he not only brought on himself much reproach, but derived a large measure of his strength and influence. On the subject of sectarianism, his logic was precisely that which every quack employs to bring his nostrums into use. He expatiates earnestly on the inefficiency of the regular medical practice. There are some diseases for which physicians have no remedy; for many others their prescriptions are sadly and confessedly unsuccessful; and, in not a few cases, their drugs have proved pernicious. Physicians of the greatest wisdom and experience have lamented the imperfection of medical science, and the uncertainty of the healing art. These evils and admissions are paraded and duly magnified before the public, by the empiric, who proclaims his certified sovereign panacea, while the credulous, and those who have despaired of aid from science, are caught by the specious artifice. The evils of sectarianism were obvious and confessed. The division of Protestant Christendom into numerous rival sects, spending their time, wasting their energies, embittering their spirits, and affording sport for their adversaries, by their subtle and profitless controversies, has long been its reproach, its curse, and its blight. It is an evil second in magnitude only to the religious uniformity, which, resembling the quiet of the cemetery, is the offspring of bigoted and intolerant despotism. Of course, in these remarks, reference is had to the evils growing out of the condition of the Christian world. The mischiefs of sectarianism were delineated by Mr. Campbell, certainly, with no fear of exaggeration. All its legitimate evils were charged upon it; and many which with equal plausibility might have been ascribed to other causes. From all these evils he promised a certain and speedy deliverance. The "ancient Gospel," or the Gospel as expounded at Bethany, was a remedy for all these disorders. The plan of relief was perfectly simple. Nothing was necessary to abolish sectarianism, and its bitter fruits, and so secure the perfect union of all Christians, but the belief of *one fact*—that Jesus is the Messiah ; submission to *one institution*—immersion, for the remission of sins ; and a steady conformity to the apostles' doctrine. The scheme was defective, visionary, and utterly inefficacious ; but it was plausible—it promised relief from evils seen, felt and lamented—it seemed to be the only prospect for relief presented—and many, cheated by the illusion, gladly embraced it.

Another cause which favored the progress of the reformation was the prevalence of hyper-Calvinistic, or antinomian views in many Baptist churches. Having adopted, in its main points, the Calvinian theology, they were led by their system into speculations as unpopular as they were sterile. To free them from objections and render them acceptable to their auditors, the pastors spent a large portion of the time devoted to pulpit labors in their discussion ; and what occupied so much of their thought grew into most exaggerated importance in their estimation. They seemed to think that they were called to the ministry for no other purpose than to proclaim and vindicate a few abstruse and barren points of the Calvinistic creed ; but their ministry, excepting to a few indoctrinated zealots, was not pleasing. The people generally becoming disgusted with such dry, and unsatisfying speculations, were ready to attend on any ministry which promised them a more palatable, if not a more nutritious diet. In churches of this sort Mr. Campbell found his way prepared before him.

His opposition to Christian missions, and other benevolent enterprizes, gained him many friends. The antinomian Baptists were, almost without exception, hostile to all combined and self-denying efforts among Christians for spreading the knowledge of the Gospel—a hostility derived, in part, from their peculiar doctrinal opinions, and, it seems not uncharitable to judge, in part, from their covetousness. They were delighted to find that they had in Mr. Campbell, a champion in their cause, so zealous and distinguished ; and, though their doctrinal sentiments were antipodal to his, yet this agreement on a very important point, as they deemed it, disposed them to pass the most favorable judgment on him, and his system. Nor was this pleasure limited to antinomian Baptists. Mr. Campbell's ridicule of missions, and kindred efforts, was too much in harmony with the selfishness of human nature, and the money-loving propensity of the age, not to awaken sympathy, and call forth admiration. An intelligent correspondent of the Christian Baptist thus addressed him : "My dear sir, you have begun wrong, if your object is reformation. Never attack the principle which multiplies the number of Bibles, or which promotes the preaching of the Gospel, or the support of it, if you desire Christianity to prevail. As I informed you when here, I repeat it again, your opposition to a preached Gospel, to the preachers and Bible societies, secures to you the concurrence of the covetous, the ignorant, the prayerless and Christless Christians. Should they have had any religion, they cease to enjoy it as soon as they embrace your views." Chn. Bap., 70.

Mr. Campbell's opposition to the clergy had much to do with the progress of the Reformation. Ministers of the Gospel have in all ages and countries, and under all the names by which they have been distinguished, had to bear a large share of the "reproach of Christ." Whoever ridicules them, throws suspicion on their motives, or, in any way, undermines their influence, with whatever pretence, is sure to win the smiles, and receive the plaudits of a certain class of persons, among whom, it is sad to say, may be found professing Christians. Mr. Campbell was decidedly politic in his attacks on the clergy. While he denounced them, he flattered the people. They did not need to hire priests for their instruction—they could read and expound the Scriptures for themselves—every church had within itself the means of its own edification. These sentiments were too congenial to the independence and pride of human nature not to find a cordial reception. Many who had been content to be learners, after reading a few numbers of the Christian Baptist, were elated with the prospect of becoming teachers. A Reformation which promised to sink the aristocratic populars and to elevate the masses far above their former teachers, could not fail to secure the approval and support of those who confided in its professions.

I know not how much influence Mr. Campbell's teaching derived from its Scotch peculiarities, but I know it derived some. The Scotch are remarkable for the tenacity with which they adhere to their religious opinions. A Scotchman of my acquaintance, an intelligent and worthy man—finding that Mr. Campbell agreed with him in certain unimportant, but cherished opinions, in regard to which he differed from his brethren generally, was induced to pay a favorable attention to the "ancient Gospel," and finally to become its earnest advocate.

The chief means of spreading the peculiar views of the Bethany Reformer was the Christian Baptist, —a small, cheap periodical, whose circulation was constantly increasing. To their development and defense its pages were exclusively devoted. Almost all who read it were either disgusted with its spirit and sentiments, and spurned it from them, or being gradually brought under its influence, at length, enlisted under the banner of the Reformation Mr.

Campbell, in addition to his editorial, and other literary labors, frequently made long tours in Virginia, Kentucky and Ohio, every where proclaiming to crowded assemblies the principles of his Reformation. His sermons, or "orations," as he styled them, long, and sometimes tedious, were heard by some with disapprobation, by others with serious doubts as to their usefulness, and by others still with indifference ; yet, on the whole, they contributed much to diffuse the knowledge of his principles, promote the circulation of his periodical, and multiply the number of his friends.

Nor must it be forgotten in enumerating the causes which facilitated the progress of the Reformation, that Mr. Campbell taught many important truths ; exposed some serious evils ; furnished some striking expositions of Scripture passages, which, if not original, were new to his hearers ; and labored diligently to awaken an interest in the study of the Scriptures.

It has been already stated that it was not Mr. Campbell's purpose—certainly not his avowed purpose—to form a new sect, but to abolish all sects. If he did not perceive, he was the only intelligent observer of his course who did not perceive, its direct and inevitable tendency to produce that result. His spirit was eminently sectarian. What is sectarianism, but an undue confidence in the soundness of our views of Scripture truth, an excessive partiality for the party concurring with us in these views, and the lack of candor, tenderness, and forbearance towards those who dissent from them? When tried by this standard, no enlightened and unbiased reader of the *Christian Baptist* can doubt that Mr. Campbell's sectarianism was unmitigated. Within the wide range of Christian literature there cannot be found a work more intolerant, proscriptive, and caustic. Love is the very soul of piety, and the moving principle in every well-directed effort at reformation; and this principle will develop itself in gentle words, candid admissions, and a due regard to the feelings and motives of opponents, as well as in a faithful, earnest exhibition of divine truth. If Mr. Campbell's object was to avoid the formation of a new sect, his course was most impolitic. Instead of commending what was good, enduring minor evils, and kindly seeking to correct the serious errors in the different Christian sects; he censured their views and practices with little discrimination, and unsparing causticity, proclaiming that they were all in Babylon, and their religion not much better than paganism; and justified his severity by the example of Luther in contending against the Papists, and of Christ in condemning the Scribes and Pharisees. Never did any leader more perfectly succeed in infusing his own spirit into his followers, than did Mr. Campbell. With not a tithe of his genius, learning, or information, they did not yield to him a hair-breadth, in the strength of their conviction, that their new religious views were Scriptural. Many of them were almost in an ecstacy that having been so long in the darkness of Babylon, a light, so effulgent and vivifying, should have suddenly shined upon them. A shadow of suspicion that, after all, they might misinterpret the Scriptures seemed never to have darkened their minds. A fact may serve to illustrate their spirit. A girl of my acquaintance, still in her teens, quite illiterate, and possessing no uncommon genius, had been immersed for the remission of sins. On meeting her, I found that she had entered fully into the spirit of the Reformation. I inquired of her, whether she was satisfied that her new views were correct. She replied, "I can't be wrong—I follow the Book." I answered, "I acknowledge that the Bible is an infallible guide; but I am not quite certain that you are an infallible interpreter of it." Our conversation was continued for some time, and I could not, by any argument or appeal, extort from her the confession that she might possibly misinterpret the Scriptures. "I follow the Book, and can't be deceived," was her unchanged reply. I remember a similar case. A Reformer invited me to his house for the ostensible purpose of seeing his sick wife, but for the real purpose, as it appeared, of affording me an opportunity of learning the principles of the Reformation. He could not read, but had a young daughter, who entered fully into his spirit and views, that was more fortunate in this respect, than her father. The Reformer called on his daughter to read certain portions of Scripture which had been selected for the occasion, and she complied with an air and manner which indicated how deeply she thought I was indebted for her kindness. He then commenced an oration, to which I listened without reply, and without a smile, though I found it difficult to maintain my gravity, until, my edification having ceased, I abruptly took my leave. I should not deem it proper to mention these particular cases, were I not satisfied that all acquainted with the early history of Campbellism will perceive in them life-like portraitures of many, not all—for some were modest, courteous, and dignified—of the primitive Reformers. I greatly misjudge if the early disciples of Mr. Campbell, (I do not use the phrase opprobriously,) were not, for the most part, restive, contentious, and factious. How could they be otherwise? They read the Christian Baptist, had strong confidence in the wisdom and piety of its editor, imbibed its spirit, adopted its principles, clothed themselves with the armor which it furnished, entered heartily into all the schemes which it advocated for the destruction of creeds, the overthrow of the clergy, the arrest of benevolent operations, and, in short, the "restoration of the ancient order of things" set up, or brought to light at Bethany; and aimed to a, prove themselves worthy followers of an illustrious and undaunted leader.

The Baptists, at least in Virginia, were unprepared for the conflict which came upon them. Their pastors, mostly plain men, with limited education, and earnest piety, had restricted their public instructions to the fundamental principles of Christianity, and were unfitted by their lack of early training, and by their confirmed habits, for polemic discussions. The members of the churches had inherited their religious opinions from the fathers of an earlier period, and held them sincerely without a suspicion that they could be controverted. They received the Bible in the common version, as their creed, and read it, mainly to be comforted by its promises, and guided by its precepts, not doubting that all their doctrinal views were clearly contained in it. It were useless to maintain that the Baptists were faultless in the controversy. They sinned far less than they were sinned against, but they were not without sin. They sometimes judged when they should have investigated, condemned when they should have debated, resorted to the exercise of authority when they should have used kind persuasion, and failed to distinguish between the factious and the misled.

In the year 1832, events were drawing to a crisis in the Baptist denomination in Virginia and some of the Western States. A party had been formed in the churches, respectable for their number, and quite formidable by the aggressive spirit which actuated them. They adopted the peculiar sentiments and practices advocated by Mr. Campbell in the Christian Baptist, and its successor, the Millennial Harbinger. They styled themselves *Reformers*, but by their opponents, they were styled *Campbellites*. They were exceedingly active in making converts, and in numbering and marshalling their forces. In this state of things it was impossible but that strife, irritations, alienations, and divisions must ensue. Mr. Campbell had for several years been sowing the seed of sectarianism, and now he was about to reap the harvest.

What was to be done in this crisis? The Reformers, with Mr. Campbell at their head, were violently opposed to separation from the Baptists, and were ready, to a man, to fight for peace. It can hardly be doubted that this desire of union sprang from policy rather than love. They were willing to remain for a time in Babylon, that they might extricate others from its smoke, vassalage, and degradation. Knowing themselves to be in a hopeless minority, they were desirous to be permitted to avail themselves of Baptist pulpits and presses for the propagation of their principles. But a division was inevitable. It existed in fact—a division in sentiment, affection, interest, and aim—and it only remained to be carried out in form.

Had the churches a *right* to expel the Reformers?

The power of expelling factious and disorderly members seems to be indispensable to the purity, peace, and prosperity of the churches, and this power is distinctly conferred in the Scriptures. "Now, I beseech you, brethren, mark them which cause divisions and offences contrary to the doctrine which ye have learned; and avoid them." Rom xvi. 27. It is true, the Reformers maintained that their teachings and efforts were in harmony with the apostolic doctrine—indeed, that their chief object was to restore that long-lost doctrine—but Christ had solemnly devolved on the churches to which the innovators belonged, the duty of deciding these points. Their decision might be wise or unwise—might be dictated by sectarian bigotry, or an honest and enlightened regard to truth—but on them devolved, by divine appointment, the duty and responsibility of making it; and from their decision there was, according to their established polity—a polity approved by the Reformers—no appeal. That there are occasions which call for the exercise of this right on the part of churches, none can deny. Members may adopt principles so utterly at war with the Gospel, evince a spirit so repugnant to the spirit of Christ, and pursue a course so manifestly factious and schismatic, as to leave no doubt of the propriety of their expulsion from church fellowship.

Whether the churches should exercise their authority in putting the Reformers out of their communion, was a question environed with difficulties—a question involving alike the rights of individuals and of churches—the maintenance of truth and order—and the prosperity of the Redeemer's cause. There were grave and weighty reasons against the separation. A schism in the churches was greatly to be deprecated. Many of the Reformers were good men—converted and trained up among the Baptists—adopting Mr. Campbell's views only in part, and imbibing his spirit in widely different measures—from whom it was painful to separate. A division could not take place without giving rise to perplexing questions concerning the right of property, and greatly increasing the strife and irritation already prevailing, to the mortification of the godly, and the reproach of Christianity. To these considerations must be added, that however sound the reasons for their exclusion, the Reformers would not fail, by the cry of persecution, to enlist the sympathies of a party in their favor, and to bring odium on their opposers. On the other hand, the reasons for a separation were overwhelming. In many churches, the parties had taken their grounds, and in the constant, earnest, and painful strife about the Reformation, the true ends of church fellowship were almost forgotten The Reformed ministers were zealous in disseminating their principles in all the churches to which they could gain access, and baptizing into their new faith such converts as they could find or make, not only in their own congregations, but in those of non-Reforming pastors. Meetings of the Reformers were called and held to promote the interests of the Reformation. With this Reformation the Baptists had no sympathy, believing it to be pugnacious in spirit, unsound in theory, and barren in the fruits of piety. It was utterly impossible that parties, so discordant in views, so alienated in affection, and of such opposite aims, should dwell together in unity. To perpetuate the union, under such circumstances, was to perpetuate strife, and heart-burnings, and entail on the churches inefficiency and ruin. Moreover, the principles advocated by the Reformers, were deemed by the Baptists to be, not only erroneous, but of pernicious influence, and such as they could not countenance without recreancy to the cause of Christ.

It is not proposed to furnish a history of the painful separation which took place between the Reformers and Baptists in several of the Southern, and most of the Western States. The details of the event would fill a large volume. Every association and every church infected with Campbellism has its peculiar history. The conflict was, in many respects, everywhere the same—maintained with the same spirit, carried on with the same weapons, and producing the same results, differing, however, widely in degree its details being in no two places the same. Here the hottest contest was in the association—there in the churches; here the Baptists were in the majority, ejecting the Reformers, and retaining possession of the property—there the Reformers were in the ascendant, and the Baptists under the necessity of relinquishing their interest in the property, and withdrawing from the communion of the Reformers; here the battle was fierce, and the separation was attended with painful exasperation—there mild counsel prevailed, and the division occurred in a gentler and more forbearing spirit.

As a specimen of the course pursued by other bodies, I will give a sketch of the action of the Dover Association—then the largest association of Baptists in the world—in regard to Campbellism; and I select this because I happen to be best acquainted with it. In the autumn of 1832, this body convened at Four-Mile Creek meeting-house, in Henrico County, Va., not far from the city of Richmond. The Reformation excitement had reached its height. Several of the churches belonging to the body had been split asunder, and others were in a distracted and unhappy condition. All eyes were turned to the Association for advice in this time of trial. The judicious and venerable R. B. Semple, so long the Moderator of the Association, was absent, having recently been called to his reward. The subject which had caused such painful anxiety, was referred to a select committee, consisting of Elders John Kerr, James B. Taylor, Peter Ainslie,

J. B. Jeter, and Philip Montague. The committee in due time made the following report:

"The select committee appointed to consider and report 'what ought to be done in reference to the new doctrines and practices which have disturbed the peace and harmony of some of the churches composing this association,' met at the house of Elder Miles Turpin, and having invited and obtained the aid and counsel of Elders Andrew Broaddus, Eli Ball, John Micou, William Hill, Miles Turpin, and brother Erastus T. Montague, after due deliberation, respectfully report the following preamble and resolution for the consideration and adoption of the association.

"This association having been from its origin, blessed with uninterrupted harmony, and a high degree of religious prosperity, has seen with unspeakable regret, within a few years past, the spirit of speculation, controversy and strife, growing up among some of the ministers and churches within its bounds. This unhappy state of things has evidently been produced by the preaching, and writings of Alexander Campbell, and his adherents. After having deliberately and prayerfully examined the doctrines held, and propagated by them, and waited long to witness their practical influence on the churches, and upon society in general, we are thoroughly convinced that they are doctrines not according to godliness, but subversive of the true spirit of the Gospel of Jesus Christ—disorganizing and demoralizing in their tendency ; and, therefore, ought to be disavowed and resisted, by all the lovers of truth and sound piety.

"It is needless to specify, and refute the errors held and taught by them ; this has been often done, and as often have the doctrines, quoted from their writings, been denied, with the declaration that they have been misrepresented or misunderstood. If after more than seven years' investigation, the most pious and intelligent men in the land are unable to understand what they speak and write, it surely is an evidence of some radical defect in the things taught, or in the mode of teaching them. Their views of sin, faith, repentance, regeneration, baptism, the agency of the Holy Spirit, church government, the Christian ministry, and the whole scheme of Christian benevolence, are, we believe, contrary to the plain letter and spirit of the New Testament of our Lord and Saviour.

" By their practical influence, churches long blessed with peace and prosperity, have been thrown into wrangling and discord—principles long held sacred by the best and most enlightened men that ever lived or died, are villified and ridiculed as 'school divinity,' 'sectarian dogmas,' &c. Ministers, who have counted all things but loss, for the excellency of the knowledge of Christ Jesus, are reprobated, and denounced as 'visionary dreamers,' 'mystifiers,' 'blind leaders of the blind,' 'hireling priests,' &c., &c. The church in which many of them live, and from which they call it persecution to be separated, is held up to public scorn as 'Babylon the mother of harlots, and abominations of the earth.' The most opprobrious epithets are unsparingly applied to principles which we think clearly taught in the Word of God, and which we hold dear to our hearts. While they arrogate to themselves the title of 'Reformers,' it is lamentably evident, that no sect in Christendom needs reformation more than they do.

"While they boast of superior light and knowledge, we cannot but lament, in their life and conversation, the absence of that 'wisdom that is from above, which is first pure, then peaceable, gentle, and easy to be entreated, full of mercy and good fruits, without partiality, and without hypocrisy.' In fine, the writings of Alexander Campbell, and the spirit and manner of those who profess to admire his writings and sentiments, appear to us remarkably destitute of 'the mind that was in Christ Jesus,' of that divine love 'which suffereth long, and is kind, envieth not, vaunteth not itself, is not puffed up, doth not behave itself unseemly, seeketh not her own, is not easily provoked, thinketh no evil.' Wherever these writings and sentiments have to any extent, been introduced into our churches, the spirit of hypercriticism, 'vain janglings and strife about words to no profit, but to the subverting of the hearers,' have chilled the spirit of true devotion, and put an end to Christian benevolence and harmony.

"If the opprobrious epithets, and bitter denunci ations, so liberally heaped upon us by Mr. Campbell and his followers, are deserved, they as pious and honorable men can not desire to live in communion with us; and if they are undeserved, and designedly slanderous, this of itself would forbid our holding them in Christian fellowship. If, indeed, they have found the long lost key of knowledge, and are the only persons, since the days of the apostles, who have entered and explored the divine arcanum, it is due to themselves—to purblind Christendom—to the world—to truth—to God, that they should, in obedience to the divine command, clothed in the shining garments of truth and righteousness, walk out of 'Babylon,' and concentrating their light, exhibit a true sample of the 'ancient order of things;' and diffuse around them a blaze of 'love, joy, peace, long-suffering, gentleness, goodness, faith, meekness, temperance.' Until they do this, grave and thinking men will doubt their high pretentions, for 'by their fruits ye shall know them.' It would seem that conscientious, unobtrusive, holy men, whose hearts are sickened with the depravity of the times, and who mourn a sad and general departure from truth and holiness, would voluntarily come out from 'the present corrupt order of things,' and holding sweet communion with one another, and with their God, let their light so shine that others seeing their good works, might be induced to glorify their Father in heaven ; but, alas ! they appear to be a strange anti-sectarian, dogmatical sect, who live only in the fire of strife and controversy, and seek to remain in connexion with the existing churches, that they may with the greater facility obtain materials for feeding the disastrous flame.

"In every aspect of the case then, a separation is indispensably necessary. The cause of truth and righteousness requires it—the best interests of all the parties concerned demand it.

"We, therefore, the assembled ministers, and delegates of the Dover Association, after much prayerful deliberation, do hereby affectionately recommend to the churches in our connection, to separate from their communion all such persons as are promoting controversy and discord, under the specious name of 'Reformers.' That the line of distinction may be clearly drawn, so that all who are concerned may understand it, we feel it our duty to declare, that whereas Peter Ainslie, John Du Val, Mathew W. Webber, Thos. M. Henley, John Richards, and Dudley Atkinson, ministers within the bounds of this Association, have voluntarily assumed the name of 'Reformers,' in its party application, by attending a meeting publicly advertised for that party; and by communing with, and otherwise promoting the views of the members of that party, who have been separated from the fellowship and communion of regular Baptist churches—therefore

"*Resolved*, That this Association cannot consistently, and conscientiously receive them, nor any other ministers maintaining their views, as members of their body; nor can they in future act in concert with any church, or churches, that may encourage or countenance their ministrations."

This preamble and resolution, prepared by Elder John Kerr, pastor of the First Baptist church in the city of Richmond, was approved by all the members of the committee, excepting Mr. Ainslie, who was a Reformed preacher, and named among those, whose excision was proposed by the report, and also by all the brethren whose counsel was sought by the committee. The report was adopted by the association, without discussion, and with few dissentients. The delegates had been selected and sent to the meeting for the purpose of adopting, if practicable, effective measures for allaying the pernicious excitement in the churches and were prepared to act promptly and decidedly Their action, whether wise or unwise, was adopted after careful deliberation, earnest prayer for divine guidance, and with much anxiety for its result, and it received the cordial approbation of the churches.

It was not to be expected that the decision of the association would be acceptable to Mr. Campbell, and the Reformers. They viewed themselves as the objects of a most unchristian and cruel persecution. Mr. Campbell stigmatized the report, adopted by the association, as the "Dover Decree," and thus discoursed of it in the Millennial Harbinger, Vol. 3, page 573.

"What a dangerous matter it has become, to think differently from Messrs. Kerr, Ball, Broaddus, and Erastus Montague! How perilous to view sin, faith, baptism, &c., differently from these 'keepers of the faith' of Virginia. This alone exposes a person to the greatest anathema in the power of Virginia Baptists. They can do no more in Virginia, as yet, than treat a dissentient as they would a murderer, or a vile adulterer. The committee or managers of the *bull* of excommunication, can neither banish, burn, nor imprison those who differ from their views of sin, faith, and baptism. There is no Patmos, jail, or pillory known in Virginia law, for those who think differently from John Kerr or Eli Ball. But they can place Peter Ainslie, John Du Val, M. B. Webber, T. M. Henley, John Richards, and Dudley Atkinson in the same society, as respects the Lord's table, with all the inmates of the penitentiary, now under the care of my friend Col. C. S. Morgan; yes, they can tell all the sects in Virginia, that they view these virtuous and exemplary men as unfit for the communion of Eli Ball and John Kerr, as were the infamous actors in the Southampton insurrection. We ask what difference have they made? What more could they do than exclude such from the kingdom of heaven? and do they not teach that the kingdom of heaven is theirs? If they think that what they have bound on earth is bound in heaven, where stand these anathematized preachers? Are they blotted out of the book of life? But perhaps they will say, that what they have loosed on earth in the house of Miles Turpin, is not loosed in heaven! Nor can they pray to the Lord to ratify in heaven what they have done on earth! What a farce this is! And how will they answer to the Lord for casting out of his church on earth (as they call the Dover Association) those whom they have every reason to think are esteemed as much the children of God as themselves?"

Many other things of like spirit and quality did Mr. Campbell pen and publish; and his adherents echoed and re-echoed his denunciations of the Dover Association, with most vehement zeal. Had they been fined, imprisoned, scourged, outlawed, branded, and exposed to a terrible martyrdom, they could not have made a greater outcry against their shameless and cruel persecutions, than they did for being put out of the communion of churches, which, in the ardor of their zeal for Reformation, they had often pronounced to be priest-ridden, corrupt, and in Babylon. They gloried in being, as they supposed, martyrs in the cause of truth and righteousness. Thus writes one of the excinded preachers—

"The long agony is over. The Dover Association has assumed the awful responsibility of producing a faction; consequently, a sect. We feel much relieved as respects ourselves. Only three or four of the Reformers attended the Association, as we had no objection to being a separate people, if the Baptists were resolved on taking to themselves this act of rebellion against Jesus Christ our Lord. I venture to say, no intelligent friend of Reform is displeased with it. *For myself, I feel highly honored in being made the first martyr in old Virginia in the present Reformation.* My Christian character has been gibbeted (though yet I live) for adhering to the sayings and doings of Jesus Christ and his apostles. *Philip Montague* has conferred this honor upon me. It is the highest I ever expect to enjoy in time—worth all the D.D.'s that ever were issued from all the seminaries in the world." Mill. Har., vol. 4, p. 13.

More than twenty years have passed since the Dover Association adopted the report of its committee condemning Campbellism. Let us now endeavor to take a calm and candid review of the measure. The report contained some unguarded and unnecessarily harsh expressions. Its author, whose temperament was naturally ardent, had been greatly annoyed and excited by the prevalence of Mr. Campbell's peculiar views in the church of which he was pastor, and the secession of a large and respectable party adopting them, from the main body. The report was evidently written under the influence of this excitement ; and the committee and the Association partook too much of the same feeling, to scan the document with severity. The doctrines taught by Mr. Campbell were declared to be "*demoralizing* in their tendency ;" and of the party embracing them, it was affirmed that "*no sect* in Christendom needed reformation *more* than they." On calm reflection, these expressions were generally admitted to be unjust. Whatever may be the ultimate influence of Campbellism on piety and morals, it must be conceded, that it gives no countenance to immorality. And while it can hardly be denied that the party embracing the system needed reformation, it is but fair to admit that there are Christian sects which need it "*more* than they." These expressions were subsequently expunged or modified by the Association. The amiable and clear-headed Moderator of the Association, the Rev. A. Broaddus, who undertook the vindication of the report from what he deemed the "unfair representation" of it by Mr. Campbell, made the following admission—

"In the report of the committee, (drafted by the chairman) there are some few expressions which, in my view, might have been advantageously omitted, or exchanged for others ; the instrument might thus have retained all its force, without any tinge of acrimony or harshness."

Let us now examine the other side of the case. Mr. Campbell and his friends maintained that the Association in its action not only transgressed the law of Christ, infringed the religious liberty of individuals, and were guilty of flagrant persecution, but plainly transcended its constitutional authority. It had no right, it must be conceded, to interfere in the government or discipline of the churches. It was simply an *advisory council.* It possessed the unquestioned and unquestionable right of *advising* the churches in all matters pertaining to their peace and prosperity. This right the members of the Association exercised, in an important matter, to the best of their judgment, and at the earnest request of the churches. They did not counsel hastily, nor without deliberation, nor without a deep sense of their responsibility to Christ, nor without prayer for divine guidance. Their advice was in the following words—" We, therefore, the assembled ministers and delegates, of the Dover Association, after much prayerful deliberation, do hereby affectionately recommend to the churches in our connection, to separate from their communion, all such persons as are promoting controversy and discord, under the specious name of Reformers." They might err in the counsel which they gave, but so might their opponents in judging of it. The churches might receive or reject their advice at pleasure. The Association had no power to enforce its counsel, except moral power. Thus far its action certainly did not exceed the limit of its admitted authority. But the ministers and delegates of the Association declared that they could not "consistently and conscientiously receive" certain individuals named, "or any other ministers maintaining their views, as members of their body." The Association had the admitted authority, for such reasons as they deemed valid, to expel a church from the body. In naming certain ministers, with whom in future they could not consent to co-operate, they did not exclude them from the churches of which they were respectively members, nor interfere with the discipline of those churches; but simply announced to the churches, that believing these ministers to be unsound in doctrine, and their labors and influence subversive of the harmony and prosperity of the churches, they would exercise their constitutional authority in excluding from their fellowship such churches as should continue to "countenance their ministrations." The design of the Association was to draw clearly "a line of distinction" between themselves and the Reformers; and the measure adopted was admirably suited to secure the object. In a very short time, and with less irritation than for several years had been existing, the parties were clearly separated.

It is proper to permit Rev. A. Broaddus, the most logical and formidable of Mr. Campbell's opponents, and one of the mildest and most courteous of controversialists, to vindicate the action of the Association, from the unfair representations, and severe animadversions contained in the Millennial Harbinger.

"But to the more particular object of this communication—the light in which Mr. Campbell has endeavored to place the conduct of the Association, in adopting this measure. Let us hear him. 'They can do nothing more in Virginia, as yet, than treat a dissentient as they would a murderer or a vile adulterer. The committee, or managers of the *bull* of excommunication, can neither banish, burn, nor imprison those who differ from their views of sin, faith, and baptism. There is no Patmos, jail, or pillory, known in Virginia law, for those who think differently,' &c.

"Now, I really should wonder, if it were not that something similar had been intimated at other times—I really should wonder—yea, and still I cannot help wondering—that Mr. *Campbell* did not think this beneath him! this politic resort—this most unfair and injurious attempt to enlist the prejudices of his readers against the Association, by charging them, as he obviously does, by implication, with a disposition to persecute those who differ from them;—to persecute them even to imprisonment, to exile, and to death ;—restrained only by the want of power from inflicting these punishments ! Such is the construction which every candid and intelligent reader must put on his expressions ; and on every candid and intelligent reader, I now call, to judge of the force and validity of this charge.

"What is the ground of this charge ? Why, the Association has cut off 'these virtuous and exemplary men' from fellowship in our body : *ergo*, the Association would imprison, banish, or burn them, if the power were not wanting ! This then is the position which arises from such reasoning :—A declaration of non-fellowship is sufficient proof of a disposition to imprison, banish or kill ! This, I say, is the position resulting from a charge established on such ground ; and on the same ground, no ingenuity of man can fairly make out, how the act of exclusion can be performed by a church, without incurring the same charge. The principle assumed is the same in every case, and thus, when we exclude from fellowship, we do of course give evidence of a disposition to imprison, to banish, to burn ; and then, to sanction exclusion from fellowship, is, in effect, to sanction the popish excommunication,—where the thunders of the Vatican are hurled at the head of the devoted victim, and temporal pains and punishments are inflicted on him.

"But I have one more argument on this case—the

argumentum ad hominem—or an argument applying to the assailant's own views. Reader, attend!

"Let us view the charge against the Association. They have gone as far as they could go. What then? Why, they would go much farther, it seems, if they had power. 'The committee, or managers of the *bull* of excommunication, can neither banish, burn, nor imprison those who differ from their views of sin, faith, and baptism:' which amounts to this: The Dover Association has passed a resolution of non-fellowship with the people called 'Reformers;' and therefore would imprison, banish or burn them, if they had the power. Now, mark well, I beseech you, reader, and see if the argument does not come home to Mr. Campbell in all its force. Mr. Campbell (be it remembered) is not an open communionist. Well; Mr. Campbell passed a resolution of non-fellowship with all Pædo-baptists: he has gone as far as he can; and therefore—what shall I say?—he has given evidence that he would imprison, banish, or burn them, if he had the power. 'But I don't believe it,' you say. Neither do I;—far from it! But is not the argumentum ad hominem fairly applied? What a pity it is that my friend could not have had charity enough to believe the committee, or the Association, might declare non-fellowship with people, whom they would neither burn, banish, nor imprison; nor indeed injure in any way whatever."

It is but justice to Mr. Campbell to note that in replying to this spirited vindication of the exscinding act of the Association, (of which only a part has been quoted,) he felt constrained to disavow the consequence so logically deduced by Mr. Broaddus from the expressions in the Millennial Harbinger. "In one word," said he, "I do not think that any of the Virginia Baptists would burn myself or brethren; but unless they would burn, or banish, or otherwise inflict civil penalties upon us, what more can they do than what they have done?" And, it may be asked, with equal pertinency, believing that the peace and prosperity of the churches demanded the exclusion of the Reformers from their fellowship, what *less* could they have done than they did do? They condemned the principles, and deplored the mischievous effects of the so-called "Reformation," and aimed, with as little irritation as possible, to produce the desired separation; but carefully abstained from any imputation on the moral character of the Reformers. If a few unguarded and acrimonious expressions escaped them, they might surely find an apology, if not a justification, in "the spirit that breathes, and words that burn" in the pages of the Christian Baptist and Millennial Harbinger.

Not long since a member was excluded from a Baptist church. He was a man of irreproachable moral character, but, having become a *Spiritualist*, as the believers in spirit rappings are called, he denied the inspiration of the Scriptures, human depravity, the divinity and atonement of Christ—in fine, all the distinctive principles of the Gospel. He claimed to be judged not by his opinions, but his works. "Not opinions, but *deeds*," he insisted, "should be the great test of character." Yet, he was expelled, and most righteously, from the fellowship of the church. Now, on the principle adopted by Mr. Campbell, this was rank persecution. "What a dangerous matter," the Spiritualist might plausibly, and in the language of Mr. Campbell, say, it is "to think differently from" the church. "Liberty, religious liberty, that liberty which alone deserves the name, . . . has expired in" it. "They can do no more . . as yet than treat a dissentient as they would a murderer or a vile adulterer. They can place 'me' in the same society, as respects the Lord's table, with all the inmates of the penitentiary ; . . . . yes, they can tell all the sects . . . that they view" me, though "virtuous and exemplary, . . as unfit for" their "communion as the infamous actors in the Southampton insurrection." Mill. Har., Vol. 3, p. 573.

The separation, though painful at first, afterwards tended to diminish the evils which had sprung from the controversy and strife produced by the Reformation. The parted combatants, finding fewer causes of exacerbation, soon began to lose the heat and violence created by the conflict. The Dover Association, though she lost several churches, and many respectable church members, continued her almost unimpeded course of prosperity and usefulness. Her losses were soon repaired; and even in congregations where the Reformation seemed to have acquired the greatest influence, her success was not long delayed. Meantime the Reformers enjoyed a privilege which without the separation they could not have enjoyed—the privilege of illustrating, by the loveliness of their spirit, the fervor of their devotion, the sanctity of their lives, their elevation above the world, and the success of their ministrations, the superiority of the "ancient Gospel" over sectarian dogmas and mystic theology—of the "ancient order of things" over the corruptions of Babylon—in short, the real value of that Reformation, whose pretensions were so lofty, whose spirit was so warlike, and whose influence among the sects was so exciting and painful.

Mr. Campbell now found himself at the head of a sect—yes, of a *sect*. The Reformers were a Sect according to the definition of Noah Webster:—"SECT—A body or number of persons united in tenets, chiefly in philosophy and religion, but constituting a distinct party by holding sentiments different from those of other men; a denomination." Did not the Reformers unite in maintaining certain religious tenets? and were they not distinguished by these sentiments from every other party? They were a sect in the Scripture sense of the term. The word "sect," or "heresy" as the Greek term "αἵρεσις," is rendered in the New Testament, signifies a party, or persons choosing and maintaining peculiar opinions. It was among the Jews, not a term of reproach, but of distinction. They called Christians a "sect," or party; and this sect they knew was every where spoken against. Acts 28 : 22. It must be added that the Reformers were a "sect" in the sense in which Mr. Campbell so frequently employed the term. They had all the attributes, and, eminently, the spirit of a sect. Their claim to be considered "*The Church*," and by eminence "*The Christian Church*," was as baseless, and far more preposterous, than the same claim vauntingly set forth by some older and more venerable, if not more worthy, sects. Did Christ have no church on earth from the commencement of the Romish apostacy till the beginning of the "current Reformation?"

Of this sect Mr. Campbell was the *head*—not by appointment, nor in form, but in fact, and by merit. His learning, zeal, energy and influence clearly marked him out for the position; and it was accorded to him without dissent, without envy, heartily, and almost unconsciously. The sect was the product of his own labor. It bore strikingly the impress of his own character. Not one among the

Reformers could encounter him in debate, nor resist the weight of his authority, nor add a beam to the light which he shed. His word was the law of the Reformation ; and it derived its force from the unwavering conviction among all the Reformers that it was in perfect harmony with the Word of God. From Maine to Georgia, and from the Atlantic coast to the Far West, the same words and phrases —"a pure speech"—" the language of Canaan"— were current among them ; and every portion of the circulating medium bore the unmistakable impress of the Bethany mint. Meet a Reformer, where you might, or under whatever circumstances, he would soon utter some peculiar word or phrase which would reveal to you, without doubt, his religious opinions, and party preference.

The churches organized, under the influence, and by the direction of Mr. Campbell, did not differ materially in form and discipline from the Baptist churches. Of course, the Babylonish practice of hearing experiences before baptism was repudiated ; and all persons applying for membership in these churches, or who could be persuaded to accept the privilege, were received promptly, on professing their belief that Jesus of Nazareth is the Messiah, and on being immersed for the remission of sins. Every church had a plurality of bishops, or elders, chosen from its own body ; and its government soon passed from the hands of the brotherhood to those of the eldership, with limitations, into which I need not stop to inquire. The churches met for worship and edification every Lord's day, even in the most sparsely peopled neighborhoods—a practice worthy of commendation—and broke bread, or partook of the Lord's supper, as a part of the instituted worship of Christ, at every meeting—a practice, which, though neither commanded, nor enforced by any clear apostolic example, contravenes no law of Christ, and should excite no opposition.

CAMPBELLISM IN ITS PRINCIPLES.

It would seem to be impossible for any person admitting the inspiration and authority of the Scriptures, and drawing his principles from them, not to agree with other Christians in many tenets. It is a redeeming quality in Campbellism that it uniformly professes a profound respect for the teaching of the Bible. Mr. Campbell holds many, and most important principles, in common with all Christians. Nobly did he vindicate the authenticity and inspiration of the Scriptures, and the vital principles of Christianity, in his debate with Robert Owen, of Scotland, the champion of infidelity; and by that service entitled himself to the gratitude and commendation of the friends of morality and social order. Mr. Campbell holds many truths in common with all Protestants; and in his discussion with Bishop Purcell, of the Romish communion, maintained them with signal ability, and fully justified his ciaim to be classed among the able defenders of Protestantism. The "*Debate on the Roman Catholic Religion*"—a small volume—has not received at the hands of the Protestant public the favor which it justly merits. Mr. Campbell embraces some views in common with Baptists. Whatever evils he may have done them, directly and indirectly—and they have been neither few nor small—he should have due praise for his indefatigable efforts to restore the apostolic baptism, or the immersion of believers, to expose the traditionary origin of infant baptism, and to show that the primitive churches were composed exclusively of baptized believers. He gave great prominence in his teaching to a few principles and practices which were deemed important, but not particularly insisted on by the ministers of the Baptist denomination. Several points in regard to which he differed from them are of very little moment, and would have attracted but slight attention, had they not been parts of a system fraught with agitation and mischief. Some of the principles embraced by him, and laid at the foundation of his Reformation, were not only different from those entertained by the Baptists, and evangelical Christians generally, but were without Scriptural authority. Some of these it is proposed particularly to examine. No intentional injustice will be done to him or his principles. His opponents and reviewers have, with perhaps no exception, been accused of misrepresenting his views; and I fear that I may subject myself to the same accusation. But, I am anxious to diminish rather than widen the breach between the Baptists and the Reformers. And this must be effected, if effected at all, neither by exaggeration nor concealing their differences, but by a fair, kind, faithful and logical examination of them. I design, therefore, to discuss with as much care and fullness as the prescribed limits of my treatise may permit, a few of the distinctive, and most objectionable *Principles of Campbellism.*

THE INFLUENCE OF THE HOLY SPIRIT IN CONVERSION.

This subject is one of vital importance in the Christian system. The admission or denial of the reality and efficiency of this influence constitutes the main difference between evangelical and rationalistic theology—between intelligent living piety, and heartless, self-sufficient formalism. Almost every Christian sect, holding grossly erroneous principles, has included among its errors the denial or perversion of the doctrine of the spirit's influence. Mr. Campbell in his debate with Rev. N. L. Rice, admitted that the subject is "of transcendent importance to the Christian"—page 611. I would, therefore, enter on its investigation, profoundly conscious of my liability to err, and earnestly seeking wisdom "of God, that giveth to all men liberally, and upbraideth not."

On no subject have the opponents of Mr. Campbell, and the Christian public generally, found it so difficult to understand and represent his views as on this important point. That Mr. Campbell may have full justice, I will make copious extracts on this subject from his voluminous works, especially from a "Dialogue on the Holy Spirit," between "*Timothy*," representing the doctrine of the Reformation, and "*Austin*," a very docile inquirer, on the point of embracing the new doctrine, contained in a work entitled "*Christianity Restored*," issued from the Bethany press, in the year 1835.

"It is a moral revolution, a moral reformation, a moral change, which is essential to the salvation of men. The means therefore must be moral, unless we can think that physical causes can produce moral effects." p. 346.

"We have two sorts of power, physical and moral. By the former we operate on matter—by the latter upon mind. To put matter in motion we use physical power, whether we call it animal or scientific power; to put minds in motion we use arguments, or motives addressed to the reason and nature of man."

"Motives are arguments; and the strength of an argument is its power to move. Arguments are said to be strong or weak, according to their power to move."

"Because arguments are addressed to the understanding, will, and affections of men, they are called moral, inasmuch as their tendency is to form or change the habits, manners, or actions of men.

Every spirit puts forth its moral power in words; that is, all the power it has over the views, habits, manners, or actions of men, is in the meaning and arrangement of its ideas expressed in words; or in significant signs addressed to the eye or ear." pp. 347, 348.

"*The argument is the power of the spirit of man, and the only power which one spirit can exert over another is its arguments.* How often do we see a whole congregation roused into certain actions, expressions of joy or sorrow, by the spirit of one man. Yet no person supposes that his spirit has literally deserted his body and entered into every man and woman in the house, although it is often said he has filled them with his spirit. But how does that spirit located in the head of yonder little man, fill all the thousands around him with joy or sadness, with fear and trembling, with zeal or indignation, as the case may be? How has it displayed such power over so many minds? *By words uttered by the tongue; by ideas communicated to the minds of the hearers.* In this way only can moral power be displayed.

"From such premises we may say, that all the moral power which can be exerted on human beings, is, and of necessity must be, in the arguments addressed to them. No other power than moral power can operate on minds; and this power must always be clothed in words addressed to the eye or ear. Thus we reason when revelation is altogether out of view. And when we think of the power of the Spirit of God exerted upon minds or human spirits, it is impossible for us to imagine, that that power can consist in anything else but words or arguments. Thus in the nature of things we are prepared to expect verbal communications from the Spirit of God, if that Spirit operates at all on our spirits. As the moral power of man is in his arguments, so is the moral power of the Spirit of God in his arguments." p. 349.

"*As the spirit of man puts forth all its moral power in the words which it fills with its ideas; so the Spirit of God puts forth all its converting and sanctifying power, in the words which it fills with its ideas.* . . . . If the Spirit of God has spoken all its arguments; or, if the New and Old Testament contain all the arguments which can be offered to reconcile man to God, and to purify them who are reconciled, then all the power of the Holy Spirit which can operate on the human mind, is spent; and he that is not sanctified and saved by these, cannot be saved by angels or spirits, human or divine." p. 350.

"We plead *that all the converting power of the Holy Spirit is exhibited in the Divine Record.*" p. 351.

"Hence it follows, that *to be filled with the Spirit*, and *to have the Word of Christ dwelling richly in one*, are of the same import in Paul's mind; and as a means to this end, Christians were to abound in singing psalms, hymns, and spiritual songs." p. 360.

"All the power of God or man is exhibited in the truth which they propose. Therefore, we may say, that if the light, or the truth, contain all the moral power of God, then truth alone is all that is necessary to the conversion of men, for we have before argued and proved, that the converting power is moral power." p. 362.

"*Assistance to believe!* This is a metaphysical dream. How can a person be assisted to believe? What sort of help? and how much is wanting? Assistance to believe must be either to create a power in man, which he had not before, or to repair a broken power. . . . . The Holy Spirit was not given until the day of Pentecost. Hence if the Holy Spirit aided men to believe in Jesus Christ, it must have been subsequent to that date." pp. 364, 365.

"Can men just as they are found when they hear the Gospel, believe? I answer boldly, yes—just as easily as I can believe the well-attested facts concerning the person and achievements of General George Washington. I must hear the facts clearly stated, and well authenticated, before I am able to believe them. The man who can believe one fact well attested, can believe any other fact equally well attested." Chn. Bap., 529.

"Paul acts the philosopher fully once, and, if we

recollec: right, but once, in all his writings upon this subject. It has been for many years a favorite topic with me. It is in his first epistle to Timothy, 'Now the end of the commandment (or Gospel) is love out of a pure heart—out of a good conscience—cut of faith unfeigned.' Faith unfeigned brings a person to remission, or to a good conscience; a good conscience precedes, in the order of nature, a pure heart; and this is the only soil in which love, a plant of celestial origin, can grow. This is our philosophy of Christianity—of the Gospel. And thus it is the wisdom and power of God unto salvation. We proceed upon these as our axiomata in all our reasonings, preachings, writings—1st, unfeigned faith; 2d, a good conscience; 3d, a pure heart; 4th, love. The testimony of God apprehended, produces unfeigned or genuine faith; faith obeyed, produces a good conscience. This Peter defines to be the use of baptism, the answer of a good conscience. This produces a pure heart, and then the consummation is love—love to God and man." Christian System, 246.

It would be easy to multiply quotations of this kind; but the above will suffice to give clear and just views of Mr. Campbell's theory of the influence of the Holy Spirit in the conversion and sanctification of men. There can be no mistake in reducing the system to the following propositions.

A moral change is essential to the salvation of

men—This change can be effected only by moral power—All moral power is in arguments, or truth, addressed to the mind by words, or other signs, equivalent to words—All the converting power of the Holy Spirit is in the words which he addresses to men in the Scriptures—Men need no divine or supernatural aid to exercise saving faith in Christ; but can believe in him as easily as they can believe the well attested history of General Washington. This faith does not imply the existence of love, but brings a person to remission, or a good conscience, through baptism; to a good conscience succeeds a pure heart; and from a pure heart flows love—And, finally, to be filled with the Spirit is equivalent to being filled with the word.

Of several positions in this scheme I disapprove; but shall, for the present, confine my remarks to its principal error—viz., *that all the converting power of the Holy Spirit is in the written word, which he has indited and confirmed.*

It is desirable to divest this subject of all extraneous matter. I fully concur with Mr. Campbell in the opinion that a moral change is necessary to the salvation of men. With all that he has written of the inspiration and importance of the Scriptures, and of their adaptation to promote the salvation of men, I heartily agree. I do not think, more than he, that any new faculty is given, or any old faculty (understanding by the term physical, not moral power,) is repaired in conversion. It is freely admitted that the Spirit operates through the word in the conversion and sanctification of men. But I understand Mr Campbell to maintain that the influence of the Spirit in the work of conversion is limited, and of necessity, to the simple presentation of arguments, motives, truth, to the minds of men, by means of words, and other signs—that all the power of the Spirit in the conversion of men is in *moral suasion*. This he does explicitly teach, if words have any definite import. By physical power we operate on matter—by moral power on mind. "All the moral power which can be exerted on human beings, is, and of necessity must be, in the arguments addressed to them." The illustration employed by Mr. Campbell would seem to preclude the possibility of misunderstanding his views. The influence of an orator over his hearers is not exerted, by the entrance of his spirit into them, but "*by words uttered by the tongue; by ideas communicated to*" *their minds*. Of precisely the same nature is the influence ascribed by Mr. Campbell to the Spirit in the conversion of men. "*As the moral power of man is in his arguments, so is the moral power of the Spirit of God in his arguments.*" The Spirit of God exerts a moral influence in conversion exactly like that which men exert in controlling the actions or emotions of one another, but stronger in proportion as his arguments are clearer, fuller, weightier, and more pertinently expressed. But the Spirit can do no more than reason, expostulate, and present motives.

"If the New and Old Testament contain *all the arguments* which can be offered to reconcile man to God, and to purify them who are reconciled, *then all the power of the Holy Spirit which can operate on the human mind is spent*; and he that is not sanctified and saved by these, *cannot be saved* by angels or *spirits*, human or *divine*."

I should deem it needless to labor this point so carefully, did I not know that Mr. Campbell and his friends have almost constantly charged his opponents with falsely stating his views on this very subject. These were the views of "the agency of the Holy Spirit" against which the "Dover Decree" was levelled. Elder A. Broaddus in the "Appendix" to the "Extra Examined," published in 1831, thus wrote:—"In few words, then, Mr. Campbell's view, in regard to Divine influence, appears to me to be in substance as follows—The canon of Scripture being closed, the actual work of the Spirit is done; but the word of truth being dictated by the Holy Spirit—the influence of that word may be termed the influence of the Spirit: and this is all the Divine influence that is *exerted*. And then, God's Spirit, which is a Holy Spirit, being in his word, as my spirit (for example) is in my writings—in receiving the word we receive *a* holy spirit:

and this is all the Holy Spirit that *is received.*' p. 48. Such were the views entertained by this astute and ingenuous writer, of Mr. Campbell's doctrine on the influence of the Spirit. This "Appendix" was noticed by the Editor of the Harbinger in several Nos. of the Dialogue on the Holy Spirit, between Timothy and Austin; and, for a wonder, Mr. B.'s statement of the doctrine was not called in question.

Mr. Campbell maintains, *or did maintain, that all the converting power of the Holy Spirit is in the arguments or motives which he presents to the mind in the written Word.* On this point I take issue with him. I maintain *that there is an influence of the Spirit, internal, mighty, and efficacious, differing from moral suasion, but ordinarily exerted through the inspired Word, in the conversion of sinners.* Whether this influence shall be called *moral*, from the effect which it produces, *physical*, from the energy which is put forth in it; or *spiritual*, from the nature of the agent who exerts it, I have no wish to decide. It is for the reality and importance of this influence, not for its name, that I contend.

The principal argument adduced by Mr. Campbell in support of his theory of conversion, is purely *metaphysical*. All power, he says, is either physical or moral—by physical power we operate on matter, and by moral power on mind A physical power cannot produce a moral effect. "And when we think of the power of the Spirit of God exerted upon minds or human spirits, *it is impossible for us to imagine*, that that power can consist in any thing else but words or arguments." The gist of Mr Campbell's logic seems to be this—We cannot comprehend any power of the Spirit of God in conversion, except that consisting in words or arguments: *therefore*, it does not exist. What is this, but to deduce a most unwarrantable conclusion from his own ignorance? It were a sufficient reply to this reasoning, to quote the words of the Saviour—"The wind bloweth where it listeth, and thou hearest the sound thereof, but canst not tell whence it cometh, nor whither it goeth, so is every one that is born of the Spirit." John 3 : 8. But we have more to say on this subject. To affirm, as Mr. Campbell does, "that if the Holy Spirit has *spoken all its arguments*, . . . then *all the power* of the Holy Spirit which can operate upon the human mind *is spent*," is a bold assumption. When a man has uttered all his arguments and persuasions to influence his fellow, his power may be exhausted; but when the *Infinite Spirit* has spoken all his arguments and persuasions for reconciling proud, perverse and stupid men to Christ, is his power spent? Is there nothing more that he can do? Are his resources exhausted? Has he thus limited himself? Has Mr. Campbell any authority for prescribing this limit to his power? The truth is, this assumption is as *unphilosophical* as it is unscriptural. God created the human spirit—has access to it—is perfectly acquainted with all its springs of emotion and of action—and can, in ways unknown to us, and without contravening the laws of its being, influence, impress, and guide it. He that made, can certainly renew the spirit of man, with means, or without them, as he pleases. It is no less the dictate of reason than of revelation, that "the king's heart," and consequently the heart of every other man, "is in the hand of the Lord, as the rivers of water; he turneth it whithersoever he will."

The assumption that the Spirit can operate on the soul of man in conversion only by arguments, or words, is, not only unphilosophical, but contrary to *divinely recorded facts.* It is not true that physical power cannot produce a moral effect. God created man, not by arguments or words, but by the direct exercise of physical power, in his "own image"—which image comprehended "righteousness and true holiness." Was not this a moral effect produced by a physical cause? Christ was created holy. "The Holy Ghost shall come upon thee," said the angel to Mary, "and the power of the Highest shall overshadow thee: therefore that holy thing which shall be born of thee, shall be called the Son of God." Luke 4: 35. Was not the holiness of the infant Redeemer a moral quality? And was not this effect produced, not by arguments, persuasion, or words, but by the "power," the physical "power of the Highest?"

The assumption under consideration is incompatible with the salvation of infants. They enter into the world, as Mr. Campbell admits, with depraved hearts. Dying before they attain to years of intelligence, they must enter heaven with their moral natures unchanged, which is impossible; they must be renovated by death, which is a mere figment; they must be renewed by the Holy Spirit without the Word, the possibility of which Mr. Campbell cannot conceive; or, they must be lost. I do not charge him with admitting this consequence; but it appears to be logically deduced from the position which he assumes, and all his ingenuity has not enabled him to escape from it.

Mr. Campbell's assumption is wholly at war with the Scripture doctrine of Satanic influence. Satan and other evil spirits are represented in the Bible as exerting a mighty moral influence for the destruction of men. They tempt, deceive, enslave, and degrade mankind. Satan is a mighty prince, and at the head of a great, spreading empire. But how do the evil spirits exert an influence over the minds of men? By arguments, or motives, addressed to them by words, oral or written? Certainly not! But by a direct, internal, and efficient influence. Can Mr. Campbell comprehend it? Will he reject the doctrine because he cannot? Or will he concede to Satan and his angels, a power which he denies to the Spirit of God?

Before quitting this subject, another point demands notice. No writer has so bitterly denounced metaphysical speculations, and mystic theology as Mr. Campbell. One great object of his Reformation was to rescue the Scriptures from the glosses of sectarian theorizers. I must say, that I have met with no writer on the agency of the Spirit in conversion, who has indulged so much in metaphysical disquisition, labored so hard to establish a theory, or drawn such momentous consequences from his own fine-spun speculations. In his writings on this delicate and vital subject, he is far from confining himself to "a pure speech," of "speaking of Bible things in Bible terms," and shows no peculiar desire to be guided by the plain and obvious import of Scripture language; but taxes his psychological lore, and dialectic skill, to establish an ingenious theory drawn from, no matter what source—but not from revelation. True, he apologizes for his seeming inconsistency. He only opposes his enemies with their own weapons. He plunges into metaphysics to extricate others from their labyrinth. The apology does not seem to me to be satisfactory. If Mr. Campbell uses the "speech of Ashdod," why may not others? How are we ever to be rescued from metaphysical subtleties, if those who profess to reform the abuse are most guilty of it?

I have endeavored to show, and, I think, have shown, that the doctrine that the Holy Spirit can operate on the mind in conversion *only* by argument or persuasion is a mere assumption, unphilosophical in itself, contrary to divinely attested facts, and pregnant with a most serious consequence. I would not, however, press this argument to an illegitimate extent. It does not follow that because the Spirit *can* operate on the mind, in other ways than by *moral suasion*, that he *does* so operate. This point must be established by other considerations.

I will now proceed to offer direct arguments against *Mr. Campbell's theory of conversion.*

1. *It overlooks, or at least, under-estimates, the inveteracy of human depravity.*

The Spirit of inspiration has drawn the picture of man's moral corruption in gloomy colors. He is utterly depraved—fleshly, sensual and impure. "That which is born of the flesh is flesh." John 3: 6. He is without spiritual life, without holiness, without moral worth—"dead in trespasses and sins." Eph. 2 : 1. He is alienated from God, and opposed to his law, and consequently to truth and righteousness. "Because the carnal mind is enmity against God : for it is not subject to the law of God, neither indeed can be." Rom. 8: 7. This depravity pervades, and controls the whole man—

blinding the mind, perverting the affections, stupifying the conscience, making rebellious and obstinate the will, and prostituting the members of the body as the instruments of sin. And this moral corruption of human nature is universal. "For all have sinned and come short of the glory of God." Rom. 3: 23.

It is proposed to make man, thus corrupt, obstinate and debased, a friend of God, humble, obedient, and meet for heaven—in short, "a new creature," from whom "old things have passed away," and to whom "all things have become new." 2. Cor. 5: 17. I do not charge Mr. Campbell with denying the doctrine of human depravity; but his theory of conversion does not provide for the accomplishment of a moral renovation, at once so difficult, and so important.

How, according to his scheme, is this great moral change to be effected? Simply by the presentation of arguments, truth, and persuasion, to the mind by words, or other signs. When the Spirit has presented all his arguments, he has spent all his power. Of this scheme several things may be observed.

First. It is oblivious of the chief difficulty in conversion. Mr. Campbell maintains that "the arguments which are written in the New Testament" must be "*understood*" in order to exert their influence on the human mind. Chn'ty. Restored, p. 350 To understand these arguments requires attention, candor, and a spiritual discernment. Men attend readily to what they delight in, and believe easily what is congenial with their tastes ; but the "natural man," the unrenewed, sinful man—has a deep-rooted aversion to divine truth. This aversion is an element and a proof of his depravity. He may hear or read the arguments contained in the Scriptures, through curiosity, politeness, or a captious spirit ; but to expect of him a candid, serious, docile and obedient attention to them, is to expect to "gather grapes of thorns, or figs of thistles." "*For every one that doeth evil hateth the light, neither cometh to the light, lest his deeds should be reproved.*" If divine truth must be understood in order to be efficacious ; and if it must be candidly examined, before it can be understood ; and if *every evil doer*, hating the light, or divine truth, refuses to come to it, or consider it, how, on Mr. Campbell's theory, can any soul of man be saved ? But the scheme which I advocate—the Scriptural scheme —makes provision for overcoming this difficulty. God, by the gracious, inward, efficacious influence of his Spirit, prepares the heart for the reception of the Gospel. "Whose heart," that is, Lydia's heart, "the Lord opened, that she attended unto the things which were spoken of Paul." Acts. 16: 14. This woman "worshipped God," as did all the Jews, and Jewish proselytes ; but there is not the slightest proof that she was pious. The very reverse is clear. Her heart was closed against the Gospel, else there had been no need for God to open it. She hated the light, neither would come to it. "The Lord opened," or inclined, her "heart" to attend "to the things which were spoken of Paul." Mr. Campbell is of opinion that the Lord opened Lydia's heart by the miracles which were wrought in confirmation of the Gospel. Chn'ty Restored, p. 354. Of this there is neither proof nor probability. There was no miracle wrought on the occasion. Miracles were utterly insufficient to awaken an obedient and saving attention, like that which Lydia gave, to the Gospel. John 11 : 47. The Lord opened the heart of this woman of Thyatira—really and effectively opened her heart, by a process which is not explained. As the result of this process she attended, promptly, honestly, and obediently to Paul's Gospel; and but for this process, the apostle, though he had spoken as an angel, had spoken without success.

Secondly. Suppose this great difficulty obviated, the sinner's attention arrested, and truth brought clearly before his mind, *would knowledge of divine truth, without the special influence of the Spirit, secure his conversion?* If ignorance is the only evil with which the Gospel has to contend, then obviously the illumination of the mind is all that is necessary for its removal. But ignorance, though it may be in itself criminal, is rather the effect than the cause of man's depravity. There is a corrupt disposition which blinds the understanding. "This is the condemnation, that light is come into the world, and men loved darkness rather than light, because their deeds were evil." John 3 : 19. The love of darkness—which signifies ignorance or error—is the very root of man's depravity. This love implies an aversion to light, truth, and holiness, and is the cause of the prevalent ignorance of divine things in the world. Conversion includes a cordial approbation of divine truth. 2 Thess. 2 : 10. Now, can arguments, however clear and weighty—persuasion, however earnest and tender—and words, however fitly chosen and expressive, change the tastes and dispositions of the soul? Man hates Christ, not because he is ignorant of his character, but because of the contrariety in their tastes and dispositions; and it is proposed to change this hatred into love, simply by giving man clearer views of the qualities which excite his aversion. Man is opposed to the divine law, because it is pure, spiritual, and inflexible; and it is proposed to overcome this opposition by revealing to him more fully its hated qualities. Man is averse to the light; and it is proposed to subdue this aversion by increasing its splendor. I cannot but suspect the inefficacy of this scheme of conversion. Sinful man needs something more than light—more than arguments, persuasion, words—for his moral renovation. "The wicked . . will not listen to the voice of charmers, charming never so wisely." Ps. 58 : 5.

Thirdly. The theory under discussion is contradicted by numerous well authenticated facts. If all the converting power of the Spirit is in the arguments addressed by him in words to the mind ; then it follows that every minister of the Word must be successful in converting souls to Christ, in proportion to the distinctness with which he presents the arguments of the Spirit to the minds of his hearers. The same measure of power must, under similar circumstances, produce similar results. But does this conclusion agree with the experience and observation of Christian ministers? But I need not appeal in this argument to questionable evidence. Christ was an unrivalled preacher of the Gospel. Mark 1 : 1. Never man spake as he did. For the weight of his arguments, the clearness of his illustrations, the simplicity and force of his style, the fervency of his spirit, the dignity of his manner, the adaptation of his discourses to the circumstances and necessities of his hearers, indeed, for every excellence which could render his ministry attractive, luminous, and successful, he stands alone. Prophets and apostles gave him homage as the "Light of the world." If all the converting power of the Spirit is in moral suasion, we might certainly infer that such a teacher as Christ would be eminently successful in winning souls. But what was the result of his ministry? It was *unsuccessful*—not wholly so—but it produced no such results, as from his preëminent qualifications might have been expected—no great moral revolution, and no extensive revival of true religion. His ministry seems to have been less effective than that of John the Baptist. Matt. 3 : 5, 6. More persons were probably converted by the preaching of Peter and the other apostles, on the day of Pentecost, than by the ministry of Jesus during its whole period. The Apostle Paul quotes from Isa. 65 : 2, a prediction of the manner in which the Messiah's ministry would be treated among the Jews. "But to Israel he saith, All day long I have stretched forth my hands unto a disobedient and gainsaying people." Rom. 10: 21. This prophecy was strikingly fulfilled in the history of Jesus. He was earnest and diligent in teaching. "All day long I have stretched forth my hands." He uttered such arguments as should have convinced, and such entreaties as should have moved, his hearers; but they were "disobedient and gainsaying." The arguments, motives, and words of the Saviour, were eminently suited for their conversion; but the converting power of the Spirit was not present—was withheld in wisdom and righteous judgment.

2. *Mr. Campbell's theory of the Spirit's influence is incompatible with prayer for the conversion of sinners.*

I do not charge him with denying, or questioning,

the propriety of such prayer. On the contrary, he insists that it is obligatory, and practices it. Still his theory and his practise are inconsistent. If all the converting power of the Spirit is in the written Word, then all that can be done for the conversion of sinners is to place the Word before their minds. The Spirit indited and confirmed the Word, and in that Word put forth all his moral or converting power. On Christians now devolves the duty of presenting the arguments, truths, and motives, contained in the written Word, to the minds of sinners. When all the arguments contained in the Old and New Testaments are brought before their minds, "then all the power of the Holy Spirit which can operate upon" them "is spent," and if they are "not sanctified and saved by these," they "cannot be saved by angels or spirits, human or divine." Why then pray for the conversion of sinners? Will the Spirit reveal the Word to their minds? or incline their hearts to receive it? Can any thing be added by the Spirit to its power and efficiency? Prayer for any blessing implies the power of God to bestow it. When we pray for our daily bread, it is implied that God so governs the seasons as to send rain or drought, fruitfulness or famine. When we pray that the sick may be healed, it is implied that God has such a control over man's physical nature, that he can, without a miracle, cure his diseases. So when we pray for the conversion of sinners, if we pray intelligently, we ascribe to the Holy Spirit the power to convert them. And this power is not inherent in the Word, any more than the power that wields a sword, is inherent in the sword. The Word is the instrument, but the Spirit is the agent of conversion. The Spirit gives efficiency to the Word, opening the mind to receive it, impressing it on the heart, and developing its excellence in the life.

3. *Mr. Campbell's theory of conversion is inconsistent with the introduction of the Millennium.*

I will permit him to define what I mean by the *Millennium*. "There is reason, clear, full, and abundant, to justify the expectation that the reign of favor, or the government of Jesus Christ, shall embrace, under its most salutary influences, the whole human race ; or that there are plain, literal, and unfigurative, as well as figurative and symbolic representations, in both Testaments, which authorize us to expect a very *general*, if not a *universal* spread of evangelical influences, so that the whole race of men, for a long period of time, shall bask in the rays, and rejoice in the vivifying power of the Sun of Righteousness." Mill. Har. vol 1, p. 54. This consummation, described in the glowing language of prophecy, has been the grand object of the hopes, prayers, and labors of the saints in all ages. Whatever contributes to hasten this glorious period must, if its tendency is perceived, awaken universal delight among the lovers of Christ. Every principle, theory, or practice, which is inharmonious with its introduction is erroneous. So Mr. Campbell very properly teaches. "In detecting the false Gospels, nothing will aid us so much as an examination of their tendencies, and a comparison of their effects with what the Millennium proposes. The gospel of no sect can convert the world. This is with us a very plain proposition ; and if so the sectarian gospels are defective, or redundant, or mixed." Mill. Har. vol. 1, p. 7 With the sectarian gospels I have now no concern : I wish to inquire whether the "ancient Gospel," furnishes any ground to hope for the introduction of the Millennial glory. I propose to try it by the rule which Mr. Campbell himself has prescribed.

The Scriptural canon was completed nearly eighteen centuries ago. Christianity was clearly revealed, perfect in all its parts, and confirmed by indubitable testimonies. The inspired record, according to the teaching of the Bethany Reformer, contains all the arguments of the Holy Spirit for reconciling men to God ; in this all his moral, or converting power is exhibited. Christ commissioned his apostles to go into all the world, and proclaim the Gospel to every creature. From the apostolic times to the present day, the servants of Christ, with the Old and New Testaments in their hands, have been laboring to convert the world to Christ What has been the success of their efforts ?

Three-fifths of the world are still shrouded in the gloom of paganism. Mohammedanism sways its hundred millions of intelligent, immortal beings. The ignorance, superstition, and spiritual domination of Popery overspread the half of Christendom. The Greek church, little less corrupt and intolerant than the Romish, divides the remaining half with Protestantism. The various sects of Protestants, in the estimation of Mr. Campbell, stand in not much less need of conversion than the heathen. Such was the moral condition of the world when the "current reformation" began. Then Mr. Campbell and his associates, disinterred the "ancient Gospel" from the accumulated rubbish of past ages. "About the commencement of this century," this is his account of the matter, "finding that notes and comments, that glosses and traditions, were making the word of God of little or no effect —I say, the pious of several of the great phalanxes of the rival *Christian* interests did agree to unmanacle and unfetter the testimony of God, and send it forth without the bolsters and crutches furnished by the schools ; and this, with the spirit of inquiry which it created and fostered, has contributed much to break the yoke of clerical oppression, which so long oppressed the people,—I say *clerical* oppression ; for this has been, and yet is, though much circumscribed, the worst of all sorts of oppression." Mill. Har., vol. 1, p. 4. Well, does the disinterred Gospel, or the unmanacled and unfettered testimony of God, furnish any more cheering indications of the Millennial dawn than the sectarian Gospels? Its most sanguine advocates will hardly claim that it does; or if they should, the futility of the claim must be apparent to all the world. I shall, in another place, examine more particularly the tendency and influence of Campbellism. I will merely affirm, what I suppose none acquainted with its progress will deny, that the proclaimers of the "ancient Gospel" have found from experience that all the arguments which they can adduce from the inspired word—all the moral suasion which they can bring to bear on the minds of men—prove deplorably inefficient in their conversion. Churches organized according to the "ancient order of things," enjoying all the light that emanates from Bethany, blessed with the unmanacled testimony of God, without "bolsters or crutches," free from "*clerical* oppression," and favored with the ministrations of reformed pastors, of their own selection, have, in many cases, become cold, worldly, and inefficient; in others, have fallen into strife, and been weakened by divisions; in some, have nourished in their bosoms the most deadly errors; in not a few, have withered and perished; and, if any of them have enjoyed uninterrupted, Millennial prosperity, their history is yet to be made known to the world. I do not write these things to disparage the Reformers. I intend no invidious comparison between the fruits of the "ancient Gospel" and of the "sectarian Gospels." I am sorry that the history of the Reformation should bear so close a resemblance, in its dark and unpromising features, to the history of the numerous Christian sects. The above facts have been stated simply because they are essential in the prosecution of the argument.

How, in view of the above facts, is the Millennium to be introduced? Not by the "sectarian Gospels," says Mr. Campbell. Not by the slow, imperfect and feeble progress of the Bethany Reformation. He that hopes for such a result from it does not need to be reasoned with. It is most manifest that the Millennium cannot shed its blessings on the world without some new agency, or influence, or some great increase of existing influences. We need expect no new revelations for our instruction—no new powers to be imparted to the human mind—and no new means of spreading the Gospel, and enlisting attention to it. How then is the Millennium to be introduced? *By an increased efficiency of the divine word.* At this point the weakness of Campbellism is revealed. It admits no provision for an increased efficiency of the divine word. Its theory of conversion is opposed to any such increase. The Holy Spirit, in the presentation of its arguments, has *exhibited* and *spent* all its converting power. All that can be done, according to this system, by men, angels, or the Holy Spirit, for the introduction of the Millennium, is to exhibit arguments or truth to the minds of men ; or, in other words, persuade them to be holy. What is this, but precisely what has been done by true ministers from the apostolic age down to the present time? And what ground is there, according to this system, to conclude, hope or conjecture, that moral suasion will, in time to come, be more efficacious than it has been in time past? The same facts and arguments must be proclaimed, in similar language, by men of like passions and infirmities, and to the same depraved, stupid and perverse race of beings, as in past ages ; and there is nothing in the theory under discussion, or the nature of the case, to justify the expectation that the fruits will materially differ in quality or quantity. It is true, the Scriptures predict a great increase of knowledge and piety in the latter days ; and Christ will certainly fulfill the prediction ; and it is because Mr. Campbell's theory of the Holy Spirit's influence in conversion, not only does not contain any provision for its fulfillment, but is clearly inconsistent with it, that it ought to be rejected. But the view of the Spirit's agency which I maintain falls in most harmoniously with the Scripture promises of a Millennium. His power is infinite. He executes the purposes of Messiah. He can impart an unction to the ministers of Christ, and increase indefinitely their zeal, diligence, fidelity and efficiency. He can dwell richly in all the saints, filling their understandings with light, their hearts with love, and their lives with his fruits. He can incline men to hear, embrace, and adorn the Gospel of Jesus Christ. In short, he possesses all the grace and energy which are requisite to secure the universal spread and triumph of the Gospel. The Millennium is to be introduced not merely by moral suasion, and providential dispensations, but by copious, general and powerful effusions of the Holy Spirit. The same Spirit which on the day of Pentecost gave signal success to the labors of Peter, and his co-laborers, will by a mighty, pervasive, and gracious agency—an agency in harmony with his own perfections, and the freedom of the human will—prepare men to receive, and spread abroad the Gospel, and thus fill the earth with the knowledge of the glory of the Lord.

"The palaces," predicted the evangelical prophet, "shall be forsaken; the multitude of the city shall be left; the forts and towers shall be for dens forever, a joy of wild asses, a pasture of flocks; *until the Spirit be poured upon us from on high*, and the wilderness be a fruitful field, and the fruitful field be counted for a forest. Then judgment shall dwell in the wilderness, and righteousness remain in the fruitful field. And the work of righteousness shall be peace; and the effect of righteousness, quietness, and assurance forever. Isa. 3: 14-17.

The direct, Scriptural proofs of the reality of this effective agency of the Holy Spirit, I shall now attempt to furnish.

4. *The theory of conversion by moral suasion is contradicted by the plain teaching of the Scriptures.*

The question under discussion is not one of metaphysics but of revelation—it is to be decided not by an appeal to philosophy, but to philology. Of the nature and operations of spirits, and of the laws which govern them, we know, and can know, but little. Profoundly convinced of our ignorance, and liability to err, on the important but abstruse subject under consideration, we should earnestly inquire, what saith the Lord? and endeavor, with childlike docility, to comprehend the import of his words.

The inspired teachers have employed the strongest terms to denote that agency, or influence of the Spirit, by which fallen man is morally renewed. If their language does not express a real, effective agency of the Spirit, more powerful than persuasion, or the mere presentation of arguments to the mind, it is difficult to conceive how such an agency could be described. They inform us simply what the Spirit does, without attempting to explain the methods of his operation—an explanation which we should probably be unable to comprehend, and which would be unprofitable even if we could. I will adduce a few passages of Scripture which teach the direct, personal agency of the Holy Spirit in conversion. These may not, in the judgment of other advocates of the doctrine, be the most pertinent or conclusive ; and I readily admit that they are not better suited to my purpose than many from which I have selected them.

Conversion is, in the New Testament, described as a *birth—a new birth—a birth of the Spirit.* "*That which is born of the Spirit is spirit.*" John 3 : 6. "*We know that whosoever is born of God sinneth not ; but he that is begotten of God keepeth himself, and that wicked one toucheth him not.*" 1 John 5 : 18. I shall here take for granted, what ought to be universally conceded, that the phrases "born of the Spirit," and "born of God," denote conversion, or the moral renovation of man—in another place I propose to examine this subject more particularly. There is a resemblance between generation, or the natural birth, and conversion. The Spirit of inspiration has employed this resemblance to elucidate the subject of man's moral renovation. In physical generation the nature and qualities of the parent are conveyed to the child. "Adam begat a son in his own likeness." "That which is born of the flesh is flesh"—that is, not merely corporeal, but depraved, corrupt, partaking of man's fallen nature, as the term flesh frequently means. So in the new birth, the nature—the moral nature —of the Spirit—of God—is conveyed to his offspring. "That which is born of the Spirit is spirit"—resembles the Spirit—partakes of his holiness—is spiritual. "Love is of God; and every one that loveth is born of God." 1 John 4 : 7. This mighty moral change is effected by the Gospel. "Of his own will begat he us with the word of truth." James 1 : 18. "The word of truth" was the instrument of regeneration—the efficiency was of God. God begat—communicated his own nature, or moral qualities, to the begotten—begat "of his own will," according to his own choice or purpose—and the Gospel was the means which he effectively used in producing the change. To ascribe this spiritual birth to the power in the word—to the force of moral suasion—rather than to the influence and efficiency of the Holy Spirit, that operates by and through the word—is as if the axe should boast itself against him that heweth therewith, or the saw magnify itself against him that shaketh it." Isaiah 10 : 15. The argument, in brief, in this—that the new, or moral birth—implying a communication of the divine nature—is effected not merely by the written word, but is ascribed to a voluntary and efficient agency of the Holy Spirit.

Conversion is termed in the Scriptures a *creation*, and described in a *variety of language of similar import.* "*A new heart also will I give you, and a new spirit will I put within you: and I will take away the stony heart out of your flesh, and I will give you an heart of flesh.*" Ezekiel 36 : 26. God promised the Israelites, his chosen people, that he would gather them out of all countries, and bring them into their own land; and having done this, he would bestow on them a far richer blessing—would do in them a work, which neither men nor angels could perform. He would "take away the stony heart out of their flesh." The "stony heart" is a hard, insensible, corrupt, impenitent heart; and this God promised to take away from them. He would do more. He would bestow on them a "heart of flesh," a "new heart," a "new spirit,"—and this language certainly imports that he would give them a tender, holy, and obedient heart. We have passages of corresponding significance in the New Testament. "*For we are his workmanship, created in Christ Jesus unto good works, which God hath before ordained that we should walk in them.*" Eph. 2 : 10. This language is exceedingly strong. The conversion of a sinner is termed a *creation.* A convert is a *new creature.* The word employed in this text to denote this renovation—"created," (κτίζω) is employed to express that exercise of power by which the universe was brought into existence. Eph. 3 : 9. Col. 1 : 16. No energy short of that which brought order out of chaos, can renew the soul of man. That soul is, in its natural state, a moral chaos—dark, void, formless; and nothing but Almighty power, and infinite grace, can restore it to life, light and beauty. "God who commanded the light to shine out of darkness" must shine into the heart "to give the light of the knowledge of the glory of God in the face of Jesus Christ." Now, I will ask any considerate and candid man, whether such language as this, which we have been examining, could have been used to denote moral suasion, without the certainty of deceiving mankind? When God takes away a "stony heart," does he merely present arguments to display the evil and danger of sin, and persuade the offender to abandon it? When he gives a "new heart"—a "heart of flesh"—does he only use arguments to induce the sinner to be penitent, holy and obedient? When he creates a man in Christ Jesus—makes him "a new creature"—does he simply address words to the eye or ear of the transgressor? As well might it be affirmed that God created the world by arguments—that he ruled chaos by persuasion. It is true, "God *said*, Let there be light: and there was light." But let no one suppose that light was the product of the words spoken.

If *language* is not ascribed to God in the act of creation, as the mere drapery of the narrative, it was uttered by him as the signal for the exercise of his creative energy. Christ, while on earth, spake to those whom he healed ; but they were healed, not by his words, but by his power. "The power of the Lord was present to heal them." Luke 5 : 17. "He—the Lord—hath made the earth *by his power* he hath established the world by his wisdom, and hath stretched out the heavens by his discretion." Jer. 10 : 12.

Conversion is described as a *resurrection from the dead.* "*But God, who is rich in mercy, for his great love wherewith he loved us, even when we were dead in sins, hath quickened us together with Christ. (by grace are ye saved).*" Eph. 2: 4, 5. The Ephesians "were by nature the children of wrath, even as others." v. 3. Their moral condition is described by the phrase "dead in sins"—a most expressive phrase, which can mean nothing less than that they were destitute of spiritual life or holiness, and were morally corrupt and helpless. From themselves there was no hope. Their deliverance was from God. It originated in his "rich mercy," and "great love." In executing the gracious scheme of their salvation, he "quickened" them, raised them from their death in sin, or infused into them spiritual life. This he did not merely by arguments or persuasion, but by the energy which raised Christ from the dead. They were quickened "together with Christ." He was raised from the dead to secure salvation to all who should believe in him. Rom.

4 : 25. As he was raised from a natural death, so they, in virtue of his resurrection, were raised from a moral death, or a death in sin. And that the Ephesians were quickened by the same power that raised Christ from the dead, is clear from the context. The Apostle prayed "the Father of glory" for them, that they might know, "what is the exceeding greatness of his power to us-ward who believe, according to the working of his mighty power, which he wrought in Christ, when he raised him from the dead," &c. 1 : 19, 20. Here it is plainly affirmed that they believed "according to the working of his (God's) mighty power which he wrought in Christ, when he raised him from the dead." The passage is thus paraphrased by Dr. McKnight, who cannot be justly suspected of an improper bias towards spiritual influence. That ye may know "*what is the exceeding greatness of his power, with relation to us*, Jews and Gentiles *who believe*, in making us alive from our trespasses and sins, (chap. 2 : 5) and in raising us at the last day from the dead, to enjoy the glories of his inheritance, *by an exertion similar to the inworking of the strength of his force, which he exerted in Christ, when he raised him from the dead*," &c. If the power that raised up Christ from the dead was exerted in quickening the Ephesians, then it is obvious that they were not converted by the mere power of words.

Before I proceed, I must meet an objection to the direct proofs which I have offered in support of the efficient agency of the Holy Spirit in conversion. It will not be denied by those who advocate the theory which I am combating, that believers are "born of the Spirit," "quickened," "created in Christ Jesus," at least after baptism. But they maintain that the Holy Spirit having indited the Word, and confirmed it by signs and miracles—and having put forth all its converting power in the arguments which it contains—that now whatsoever is done by the Word is done by the Spirit. Men are regenerated, created anew, quickened, by the arguments or motives presented to their minds in the written Word, precisely as a congregation are convinced, agitated, and put into motion by the words of an orator, and whatever is ascribed to the Word is justly ascribed to the Spirit. The Spirit has completed the instrument of conversion—the recorded Word—put it into the hands of his church to be employed by them for its destined purpose; and for all the good which they accomplish by it, he is entitled to the glory. This objection is plausible, and worthy of a careful consideration.

It is neither common nor just to ascribe to the manufacturer of an instrument the work effected by it. The instrument may be good—perfect in its kind—admirably suited to its purpose; and its maker may deserve high commendation; but nobody would deem it proper to give him the honor of the work done by it. Let me illustrate—The architect purchases tools of a manufacturer: they are of the best metal, keenest edge, and most approved patterns—he erects a tasteful house—Would any man in his senses affirm that the tool-manufacturer built the house? A daguerreotypist obtains from a factory a camera obscura, and all the appliances necessary for practising his art, and succeeds in obtaining an accurate likeness of the President of the United States. What would you think of the fidelity of a reporter who should affirm that Daguerre had taken a very exact likeness of the President? Or, would you be more favorably impressed with his discrimination and truthfulness, if he should publish that the maker of the camera obscura had succeeded in taking the picture? But if the manufacturer of an instrument is the agent who uses it, then he is, in the fullest sense, the author of all the effects produced by it. Whatsoever is done by the instrument, he does; and he is justly entitled to the credit of it.

Let me now apply the illustration.—The written Word is the instrument, divinely fitted and appointed for the conversion of sinners. This instrument, completed in the apostolic age, has been committed to the hands of the church to be by them employed for its appropriate purpose. It is their duty to translate the Word, print, circulate, expound, and enforce it, call the attention of men to it, and exemplify in their lives its efficiency and loveliness. If the Spirit is the Agent—the all-pervading and mighty Agent—who uses the Word, and the ministers of it, as suitable instruments for the conversion and salvation of sinners—or, in other words, if he, through these means, puts forth a special and efficient influence for their moral renovation—then, in the fullest sense, and with the strictest propriety, he may be said to beget—new-create—quicken—the subjects of his grace ; and he is entitled to all the praise of their salvation. But if, on the other hand, he has merely furnished the means of conversion—arguments to persuade men to turn to God—and these means have been successfully employed by his servants, I do not perceive with what pertinency the strong language under consideration can be applied to his agency. Let us recur to the illustration used above. The minister of Christ is an architect. "I have laid the foundation," says Paul, "and another buildeth thereon." The arguments, facts, motives, furnished by the written Word are, to follow out the figure, the tools by which the builder carries forward his work. Now, if the Spirit merely furnishes the tools, and exerts no effective agency in rearing the edifice, can it properly be termed his "workmanship?" Mr. Campbell's theory of conversion amounts to this—*God furnishes the tools*—

we do the work. The Spirit of God, having, in the Old and New Testaments, spoken "all the arguments which can be offered to reconcile man to God," all his power "which can operate on the human mind is spent," and it now remains for the disciples, unaided by the Spirit, to carry on the work of human salvation. But orthodox Christians believe and maintain, that the written Word, ordinances, churches, ministers of the Word, and providences, prosperous or adverse, are so many means through which the Holy Spirit, infinite in grace and power, exerts a personal and efficacious influence for the conversion and sanctification of men.

"*I have planted, Apollos watered; but God gave the increase. So then, neither is he that planteth anything, neither he that watereth; but God that giveth the increase.*" 1 Cor. 3 : 6, 7. The church of Corinth is compared to a field—"Ye are my husbandry," or "field," according to McKnight's rendering. In this field the ministers of Christ were laborers together with God." v. 9. In it *Paul planted.* He was an apostle, eminent alike for piety, gifts, diligence, and fidelity in his ministrations. He was an evangelical pioneer in Corinth. Acts 18 : 8. Here he sowed or planted the seed, which "is the Word of God." Luke 8 : 11. Or, dropping the figure, he preached the Gospel with great plainness, pungency, and fervor. In the same field, "*Apollos watered.*" He was a preacher distinguished for his thorough knowledge of the Jewish Scriptures, the fervency of his spirit, the eloquence of his address, and the cogency of his reasoning. He entered into the labors of Paul and others ; and endeavored to irrigate and culture the plants which they had set. But Paul, who planted, and Apollos, who watered, were nothing, entitled to no glory, as "God gave the increase." The text teaches that the success of Gospel ministers—even the most eminent—whether in the conversion of sinners, or the improvement of saints, is of divine influence. The doctrine is according to analogy. In the vegetable kingdom, God gives the increase. The best seed, sown in the best soil, and in the best manner, will prove unfruitful, except God send sunshine, and rains, and dews, and a suitable temperature, to give the increase. The most skillful husbandman on earth, cannot make a blade of grass grow without divine aid. "That which thou sowest, thou sowest not that body that shall be, but bare grain, it may chance of wheat, or of some other grain. But God *giveth it a body* as it hath pleased him, and to every seed his own body." 1 Cor. 15 : 37, 38. It would be easy to show that the same principle pervades the animal kingdom. We might reasonably infer that this principle extends into the kingdom of grace. But on this subject we are not left to the uncertain deduction of reason. All increase in the evangelic field is of God. The piety and ability of the ministry—the truth proclaimed—the manner of publishing it—and the character of the people among whom it is preached, can furnish no guarantee of success. If Paul and Apollos were dependent on the Divine blessing and efficiency for "the increase," no minister can reasonably hope to rise above this dependence. And if the success of Gospel ministers is from God, then it follows that the inspired facts and arguments which they are authorized to proclaim are insufficient to secure it. *Planting* and *watering*, figurative terms, comprehend within their legitimate import, all the uses that can be made of the Divine word—all the methods of instructing, warning, and persuading—all that can be said and done to give efficiency to the Gospel—and yet something more is demanded to secure the increase—even the Divine blessing and energy. Indeed, so powerless is the most luminous and faithful exhibition of Divine truth, without God's coöperation, (v. 9.) that "neither is he that planteth any thing, neither he that watereth." To God be all glory!

"*Seeing ye have purified your souls in obeying the truth through the Spirit, unto unfeigned love of the brethren, see that ye love one another, with a pure heart fervently.*" 1 Peter 1 : 22. In this text the influence of the Word and of the Spirit are clearly distinguished. By nature our souls are impure, or sinful. All moral excellence lies in obeying the truth, or Gospel. (v. 25.) Conversion is obedience to the truth; and sanctification is a growing conformity to it. These positions will not, it is presumed, be disputed. The Gospel alone is not sufficient to secure this obedience, though its facts are confirmed, its arguments are weighty, and the motives by which its claims are urged are high as heaven, deep as hell, and vast as eternity. An influence distinct from, and above the truth is indispensable to the production of this obedience. The Holy Spirit exerts this influence not in revealing new truth, or creating new faculties; but in disposing the heart to receive and be guided by the Gospel. This influence is particularly described by the word of the Lord in Ezekiel—"*And I will put my Spirit within you, and cause you to walk in my statutes, and ye shall keep my judgments, and do them.*" 36 : 27.

"*For this is the covenant that I will make with the house of Israel after those days, saith the Lord; I will put my laws into their mind, and write them in their hearts; and I will be to them a God, and they shall be to me a people.*" Heb. 8 : 10. The apostle is demonstrating the superiority of the new or Gospel covenant over the old or Sinaitic. Under the old covenant God inscribed his laws on tables of stone—under the new he writes them "on the fleshly tables of the heart." God's laws are excellent—a transcript of his own character. Between the law and the Gospel there is perfect harmony.

The Gospel is designed to sustain, illustrate, and enforce the divine laws. These laws, recorded first on tables of stone, and afterwards in the volume of inspiration, are worthy to be loved, and obeyed by men. But in order to receive a due appreciation of them, and a cordial submission to their authority, a new and peculiar process is necessary. They must be put "into their mind," and written "in their hearts." It cannot be doubted that the result of this process is a knowledge of the Divine laws, delight in them, and a willingness to obey them. This process is above the power and skill of men or angels. It is God's prerogative, and one of the privileges secured by the new covenant, that he puts his laws into the minds, and writes them on the hearts of his people. The law is the stamp which, with his own hand, he impresses on the renewed soul—the soul renewed by the very act of impressing it. It is pleasing to find that on this point my views are in harmony with those of Mr. Campbell. In his *Christian System*, describing the Subjects of the Kingdom, he writes, p. 156, "They all know the Lord." "All thy children shall be taught of God." The Holy Spirit of God, writes the law of God upon their hearts, and inscribes it upon their understanding; so that they need not teach every one his fellow citizen to know the Lord, "for they all know him from the least to the greatest." Now whether this process of writing the law upon the heart, and inscribing it upon the understanding is physical or moral, I am not concerned to decide. All I maintain is, that it is not owing exclusively to the force of argument in the Divine Law, or Word, that this deep, abiding, renovating impression is made upon the heart; but to the inward, and effective agency of the Holy Spirit.

Before I close this argument on the direct testimony of the Scriptures, I must make a single remark to prevent misconception. All those portions of the inspired volume in which conversion or sanctification, in whatever terms expressed, is ascribed to God, have reference to the Holy Spirit. He is the sanctifier. In the economy of man's redemption it is his prerogative to reveal and confirm the truth, and make it efficacious in man's moral renovation. This point needs no proof.

5. *The theory of conversion advocated by Mr. Campbell, is inconsistent with the plainly revealed, and fairly conceded influence of the Holy Spirit in believers after baptism.*

That the Spirit of God dwells in the saints, or believers, as in a temple, to refresh and invigorate them, to quicken their devotions, and to make them fruitful in good works, is a truth so clearly taught in the Scriptures, and so generally admitted among Christians, that it is unnecessary to attempt to prove it. I will merely refer the reader to a few out of many Scripture proofs of it. Lev. 11, 13.—

Rom. 8: 9.—1 Cor. 6: 19.—Eph. 5: 5.—Phil 2: 13.—Gal. 5: 22-23.

Mr. Campbell admits, and maintains the efficacious influence of the Holy Spirit in believers—an influence differing not in degree, but kind, from that by which a sinner is converted. As this is a very important point, I will permit Mr. Campbell to present his views regarding it fully.

"In the kingdom into which we are born of water, the Holy Spirit is as the atmosphere in the kingdom of nature—we mean that the influences of the Holy Spirit are as necessary to *the new life*, as the atmosphere is to our animal life, in the kingdom of nature. All that is done in us before regeneration, God our Father effects by *the Word*, or the Gospel as dictated and confirmed by his Holy Spirit. But after we are thus begotten and born by the Spirit of God—after our new birth, the Holy Spirit is shed on us richly through Jesus Christ our Saviour; of which the peace of mind, the love, the joy, and the hope of the regenerate is full proof; for these are amongst the fruits of that Holy Spirit of promise of which we speak." Chn. Sys., p. 267.

I do not, I trust, misunderstand Mr. Campbell on this vital subject. He teaches that all that is done in us before regeneration—which in the Bethany dialect means "born of water," or immersion—"God our Father," not the Holy Spirit, "effects by *the Word*;"—but *after* our new birth, "the Holy

Spirit is shed on us richly through Jesus Christ our Saviour; of which the peace of mind, the love, the joy, and the hope of the regenerate is the proof." The illustration employed by Mr. Campbell seems to preclude the possibility of misunderstanding his views. What the atmosphere is to animal life, the influences of the Holy Spirit are to the new life. As the animal, after its birth, is sustained by respiration; so after we are "born of water," or immersed, we live—our new life is maintained—by "the influences of the Holy Spirit."

But to show that my interpretation of his language is in perfect harmony with what he calls the "ancient Gospel," I will furnish another extract from his writings.

"Where there is a guilty conscience there is an impure heart. So teaches Paul: 'To the unbelieving there is nothing pure; for even their mind and conscience is defiled.' *In such a heart the Holy Spirit cannot dwell.* When God symbolically dwelt in the camp of Israel, every speck of filth must be removed even from the earth's surface. Before the Holy Spirit can be received, the heart must be purified; before the heart can be purified, guilt must be removed from the conscience; and before guilt can be removed from the conscience, there must be a sense, a feeling, or an assurance that sin is pardoned and transgression covered. For obtaining this there must be some appointed way—and that means or way is immersion into the name of the Father, Son, and Holy Spirit. So that, according to this order, it is incompatible, and therefore impossible, that the Holy Spirit can be received, or can dwell in any heart not purified from a guilty conscience. Hence it came to pass, that Peter said, 'Be immersed for the remission of your sins, and you shall receive the gift of the Holy Spirit.'" Chn. Bap., 439.

According to the "ancient Gospel," if Mr. Campbell is a safe expounder of it, *immersion*—which in the "pure speech" of the Reformation, is "the regenerating act itself"—is necessary for the remission of sins; "*a sense, feeling, or assurance that sin is pardoned* is necessary for the removal of guilt from the conscience; the *removal of guilt* from the conscience is indispensable for the purification of the heart; and *the purification of the heart* is an essential prerequisite of the reception of the Holy Spirit. Immersion—the remission of sins—the removal of guilt—a pure heart—the influence of the Holy Spirit—and then love, meekness and humility, the fruits of the Spirit—is the established order in the "ancient Gospel," promulged from Bethany. I might notice many things in this order, from which I utterly dissent, but I must limit my remarks to the point in hand. Mr. Campbell does teach that there is an influence of the Spirit, after baptism, and the purification of the heart. When a man is "born of water," and his heart is purified, then the Holy Spirit dwells in him, and love, joy, and other graces attest his presence and agency. All that is done in the believer before he receives the Spirit, God his Father "effects by *the Word.*"

To do Mr. Campbell ample justice, I will permit him to explain and vindicate his views on this point.

"But the Spirit is not *promised to any persons out of Christ.* It is promised only to them that believe in and obey him. These it actually and powerfully assists in the mighty struggle for eternal life. Some, indeed, ask, 'Do Christians need more aid to gain eternal life—than sinners do to become Christians? Is not the work of conversion a more difficult work than the work of sanctification? Hence, they contend more for the work of the Spirit in conversion, than for the work of the Spirit in sanctification. This, indeed, is a mistaken view of the matter, if we reason either from analogy or from Divine testimony. Is it not more easy to plant, than to cultivate the corn, the vine, the olive? Is it not more easy to enlist in the army, than to be a good soldier, and fight the battles of the Lord; to start in the race, than to reach the goal; to enter the ship than cross the ocean; to be naturalized, than to become a good citizen; to enter into the matrimonial compact, than to be an exemplary husband; to enter into life, than to retain and sustain it for three score years and ten?

And while the commands, '*believe*,' '*repent*,' and '*be baptized*,' are never accompanied with any intimation of peculiar difficulty; the commands to the use of the means of spiritual health and life; to form the Christian character; to attain to the resurrection of the just; to lay hold on eternal life; to make our calling and election sure, &c., are accompanied with such exhortations, admonitions, cautions, as to make it a difficult and critical affair, requiring all the aids of the Spirit of our God, to all the means of grace and untiring assiduity and perseverance on our part; for it seems, 'the called,' who enter the stadium are many, while 'the chosen' and approved 'are few;' and many, says Jesus, 'shall seek to enter into the heavenly city, and shall not be able;' 'Let us labor, therefore, to inter into that rest lest any man fall after the same example of unbelief.' "

What religious teachers those are who "contend more for the work of the Spirit in conversion, than for the work of the Spirit in sanctification," I do not know. I do not think that Mr. Campbell can name a single orthodox divine, of reputation, who does not believe that the influence of the Spirit is equally and indispensably necessary in conversion and sanctification. The question whether that influence is more needed in the one process or the other, could have originated only from such metaphysical, vague and barren speculations as abound in the writings of Mr. Campbell.

But let us attend to the main point in our argument. I understand Mr. Campbell to admit the influence of the Holy Spirit after baptism. "These"—them that believe in and obey Christ—"it"—the Spirit—"*actually and powerfully assists in the mighty struggle for eternal life.*" This language is quite orthodox—scarcely distinguishable from the dialect of the *populars.* Whether this influence of the Spirit in believers, by which they are actually and powerfully assisted, is physical, moral, or indefinable, he does not inform us. He not only admits the reality of this influence, but clearly states the ground of its necessity. Conversion, he teaches, is comparatively easy; but sanctification is very difficult. "Is it not more easy to plant, than to cultivate the corn, the vine, the olive?" "The commands '*believe,*' '*repent,*' and '*be baptized,*' are never accompanied with any intimation of *peculiar difficulty.*" "We rejoice to know that it is just as easy to believe and be saved, as it is to hear or see." Chn. Bap., vol. 5, p. 221. It is quite clear that for a work so easily accomplished as conversion, no assistance of the Spirit is needed. "*Assistance to believe!* This is a metaphysical dream. How can a person be assisted to believe?" "All that is done in us before regeneration, (baptism) God our Father effects by *the Word.*" But when the sinner believes, repents, is baptized, has a feeling that sin is pardoned, has guilt removed from his conscience, and his heart purified, then "in the *mighty struggle* for eternal life," he will need and receive the actual and powerful assistance of the Holy Spirit. "The commands to the use of spiritual health and life; to form the Christian character; to attain to the resurrection of the just; to lay hold on eternal life; to make our calling and election sure, &c., are accompanied with such exhortations, admonitions, cautions, *as to make it a difficult and critical affair, requiring all the aids of the Spirit of our God*, to all the means of grace and untiring assiduity and perseverence on our part." According, then, to the "ancient Gospel," conversion is easy, and is by the Word, without any assistance from the Holy Spirit; but sanctification, or the Christian life, is difficult, and very critical, and can be carried on only by his indwelling, actual, and powerful assistance. From these views I utterly dissent. I maintain that conversion is a work no less difficult than sanctification—that the same influence which is requisite to nourish the new life, was requisite to originate it—that a man can no more repent and believe without the influence of the Spirit than he can love, rejoice, and continue to obey. I go farther, and insist that the influence of the Spirit in sanctification being admitted, it follows, as a logical sequence, that the same influence is exerted in conversion, which is but the commencement of the work of which sanctification is the progress.

Before I proceed to offer direct proofs in support of my position, I must briefly notice what Mr. Campbell has alleged in support of his views. This may be comprehended under three heads—

First. "The Holy Spirit," he affirms, "is not *promised to any persons out of Christ.*" This position I do not controvert. The Spirit is bestowed on believers, in answer to prayer, to comfort, refresh, strengthen, and guide them—in fine, to carry on within them the process of sanctification. This privilege is peculiar to Christians. But I do most widely dissent from the inference which Mr. Campbell seeks to draw from this position. His reasoning is this: The Spirit is *promised* only to believers; therefore, the influence of the Spirit is limited to believers. This reasoning is illogical. It is based on the assumption that God bestows no blessing which he does not promise. But this is not true. God's promises are all made to believers—to the obedient—to the holy. So far as I know, there is not a promise in the Bible to the ungodly, except on condition of their repentance and faith. But the Divine blessings are bestowed profusely on the bad as well as the good—the disobedient as well as the righteous. Matt. 6 : 45. God has promised the Spirit of consolation and encouragement to believers; but this truth is in perfect harmony with the doctrine that God's unpromised, free, gracious, and sovereign Spirit exerts a real, powerful, and creative influence in changing carnal, ungodly men, into humble believers.

Secondly. Mr. Campbell's next argument in support of his views, *is derived from analogy.* "Is it not more easy," he inquires, "to enlist in the army, than to be a good soldier, and fight the battles of the Lord; to start in the race, than to reach the goal; to enter the ship, than to cross the ocean; to be naturalized, than to become a good citizen; to enter into the matrimonial compact, than to be an exemplary husband; to enter into life, than to retain and sustain it for three-score years and ten?" Analogies prove nothing. It is easy for Mr. Campbell to furnish examples in which it is more difficult to prosecute than to commence an enterprise; but these examples are far from proving that it is more difficult to continue than to begin a life of piety. Moreover, the Scriptural analogies are against Mr. Campbell's views. Conversion is a resurrection. Is it easier to raise a man from the dead, than to nourish him after he is made alive? Conversion is a creation. Is it easier to create than to preserve that which is created? Conversion is reconciliation. Is it easier to reconcile an enemy, than to retain a friend? It requires the same power, and certainly no less an exertion of that power, to quicken a soul dead in trespasses and sins, than to support and nourish the new life. So analogy and reason decide ; and nothing but unbridled speculation would doubt.

Thirdly. Mr. Campbell derives another argument in support of his opinions from *the difficulty of a life of piety.* "The commands to the use of the means of spiritual life and health ; to form the Christian character, etc., are accompanied with such exhortations, admonitions, cautions, as to make it a *difficult and critical affair.*" I admit the difficulty of a life of piety ; but assuredly the difficulty includes the obstacles at the commencement, as well as those in its progress. Take for illustration the text which Mr. Campbell has misquoted in the extract above as an illustration. "Strive to enter in at the strait gate ; for many, I say unto you, will seek to enter in, and shall not be able." Luke 13 : 24. The entrance through the strait, or difficult gate, the necessity of which we are here taught, includes conversion, if it does not primarily refer to it. The exhortation was addressed to captious, unbelieving Jews, who needed to commence, before they could pursue a life of piety.

I am now prepared to offer direct proofs in support of my position.

My *first* argument respects the *power of the Holy Spirit.* It is this—if the Spirit can and does dwell in believers, "actually and powerfully" assisting them "in the mighty struggle for eternal life"—

then *he can* exert a similar influence in enlightening, quickening and renewing the ungodly. Call it moral, physical, or any other kind of power, the energy by which he assists Christians in their struggles may be exercised in giving sinners "repentance *to the acknowledging of the truth*." 2. Tim. 2 : 25.

My *second* proof is derived from the *nature* of *sanctification*. It is progressive holiness. It is beautifully described by the wise man—"The path of the just is as the shining light, that shineth more and more unto the perfect day." Prov. 4: 18. Regeneration is the commencement of holiness. Regeneration and sanctification do not denote different processes, but the same process in different stages. They resemble each other as the child resembles the man, or the dawn resembles the day. I will not now stop to defend these definitions, partly, because I presume the advocates of the Reformation will admit their correctness, and partly, because I purpose in another place to examine more particularly Mr. Campbell's use of these terms. Now to maintain that regeneration or conversion, and sanctification are the result of different influences, or processes, is about as discriminating and wise as to maintain that the dawn of day and the brightness of noon spring from different orbs. Conversion is holiness begun ; sanctification is holiness progressing ; but in both cases the holiness is of the same nature, tendency and origin. To ascribe the commencement and the progress of this renovating process to different influences, or authors, is as unphilosophical as it is unscriptural—is to adopt a visionary theory, without proof, without plausibility, and without advantage.

My *third* proof is drawn from the direct *testimony of revelation.* The Scriptures, I may remark, in general terms, ascribe conversion to Divine agency in language as clear, strong and varied as they do sanctification. The Spirit that nourishes is the Spirit that begets : the Power that preserves is the Power that creates. But on this point revelation bears explicit testimony. "Being confident of this very thing, that he which hath begun a good work in you will perform it until the day of Jesus Christ." Phil. 1 : 6. This "good work" is the work of grace in the soul—that process of moral purification by which it is fitted for communion with God. The same Agent who begins this work, in conversion, "will perform it," or "be completing it," in sanctification, "until the day of Jesus Christ." As Mr. Campbell admits that the Spirit *carries on* this good work, and as Paul teaches that he who carries it on also *began* it, it follows that the Spirit began it. By "*good work*," in this passage, Mr. Campbell understands the liberality of the Philippian Christians to the apostle Paul. To favor this interpretation, he has in his New Testament abandoned the well established translation of McKnight, which he professes to follow, and adopted that of Thompson, in the preceding verse. Instead of "fellowship in the Gospel," as McKnight has it, or "your participation in the Gospel," as Doddridge renders it, he has printed, on Thompson's authority, "your contribution for the Gospel." All the commentaries, within my reach, both Calvinistic and Arminian, are opposed to his interpretation of the sixth verse. "Some sectaries," he says, have converted this *good work*, into God's work, upon them, and have made the apostle invalidate his own exhortation to them, to work out their salvation with fear and trembling." New Trans. Appendix 32. The quotation by which Mr. Campbell aims to confirm his interpretation is singularly infelicitous. The Philippians are exhorted by the apostle to *work out their salvation*, for this very reason, that "*it is God which worketh in them to will and to do of his good pleasure.*' Phil. 2: 12–13, or as the passage is more strongly rendered in Mr. Campbell's New Testament, "*For it is God who inwardly worketh in you, from benevolence, both to will and to work effectually.* Now it is precisely this *inward, effectual working of God* in the Philippians, *both to will and to work*, which the apostle styles "a *good work*," and which, he is fully persuaded God *will perform until the day of Jesus Christ.*

My *last* remark, concerns the *honor of the Holy Spirit.* The theory which I am opposing represents the infinite Spirit as condescending to carry on, and complete a work, which was commenced, and passed through its most difficult stage, without his influence. Man without any agency except the force of argument, contained in the written Word, is converted. He attends to the Word, is enlightened by it, sorrows for his sins, abandons them, believes in Christ, or heartily receives him as a Saviour, devotes himself with delight to the service of Christ, confesses him before men, braves scorn, persecution and death in his cause, and is baptized in his name; and then, this easy part of the work, as Mr. Campbell deems it, but most difficult according to the Scriptures, having been performed, the Holy Spirit *actually and powerfully assists him in his mighty struggles for eternal life.* What is this but to wrest from the Spirit the chief glory of his work?

Mr. Campbell, in his great zeal to steer clear of all speculative theology, maintains that all theories of the Spirit's influence in conversion are equally inefficacious and worthless. He thus writes—"But who can live on essential oils? Or will the art of speculating or inferring; or will the inferences when drawn—that the Spirit without the Word, or the Word without the Spirit, or the Spirit and Word in conjunction, regenerates the human soul; I ask, will the act of drawing these inferences, or these inferences when drawn, save the soul? If they will not, why make them essential to Christianity, beneficial to be taught?" Chn. Bap., p. 269. I am no more an advocate of mere speculation and empty theory, than Mr. Campbell. The subject of the Spirit's influence has been a fruitful source of profitless theorizing and vain jangling. I fully concur with him in the opinion that preaching the influence of the Spirit, is not preaching the Gospel; and that much mischief has arisen from insisting on this influence to the neglect of the duty of repentance and faith. But whether men are converted by the Spirit without the Word, or the Word without the Spirit, or the Word and Spirit in conjunction, are not questions of mere speculation, but grave, weighty, and practical. Whatsoever is legitimately inferred from the Scriptures is a part of Divine revelation, and profitable for instruction. The belief of it may not be essential to salvation; and yet it may contribute to the growth, happiness, and efficiency of the disciples of Christ. The influence of the Holy Spirit in the conversion of sinners is not a mere theory, but a revealed truth, the belief of which is intimately connected with the progress of the Redeemer's kingdom. The doctrine of the Spirit's efficient agency in the salvation of men, teaches us our entire dependence on God for the success of our efforts—even the most vigorous and best directed—for the promotion of his cause. It is well fitted to impress upon the heart the word of the Lord unto Zerubbabel, " Not by might, nor by power, but by my Spirit, saith the Lord of hosts." Zec. 4 : 6. This Scriptural doctrine clearly understood and heartily embraced, must lead Christians to humble, earnest, and persevering prayer for the salvation of sinners. It shows them where all their strength lies, and whence all their help must come. It disposes them to give the honor of their success to its real author, inspiring them with the devout sentiment of the Psalmist, " Not unto us, O Lord, not unto us, but unto thy name give glory, for thy mercy, and for thy truth's sake." In all ages, and in all countries, the truly pious, though differing widely on other subjects, have cordially united in the belief and maintenance of the doctrine of a supernatural agency in the conversion of sinners. Under the influence of this truth they have lived, their characters have been moulded, their labors have been performed, their prayers have been presented to God, and their successes have been achieved.

Much as Mr. Campbell was opposed, in the commencement of his Reformation, to religious speculations, it was not a great while before he adopted, or elaborated, an abstruse, metaphysical theory of conversion. I will not affirm that he taught regeneration by the Word—by the force of arguments—

without the Spirit. But if he did not so teach, in his Christianity Restored, then it has not been taught by any writer within the compass of my knowledge, and I seriously question whether it has ever been taught in the English tongue. Indeed, I do not perceive how the clearest, and most discriminating author, who admits the inspiration of the Scriptures, can teach it, if Mr. Campbell has not. Now, this "*inference*," or theory, I am very far from deeming "essential to Christianity, beneficial to be taught." Nay, it is an illegitimate inference, a false theory, not "essential to Christianity," but subversive of it, not "beneficial to be taught," but most pernicious. It cuts off all hope of divine aid, and all motives to pray for it. It greatly weakens a sense of obligation to the author of salvation, if, indeed, salvation is compatible with the "inference," and leads to a cold and heartless rationalism.

I have not yet entirely disposed of the subject of the Holy Spirit's influence in the work of conversion. I have already referred to the difficulty which Mr. Campbell's opponents have found in comprehending his views on this vital point. It seems thus to have arisen. While he has denounced the popular teaching on the subject, as mystical and pernicious, and has seemed most obviously to maintain a new and peculiar theory of conversion, he has sometimes published sentences on this point to which the most rigid advocates of orthodoxy could find no objection. As early as the year 1826, Rev. A. Broaddus, over the signature of Paulinus, thus addressed him—"There are some among us possessed of strong apprehension that you are disposed to deny the existence of the regenerating and sanctifying operations of the Holy Spirit on the spirit or heart of man; and that you would ascribe all the religious effects produced in us, solely to the influence of the written Word, or the external revelation of God. . . . For myself, I have said to others, as I now say to you, that I cannot think this of you. *I have seen many things in your writings which appear inconsistent with such a sentiment.*" Chn. Bap., p. 266. We have already seen in an extract from the Appendix to the Extra Examined, published in 1831, that Mr. Broaddus had changed his opinion on this point.

That I may do Mr. Campbell full justice, I will quote from his writings a few passages in which he appears to maintain evangelical views on the agency of the Holy Spirit.

"But if any man accustomed to speculate on religion as a science, should infer from any thing which I have said on these theories, that I contend for a religion in which the Holy Spirit has nothing to do; in which there is no need of prayer for the Holy Spirit; in which there is no communion of the Holy Spirit; in which there is no peace and joy in the Holy Spirit, he does me the greatest injustice." Chn. Bap., 269.

"If any man ask me how the influence and aid of the Holy Spirit is obtained, I answer, By prayer and the Word of God." p. 329.

"From the answer above given to query first, I am authorized to say, that 'saving faith' is wrought in the heart by the Holy Spirit, and that no man can believe to the saving of his soul, but by the Holy Spirit." p. 353.

Paulinus, in an article on the influence of the Spirit, thus summed up his argument—"The substance of the leading sentiment maintained in these two essays is, that we are dependent on the influence of the Holy Spirit to render the Word effectual to our conversion and final salvation." To this the editor of the Christian Baptist replied—"Although it might appear that some of the sentences extracted from different parts of the sacred volume were not originally intended to prove the position which was before the mind of Paulinus, yet still the conclusions to which he has come will be very generally embraced as declarative of sentiments styled evangelical. If this language does not endorse the doctrine of Paulinus, it is evasive, and unworthy of a candid writer." p. 437.

"On the subject of spiritual influence, there are two extremes of doctrine. There is the *Word alone* system, and there is the *Spirit alone* system. I believe in neither. The former is the parent of a cold, lifeless rationalism and formality. The latter is, in some temperaments, the cause of a wild, irrepressible enthusiasm ; and, in other cases, of a dark, melancholy despondency. * * * There yet remains another school, which never speculatively separates the Word and Spirit, which in every case of conversion contemplates them as *co-operating ;* or, which is the same thing, conceives of the Spirit of God as clothed with the Gospel motives and arguments—enlightening, convincing, persuading sinners, and thus *enabling them* to flee from the wrath to come." Debate with Rice, p. 614.

"I would not, sir, value at the price of a single mill, the religion of any man, as respects the grand affair of eternal life, whose religion is not begun, carried on, and completed by the personal agency of the Holy Spirit." p. 614.

"I believe the Spirit accompanies the Word, is always present with the Word, and *actually and personally* works through it upon the moral nature of man, but not without it." p. 745.

I have selected these quotations partly from the early, and partly from the later writings of Mr. Campbell, taking the liberty of italicising a few terms. I could easily increase the list of pertinent quotations—but it is unnecessary.

Concerning these extracts, one of three conclusions is certain. Either, *first,* they contradict the quotations furnished in the commencement of this chapter—or, *secondly*, they must be interpreted in harmony with the theory of conversion by moral suasion, which I have already discussed—or, *thirdly*, they must be understood as agreeing substantially with the popular, evangelical doctrine of conversion by Divine influence. And these several conclusions are entitled to particular attention.

First.—Are the statements of Mr. Campbell concerning the influence of the Holy Spirit contradictory? In my judgment they are. Whether his views on the subject were confused, or differed at different times, or were carelessly and vaguely expressed, I will not say; but they appear to me to be inconsistent. "*The only power,*" says Mr. Campbell, "*which one spirit can exert over another is in its arguments.*" If this is not the "*word alone system,*" I would gladly be informed what that system is. I repeat, I must be permitted to doubt whether any man ever has taught, or ever can teach the system, if Mr. Campbell did not inculcate it in his Christianity Restored. And yet he affirms in his Debate with Rice, "There is the *Word alone* system, and there is the *Spirit alone* system. I believe in neither." In one place he says, "Before the Holy Spirit can be received, the heart must be purified." In another place he writes, "I would not value at the price of a single mill, the religion of any man,—whose religion is not *begun, carried on, and completed by the personal agency of the Holy Spirit.*" In one he represents that all that is lone in us before regeneration, that is baptism, "God our Father effects by *the Word*;" in another he maintains, that in every case of conversion the Spirit and Word *co-operate*, "enlightening, convincing, persuading sinners, and thus *enabling them* to flee from the wrath to come;" and that the Spirit "*actually and personally works* through" the Word, "upon the moral nature of man." I will not affirm these various statements are contradictory; but I do not perceive their harmony. For the sake of the argument, however, I will admit their agreement. And now I must inquire,

Secondly, Are the last recited extracts from the writings of Mr. Campbell to be interpreted in harmony with the theory of conversion by moral suasion? Are we to understand all that he has said of the *co-operation* of the Spirit and Word—of religion "*begun, carried on, and completed by the personal agency of the Holy Spirit*"—of his "*actually and personally*" working through the Word on "man's moral nature"—as meaning nothing more than that the Spirit addresses arguments, through the written Word, to sinners, to persuade them to be converted; and that having done this his resources are exhausted, his power is spent? In other words, is the actual, personal agency of the Spirit, pleaded fo' by Mr. Campbell, to be resolved into mere moral suasion? If so, the system has been already examined, and the reader must decide whether it has been satisfactorily refuted. But if Mr. Campbell rejects the doctrine of conversion by moral suasion, or by the mere presentation of the arguments of the Holy Spirit to the mind, then I remark,

Thirdly—That Mr. Campbell's teaching is in substantial agreement with the popular evangelical doctrine of conversion through Divine influence. There is no middle ground between the "Word alone," or moral suasion system, and that which ascribes conversion to the personal agency of the Spirit through the Word. This latter system is the popular evangelical system—the system universally taught, when Mr. Campbell commenced his Reformation, except by a few ultra-Calvinists, and low Arminians and formalists—the system which permeated almost all our Biblical and theological literature; our commentaries, Bible dictionaries, bodies of divinity, and popular sermons—in fine, the system which maintained a quiet, undisputed, and controlling influence in all the orthodox churches of the land. I must confirm these statements by a few quotations from popular, evangelical writers, whose reputation preceded the Bethany Reformation, and has not declined from its influence.

"The instrument of this renovation (regeneration) is 'the word of truth.' In infusing the principle of divine life into the soul, God is wont to employ the Gospel as the instrument." R. Hall, vol. 3. p. 66.

"The change which God produces in men's dispositions and actions, by the truths of the Gospel impressed on their minds, is so great that it may be called a *begetting*, or *creating* them anew." McKnight. Note on Jas. 1: 18.

"But though this Word (the Gospel) cannot beget without him (God), yet it is by this Word that he begets, and ordinarily not without it." Leighton's Works, p. 120.

"*The Word*, or *doctrine of truth*, what St. Paul calls *the Word of the truth of the Gospel*, Col. 1: 5, is the *means* which God uses to convert souls." A. Clarke's Com., Jas. 1: 18.

"In this passage St. Peter declares, that Christians are born, or regenerated, διά λογου, by means of the *Word* of God. Of course he declares, that they were not regenerated without the instrumentality of the Word of God. What is true, with respect to this subject, of the Christians to whom *St. Peter* wrote, will not be denied to be true of Christians universally." Dwight's Theol., vol. 4, p. 40-41.

"The means (of regeneration) are pointed out; *the Word of truth*, i. e., the Gospel; as Paul expresses it more plainly, 1 Cor. 4: 15. This Gospel is indeed a *Word of truth;* else it could never produce such real, such lasting, such great and noble effects." M. Henry's Com., Jas. 1 : 18.

"No regeneration, no quickening grace, no faith nor holiness, come this way (through the law,) but through the preaching of the Gospel; in and through which, as a vehicle, the Spirit of God conveys himself into the heart, as a Spirit of regeneration and faith." Gill's Com., 1 Cor. 4: 15.

"Here is a plain evidence, that the Word of God is the ordinary means of our regeneration, it being 'the word preached,' the word we are to hear, (v. 19, 22,) and 'receive with meekness,' by which the new birth is by God wrought in us, and which, saith the apostle, is able to save the soul." Dr. Whitby's Com., Jas. 1 : 18.

Even Andrew Fuller, who maintained a Divine influence in regeneration, "which is immediate, or without any instrument whatever," and in which sentiment, so far as I have observed, he stood alone, did not consider this influence as producing the whole of that change denoted by the term *regeneration*. "I admit regeneration," he says, "to be by the Word of God, and that this truth is taught by the passage in question, (1 Pet. 1 : 23,) and also in Jas. 1 : 18; nor does this concession appear to clash with the position above." Fuller's Works, vol. 1, p. 666.

Quotations of this kind might be indefinitely multiplied, from the most enlightened, pious and approved authors, showing conclusively that the doctrine in question was generally, almost universally, held by evangelical Christians, before the first number of the *Christian Baptist* saw the light. In all the "vain janglings," to which the speculations of Mr. Campbell have unfortunately given birth, I do not remember to have heard but a single individual maintain the Fullerian theory, that regeneration is *commenced* by a Divine influence, "without any instrument," and he was an earnest and faithful minister of the Gospel, whose success was, in no degree, impeded by his peculiar theory.

Now if Mr. Campbell rejects the theory of conversion by *moral suasion*, and holds that conversion is effected by the personal agency of the Spirit, through the written Word, then on this great, vital, distinctive principle of evangelical Christianty, he is found in company with our Halls, our Leightons, our Henrys, and a host of such Protestant worthies; nor does he need to be ashamed of his company. On one merely speculative point, he differs from most, or all of his brethren. They believe that this is God's ordinary, or usual way of converting sinners; the only way in which we should hope, labor and pray for their conversion; but that he is not limited to this way. In the case of dying infants, or idiots, they believe that a moral change, equivalent to regeneration, is effected by the direct, personal agency of the Holy Spirit, without the Word.

They found their belief on what seems to them to be a legitimate inference from clearly revealed truth. From this inference Mr. Campbell dissents; and maintains not only that the Spirit does not, and needs not, but *cannot* operate except through its arguments. As this point, however, is purely speculative, and as Mr. Campbell admits the salvation of dying infants, and idiots, it cannot be deemed of great importance.

Is he then to be classed among the orthodox teachers of a Divine influence in the conversion of sinners? It will, doubtless, seem as strange to many as it was of old to find Saul among the prophets. For thirty years it has been his chosen employment to denounce, by the tongue and the pen, in no measured terms, the "mystic theology," and "theoretic doctors," and to expose the pernicious effects of the popular teaching on the influence of the Holy Spirit. He claimed to have made discoveries on this subject of great importance to the world. His admirers fancied that he had shed fresh, and most satisfactory light on it. They certainly received new views of this delicate and profound subject from their erudite instructor. One of them felt impelled to reflect the light which he had received "about the Holy Spirit's operations in this metaphysical day," in the following unequivocal language, which was published in the Christian Baptist, "without note or comment." "We must first hear, then believe and reform ; then obey, that is, be immersed ; then receive the regenerating Spirit, with all its heavenly blessings promised to the believing sons and daughters of Adam. This appears to be so plainly inculcated in the New Testament, that I am astonished that I so long remained ignorant of the Gospel, when at the same time I professed to be a teacher of it. And for this discovery I am indebted to you, brother Editor." p. 544. Another coadjutor, and an accredited leader in the Reformation, thus wrote—"If they (the Samaritans) were converted before baptism, they were converted without the Holy Spirit, for they had been baptized, and yet 'the Spirit had fallen on none of them.' . . . This passage (Gal. 2: 2,) ought alone to decide this controversy about the work of the Spirit. The passages are abundant which teach the nature of the Spirit's work, and all are like the above, conclusive as to the fact, that the Holy Spirit dwells in the saints, and that *he does not come to sinners to convert them.*" Scriptural Reformation by Jas. Henshall, p. 23. But this confidence that new light had appeared was, it seems, illusory. Mr. Campbell believes as the great body of evangelical ministers in all the Christian sects, believes, that sinners are converted by the personal agency of the Holy Spirit, through the Gospel. But, surely, since the world began, have there never been so many labored arguments, so much learned criticism, so much toil, debate and strife, such a waste of ink and paper, and such a multiplication of essays, pamphlets and books, to prove what scarcely any body doubted. The public mind was excited, the Christian world was agitated, the Baptist denomination, in several states, was thrown into confusion, many of the churches were rent asunder, a new sect was formed, and the aid of earth and heaven was invoked in the contest; and for what? Why, simply because Mr. Campbell taught, what was almost universally admitted, that the Spirit in conversion operates through the Word. But what then becomes of the boasted Reformation, of which the peculiar teaching on the influence of the Spirit constituted so important an article? It turns out, if the supposition under discussion is true, that the Reformation, on this important point, is no Reformation at all. We cannot avoid being reminded of a well known fable. Surely, there were never in any previous case, such sore travail, such mighty heavings, such piteous moanings, and such swelling expectations, in a simple case of abortion.

Before I conclude my remarks on this subject, I must venture on a conjecture, which will, I fear, not prove very acceptable to Mr. Campbell and his admirers. It is this—When he commenced his career as a Reformer, his religious views were undefined and crude. His first object was to bring into disrepute the "mystic theology" of the "populars," or "clergy." He found it necessary, for the accomplishment of his purpose, to publish some theory at variance with the popular doctrine of the Spirit's influence in conversion. This new theory began to be developed about the year 1826, and was consummated, and fully revealed, in the year 1831, when Austin taught the docile Timothy, that "every Spirit puts forth its moral power in words; that is, *all the power* it has over the views, habits, manners, or actions of men, is in the *meaning* and *arrangement* of its *ideas expressed in words;* or in significant signs addressed to the eye or ear." Christianity Restored, p. 348. But after the Reformation resulted in an organized party, Mr. Campbell, to avoid the odium of his peculiar notions of the Spirit's influence, or because he found it easier to defend the popular doctrine, began gradually to modify his views, and to glide out of the theory of conversion by moral suasion, into the doctrine that conversion is by the actual, personal agency of the Holy Spirit. This modification of his views began to appear in a discussion of the subject with the Rev. J. M. Peck, and was still more apparent in his Debate with the Rev. N. L. Rice. But for Mr. Campbell to acknowledge that he had erred in the fundamental principle of his Reformation, and that after all his wanderings, and denunciations of the "popular clergy," he had been compelled to admit the truth of their teaching on this vital point, would have demanded a degree of humility and moral heroism, which the high-spirited Reformer did not possess.

I do not intend to impeach the motives of Mr. Campbell. With their moral qualities I have nothing to do. Men are influenced by considerations of which they have little knowledge. Mr. Campbell has quite a fair share of human nature in him. He does not rise above the laws which govern other frail mortals. I have simply, and, I trust, kindly sketched what appears to me to have been his course in regard to the agency of the Spirit in conversion, and the motives that probably shaped it, and the intelligent and candid reader must form his own judgment.

The Identity of Regeneration, Conversion, and Baptism.

The subject of *Regeneration*, or *Conversion*, is of vital importance in the Christian System. On other points ignorance may be harmless, but on this it may be fatal. These terms, the former figurative, and the latter literal, are almost universally employed by theologians to denote that moral renovation, by which fallen man is fitted for the service of Christ on earth, and the enjoyment of his presence in heaven. On this subject Mr. Campbell has put forth new and peculiar views. He has written on it largely. It occupies a conspicuous place in the Reformation which he has so zealously advocated. His thoughts on this topic, scattered through his numerous periodicals, extras, and larger works, would fill a ponderous octavo. I have endeavored, sincerely and diligently, to comprehend his views on the subject, but have found it very difficult to do so. If they have not been obscure, variable, and contradictory, I confess to a want of perspicacity, which he, no doubt, will be very ready to admit. That the reader may judge for himself on this point, I will present in contrast a few quotations from the accredited works of the Reformer.

1. "No man believes more cordially, or teaches more fully, the necessity of a spiritual change of our affections—a change of heart—than I do. I have said a thousand times, that if a person were to be immersed twice seven times in the Jordan for the remission of his sins, or for the reception of the Holy Spirit, it would avail nothing more than wetting the face of a babe, unless his heart is changed by the Word and Spirit of God." Debate with Rice, p. 544.

Now this is quite orthodox. No "mystic doctor" in the land could have discoursed on the subject in a more evangelical strain. But let the reader turn to the Mill. Har., vol. 1, p. 136, and he will find the following language :

"The sprinkling of a speechless and faithless babe never moved it one inch in the way to heaven, and never did change its heart, character, or relation to God and the kingdom of heaven. But not so a believer, immersed as a volunteer in obedience of the Gospel. He has put on Christ."

"The sprinkling of a speechless and faithless babe—*never did change its heart ;*" but what is true of the sprinkling of an infant is *not true* of the voluntary immersion of a believer. So Mr. Campbell seems to teach. But do I not misunderstand him? He shall have the benefit of another quotation.

"There are three births, three kingdoms, and three salvations. One from the womb of our first mother, one from the water, and one from the grave. We enter a new world on, and not before each birth. The present animal life, at the first birth; the spiritual, or the life of God in our souls, at the second birth; and the life eternal in the presence of God, at the third birth. And he who dreams of entering the second kingdom, or coming under the dominion of Jesus without the second birth, may, to complete his error, dream of entering the kingdom of glory without a resurrection from the dead." Chn. Sys., p. 233.

Whether Mr. Campbell does here teach that we enter "the spiritual life, or the life of God in our souls, *at*," not *before*, "the second birth," or birth 'from the water,' which in the terminology of the

Bethany Reformation, means simply baptism ; and whether this teaching is compatible with what he has previously admitted of the inefficacy of baptism without a change of heart, the reader must decide.

2. " And will not every Christian say, that when a person *feels* and *acts* according to the faith, or the testimony of God, he is a new creature—regenerate —truly converted to God ?" Chn. Sys., p. 259. Certainly—I know no one that disputes this point. But if *feeling and acting* according to the testimony or Word of God, constitute regeneration or conversion, why does Mr. Campbell affirm, as he does in this very volume, that " *the Holy Spirit calls nothing personal regeneration except the act of immersion ?*" p. 202. And if baptism be the only Scriptural regeneration, as he maintains in this language, how can he reconcile this position with what he teaches in his late work on Baptism ?

Among the *Questions on Infant Baptism*, we find the following—*Ques.* 103. Is baptism compared to any thing else in the Scriptures ? *A.* Yes ; to the regenerating influences and operation of the Holy Spirit. Hence we read of 'the washing of regeneration,' and of the 'baptism of the Holy Spirit.' Camp. on Bap., p. 431. But if the " Holy Spirit calls nothing personal regeneration, except *the act of immersion*," how can the Scriptures, the only medium through which the Spirit communicates with us, compare *baptism* to " the *regenerating in-*

fluences and operation of the Spirit of God?" Is immersion in water an emblem of itself?

3. "Now, as soon as, and not before, a disciple, who has been begotten of God, is born of water, he is born of God, or of the Spirit." Ch'nty Restored, p. 206. "*Begotten* of God he may be; but *born* of God he cannot be, until born of water." Mill. Har. Extra, p. 30. I have noticed this strange conceit merely to show how flatly Mr. Campbell contradicts it. Hear him—"We are not baptized because of our fleshly descent from members of any church, but because '*born from above—born of the Spirit.*'" Camp. on Bap., 390. But if we are baptized *because* we are "born of the Spirit," then clearly we are not only "begotten of God," but born of God," *before* we are "born of water." Again, the distinction which Mr. Campbell sought to establish, in the above citations, between the phrases "begotten of God," and "born of God," he, in another place, thus earnestly repudiates.—"I would not say that Mr. Rice has been sporting with the credulity of the audience in his dissertations on *begotten* and *born*. Far be it. Yet really it looks more like an attempt of that sort, than at any grave argument. Whether we shall read, 'He that believeth that Jesus is the Christ, is born of God,' or is begotten of God, must depend on the taste and discrimination of the translator, as the word is the same in the original text." Debate with Rice, p. 457.

I should find it easy to increase the list of seeming contradictions on this subject from the writings of Mr. Campbell; but the above may suffice to convince the reader that it is difficult distinctly to comprehend what he does aim to teach in regard to it. His views seem to be unsettled. What he affirms at one time, he denies at another. What he insists on in the Millennial Harbinger Extra, as of great importance, he summarily dismisses in his Debate with Dr. Rice, as mere trifling. But amid the mass of confusion and contradictions, one point is clear. Mr. Campbell insists, frequently, and in a variety of language, on the perfect *Identity of Regeneration, Conversion, and Baptism.* It is, or it was, an important article in the creed of the Reformers.

The substance of the Reformation, on this point, as developed in the Millennial Harbinger Extra, and perpetuated in the Christian System, is this—*Converts made to Jesus Christ by the apostles were taught to consider themselves pardoned, justified, sanctified, reconciled, adopted, and saved.—These terms are expressive, not of any moral quality, but of a state or condition.—This change of state is effected, not by any change of views or of feelings, nor by faith, but by an act resulting from faith—and this act is* IMMERSION, *called with equal propriety,* CONVERSION *or* REGENERATION. But let us listen to the highest authority on this point. "Whatever the act of faith may be, it necessarily becomes the line of discrimination between the two states before described. On this side, and on that, mankind are in quite different states. On the one side, they are pardoned, justified, sanctified, reconciled, adopted, and saved : on the other, they are in a state of condemnation. This act is sometimes called immersion, regeneration, conversion." Chn. Sys., p. 193. "These expressions," (immersed, converted, regenerated,) "in the apostle's style, denote the same act," p. 203. "For if immersion be equivalent to regeneration, and regeneration be of the same import with being born again, then being born again and being immersed, are the same thing." p. 200.

I may have occasion under another head to examine the above system—I shall, in this place, confine my discussion to the *identity of baptism, regeneration, and conversion.*

Before I enter on my task, I must submit a few remarks to prevent misconception.

Mr. Campbell has been frequently, but, I think, unfairly charged with teaching *baptismal regeneration.* As popularly understood, baptismal regeneration denotes a moral change, effected through the influence of Christian baptism. Some things which Mr. Campbell has written, as we have seen, seem to imply this doctrine ; and he has exposed himself to the suspicion of holding it, by quoting its advocates in support of his peculiar views ; but certainly he has not formally proclaimed it—he earnestly advocates principles at war with it. What he clearly maintains is, not that we are regenerated by baptism, but that baptism is itself regeneration, and the *only "personal regeneration."*

I do not charge Mr. Campbell with denying the necessity of a moral change preparatory to baptism. He has written equivocally, perhaps it would be better to say, obscurely, on the subject. His love of novelty, the immaturity of his views, or the blinding influence of his theory, or all these causes combined, have impelled him to record many sentences, which ingenuity, less pregnant than his own, finds it difficult to reconcile with my admission. A pity it is, that an author, destined to exert so widespread and moulding an influence in the world, should have written so carelessly and confusedly on so vital a subject.

It is also due to Mr. Campbell to admit, that in the passages under discussion, he professes to use the terms Regeneration and Conversion, not in their popular, but *Scriptural* sense. "It is not," he modestly says, "the regeneration of the schools, in which Christianity has been lowered, misapprehended, obscured, and adulterated, of which we are to write; but that regeneration of which Jesus spoke, and the apostles wrote." Chn'ty Restored, p. 257. It is to displace the "jargon of the schools," by a "pure speech," that Mr. Campbell would have us to confound regeneration, baptism and conversion.

Having made these preliminary remarks, I now take issue with the Bethany Reformer on the *Identity of Baptism, Regeneration, and Conversion.* I maintain that neither the term *regeneration*, nor *conversion*, nor *any equivalent term*, nor the *Greek words* which they properly represent, nor any of their *cognates*, are ever used in the Scriptures to denote baptism.

Regeneration.—This term as it has been already remarked, which is usually employed by theologians to denote that moral change by which man is fitted for the enjoyment of the kingdom of heaven, occurs but twice in the common version of the Scriptures. In the Greek it is παλιγγενεσίᾳ, which literally signifies a new birth, or creation. It is first found Mat. 19: 28. Whatever may be its import in this passage, it is agreed, on both sides, that it refers neither to a personal renovation, nor to baptism. This text has no bearing on the controversy. Its last occurrence is Tit. 3: 5. "Not according to works of righteousness which we have done, but according to his mercy he saved us, by the washing of regeneration, and renewing of the Holy Ghost." The phrase the "*washing of regeneration*," or according to McKnight's rendering, which Mr. Campbell prefers, "the *bath of regeneration*," is understood by him to mean *immersion*. "*Washing of regeneration*," he says, "*and immersion are therefore only two names for the same thing.*" Chn. Sys., p. 200. The phrase does not elsewhere occur in the Scriptures. That it means baptism is a mere assumption. The weight of authority is in favor of this opinion, and there is no motive, so far as this discussion is concerned, to controvert it. The assumption is, however, subversive of the position that immersion and regeneration are identical. According to the assumption it is not *regeneration*, but "the *washing* of regeneration" that means baptism. Baptism is a *washing*, or, if Mr. Campbell prefers it, a *bath*, emblematic of regeneration—alluding, as some suppose, to the cleansing of a new born infant. I need not farther discuss this point. I can adduce authority to settle this matter, of the greatest weight with the Reformers, and to which Mr. Campbell will not demur. In his Debate with Rice, he thus discoursed—"I believe that almost all, if not absolutely all, the fathers, Greek and Latin, used regeneration and baptism as representatives of the same action and event. I do not, however, approve the phraseology used by them on this subject. I call baptism 'the washing of the new birth,' rather than the new birth itself. So I think Paul most learnedly denominates it." p. 544. This point is settled. The term *regeneration is never used in the Scriptures to denote baptism.*

Here we might drop this subject, were it not that

kindred phrases, such as "born of God," "born of the Spirit," "born of water," &c., have been drawn into the controversy. It is necessary to dispel the mist that Mr. Campbell has spread over them. The Greek term, γεννάω, means to beget or generate. Its derivatives in the New Testament are generally passive, and mean to be begotten. It occurs in the writings of the apostle John fifteen times relative to a moral change. The following are the passages in which it is found—John 1 : 13. —3: 3, 6, 7, 8.—1 John 2: 29—3 : 9—4: 7—5: 1, 4, 18. Twelve times it is rendered *born*—eight times it is found in the phrase "born of God," or its equivalent—twice in the phrase "born of the Spirit," and twice in the phrase "born again." Three times it is rendered *begotten*—and every time it is contained in the phrase "begotten of God." It is once rendered *born* in connexion with water—"born of water." John 3 : 5. Twice the term is employed by the apostle Paul to denote the influence which he exerted in conversion; but this sense of the term does not affect the controversy. 1 Cor. 4: 15.—Philem. 10.

The phrases "born again," "born of God," &c., have been universally considered by evangelical Christian writers as equivalent to a *new birth*, or *regeneration.* If men are born of God they must be *re*-generated. Even Mr. Campbell, when his system is out of view, admits the soundness of this position. "To the fruits of his labors," he writes, "such a preacher with Paul may say, to Jesus Christ, through the Gospel, I have *regenerated*, or *begotten* you." Chn. Sys., p. 300. Now that these phrases (not including "born of water"), all denote not baptism, or a change of state, but a personal, moral renovation, is clear and indisputable. To ascribe to immersion what is ascribed to this divine birth would be not only false, but ridiculous. "Except a man be born again he cannot *see* the kingdom of God." Does baptism open a man's eyes? "That which is born of the Spirit is spirit"—spiritual, holy. Can such an effect be ascribed to baptism? "Whosoever is born of God doth not commit sin; for his seed remaineth in him: and he cannot sin because he is born of God." Will Mr. Campbell venture to ascribe this efficacy to baptism? "He that is begotten of God keepeth himself, and that wicked one toucheth him not." I need not say more to prove that these phrases denote a moral change; and the pertinency and force of the language for this purpose every intelligent mind must perceive.

The phrase "born of water," John 3 : 5, whatever may be its import—and I do not think it refers to baptism—cannot by any reasonable construction, or inference, justify the confounding of regeneration and baptism. Admitting that it means baptism, it is clearly distinguished from the new birth, or being "born of the Spirit," and to confound them is not to interpret, but to pervert the word of God, and that too on a most vital subject.

I have been greatly surprised to find on examination with how little caution and discrimination Mr. Campbell has discussed the subject of the new birth. Take the following passage as a specimen—"Persons are begotten by the Spirit of God, impregnated by the Word, and born of the water. In one sense a person is born of his father, but not until he is first born of his mother. So in every place where water and the Spirit, or water and the Word, are spoken of, *the water stands first.* Every child is born of its father, when it is born of its mother. Hence the Saviour put the mother first, and the apostles follow him. . . . . Now, as soon as, and not before, a disciple, who has been begotten of God, is born of water, he is born of God, or of the Spirit. *Regeneration is, therefore, the act of being born.*" Ch'nty Restored, p. 206. Had Mr. Campbell not proclaimed so frequently that his mission is to "restore a pure speech," it might easily be supposed that it is to introduce an *unintelligible jargon.* A person is *begotten of God*, and *born of water*—God is his *father*, and the *water* his mother—and this same person is impregnated by the Word. The work is begun in the Spirit, and ended, not in the flesh, but in water. "How can these things be?" "Now, as soon as, and not before, a disciple, who has been *begotten of God*, is *born of water*, he is *born of God*." With equal clearness, taste and truth, might he affirm, That "as soon as, and not before, a disciple, who has been" begotten of water, is born of God, he is born of water. Nay, the language would seem to be more in harmony with his system. "In every place where the water and the Spirit are spoken of, *the water stands first*." It is not easy to say whether this jargon partakes more of the ridiculous or of the blasphemous; yet, doubtless, its author meant it for sound theology. Now, the slightest attention to his Greek Testament, would have preserved him from this confusion of speech. He would have seen, as he subsequently saw, and confessed, that the same term is rendered in the common version, according to the taste of the translators, *begotten* or *born*; and that all arguments and deductions grounded on this distinction in the common version would be merely trifling with the ignorance or credulity of his readers. And yet, a large portion of the sophistry and crudities with which the Millennial Harbinger Extra abounds, is drawn from this shallow conceit.

Before I abandon this subject, I must submit another remark. The Greek word ἀναγεννάω which properly means to beget again, or to regenerate, is found twice in the New Testament. Once it is found in 1 Peter 1: 3, and is rendered *begotten again*. "Blessed be the God and Father of our

Lord Jesus Christ, which, according to his abundant mercy, *hath begotten us again* unto a lively hope," &c. It occurs again in the 23d verse of the same chapter, and is rendered in the common version *born again*, and by Doctors Doddridge and McKnight, with the sanction of Mr. Campbell, in his New Testament, *regenerated.* "Being born again," or "regenerated, not of corruptible seed, but of incorruptible, by the word of God," &c. Now, it is clear and unquestioned that both these texts have reference, not to baptism, but to a personal and moral renovation.

I have now shown that there is not the shadow of authority in the language of Christ, or his apostles, for confounding regeneration and baptism. They are totally distinct in their nature, design, and effects, as can be easily demonstrated.

CONVERSION.—The Greek word, ἐπιστρέφω, which means simply to *turn*, occurs with its variations, in the New Testament, thirty-nine times, and nineteen times, if I mistake not, it refers to a moral change, total or partial, or to what theologians term *conversion ;* but never to *immersion.* That the reader may form his own judgment on this subject, I will cite the passages in which the term is found. Mat. 13 : 15—Mar. 4 : 12—Luke 1 : 16, 17 ; 22 : 32—John 12 : 40—Acts 3 : 19 ; 9 : 35 ; 11 : 21 ; 14 : 15 ; 15 : 19 ; 26 : 18, 20 ; 28 : 27—2 Cor. 3 : 16—1 Thess. 1 : 9—Jas. 5 : 19, 20—1 Pet. 2 : 25.

The noun, επιστρωφή, is used but once, (Acts 15 : 3) and is properly rendered *conversion*. That these terms denote a moral renovation—the turning of a man, soul and body, to God—the evidence seems complete. "When thou art *converted*, strengthen thy brethren." "A great number believed and *turned unto the Lord.*" "Brethren, if any of you do err from the truth, and one *convert* him ; let him know, that he which *converteth* a sinner from the error of his way, shall save a soul from death," &c. That the word in these passages denotes, not the act of immersion, but a hearty turning from sin to God, or from error to rectitude, the intelligent reader needs no proof. And what the term means in these texts, it uniformly means in the places where it refers to man's moral change. Yet, read what Mr. Campbell pens in the face of these truths. "Conversion is on all sides, understood to be a turning to God." Very well! . . . "Here it is worthy of notice, that the apostles, in all their speeches and replies to interrogatories, never commanded an inquirer to pray, read, or sing, *as preliminary to his coming, but always commanded and proclaimed immersion as the first duty, or the first thing to be done, after a belief of testimony.*" The sincere "belief of testimony," or faith in Christ, necessarily implies conversion, or "coming to God." It is essential to the act, and inseparable from it. So an apostle teaches, "Whosoever believeth that Jesus is the Christ, is born of God," and consequently converted. Now, it would have been strange, indeed, if the apostles had commanded an inquirer to "pray, read, or sing, as preliminary" to that which had been already done. If when Mr. Campbell affirms that the apostles proclaimed "*immersion as the first duty, after a belief of testimony,*" he means that baptism is the first institution in which the believer is required to make a public confession of Christ, I agree with him. It does not follow, however, from this position, that there may not be other, and important duties incumbent on a believer previously to baptism. "Hence," continues the Reformer, "neither praying, singing, reading, repenting, sorrowing, resolving, nor waiting to be better, was the converting act." Perhaps not! Conversion, or turning to God, is necessarily a complex exercise, comprehending that series of inward conflicts usually termed experience. Mr. Campbell continues—"Immersion *alone* was that act of turning to God." A more gratuitous assumption was never penned. It sets at naught the laws of philology and the teaching of revelation. Neither godly sorrow, repentance unto salvation, faith that works by love, nor a readiness to suffer martyrdom for Christ, nor all these together constitute conversion; but immersion *alone*, (I give his own emphasis) is the act of turning to God. Let us hear him again. . . . "From the day of Pentecost, to the final *Amen* in the revelation of Jesus Christ, no person was said to be converted, or to turn to God, until he was buried in, and raised up out of the water." Chn. Sys., p. 209. Suppose I admit this position, is it possible that the astute Reformer does not perceive that his reasoning is illogical? Thus he reasons—None were said to be converted who were not immersed—*ergo*, immersion—*immersion alone*, is the converting act. Let us try the force of this reasoning in another case. "From the day of Pentecost to the final *Amen* in the revelation of Jesus Christ, no person was said to be" *holy* "until he was buried in and raised out of the water," *ergo*, immersion and holiness are identical. But I will furnish a more carefully fortified illustration of this argument. "From the day of Pentecost to the final *Amen* in the revelation of Jesus Christ, no person was said to" *believe in Christ*, who had not been immersed. So Mr. Campbell testifies. "The apostle—never supposes such a case as is often before our minds—a believing unbaptized man. Such a being could not have been found in the whole apostolic age." Debate with Rice, p. 509.—*Ergo*, "*immersion alone*" is the act of believing. The conclusion follows irresistibly, according to the principles of Mr. Campbell's logic.

It is no part of my purpose to reconcile the assertion that "a believing unbaptized man" "could not have been found in the whole apostolic age," with the acknowledged truth that faith was a *pre-*

requisite to baptism, that the Ethiopian treasurer confessed his *faith* in Christ, *previously* to his baptism, and that "many of the Corinthians, hearing, *believed*, and were baptized." I will leave this for Mr. Campbell to do—a task for which his ingenuity eminently fits him.

I will now notice Mr. Campbell's chief argument in support of his position.

"The commission for converting the world teaches that immersion was necessary to discipleship; for Jesus said, "Convert the nations, immersing them into the name," &c., and "teaching them to observe," &c. The construction of the sentence fairly indicates that no person can be a disciple, according to the commission, who has not been immersed: *for the active participle in connection with an imperative. either declares the manner in which the imperative, shall be obeyed, or explains the meaning of the command.*

"To this I have not found an exception:—for example—'Cleanse the house, sweeping it.' 'Cleanse the garment, washing it,' shows the manner in which the command is to be obeyed, or explains the meaning of it. Thus, 'Convert (or disciple) the nations, immersing them, and teaching them to observe,' &c., expresses the manner in which the command is to be obeyed.

If the Apostles had only preached and not immersed, they would not have converted the hearers according to the commission: and if they had immersed, and not taught them to observe the commands of the Saviour, they would have been transgressors. A disciple, then, according to the commission, is one that has heard the Gospel, believed it, and been immersed. A disciple, indeed, is one that continues in keeping the commandments of Jesus."

The principle of construction, so warmly advocated by Mr. Campbell, is simply this—Active participles, when united with a command, *invariably* express the *meaning* of the command, or the *manner* of obeying it.

Let us observe the influence of this principle in the interpretation of the commission. "Go—teach all nations,"—or *convert* all nations, as Mr. Campbell renders it—this is the command: "*immersing* them," &c. The active participle *immersing* expresses the manner of converting the nations.

This principle or rule is assumed by Mr. Campbell to be correct. He adduces the authority of no critic in its support. His only argument in its favor is a string of sentences so constructed as to agree with the rule. It is quite as easy, however, to form sentences at variance with it; and it is purely a question of taste whether in such sentences the imperative mood, or the participle should be employed. It is worthy of remark, too, that his examples in support of the rule are all in the

English language ; and his numerous criticisms, and extended discussions, furnish not the slightest evidence that the rule was based on a critical investigation of the genius of the Greek tongue, or even the slightest acquaintance with it.

I will not follow him in his labored discussions on this point—I need not—I am greatly deceived, if I cannot demonstrate by a shorter process the *absurdity* of the rule as applied to the commission. There are two Greek words in this solemn charge rendered *teach*. The first, with which we have chiefly to do, is μαθητεύσατε from μαθητεύω, which in Donnegan's Lexicon is defined, ("*act, with an accusative in N. T.,*) *to instruct.*" It may be well to examine briefly its use in the New Testament. It occurs in various forms in this volume four times. Its first occurrence is Mat. 13 : 52—"Therefore every scribe which is μαθητευθεὶς, *instructed*, unto the kingdom of heaven, is like unto a householder, which bringeth forth out of his treasure things new and old." Dr. G. Campbell, following the common version, renders it *instructed ;* and Doddridge translates it *disciplined.* There can be no reasonable doubt but that the word here means *instructed, taught, well informed.* It is found again Mat. 27 : 57, where Doctors Campbell and Doddridge concur with king James' translators in rendering it *disciple.* Joseph of Arimathea was "Jesus' ἐμαθήτευσε, *disciple.* Joseph was, according to the *usus loquendi* of Christ, and of the times, a *disciple of Jesus, without baptism*, for he was one "secretly for fear of the Jews." The word occurs, also, Acts 14: 21—"And when they had preached the Gospel to that city, and had μαθητεύσαντες *taught* many," or, according to the rendering of Doddridge, "*made a considerable number of disciples*, they returned again to Lystra," &c. The apostles, according to their custom, proclaimed the Gospel, and taught, instructed the people,—made disciples, or learners of them—but whether they baptized them does not appear. The word occurs no where else but in the commission, where in the common version it is translated *teach*, by Dr. Campbell *convert*, and by Dr. Doddridge *proselyte*. "I render the word μαθητεύσατε *proselyte*," he says, "that it may be duly distinguished from διδάσκοντες *teaching*, (in the next verse,) with which our version confounds it. The former seems to import instruction in the essentials of religion, which it was necessary adult persons should know and submit to, before they could regularly be admitted to baptism; the latter may relate to those more particular admonitions in regard to Christian faith and practice, which were to be built upon that foundation." Fam. Expos. *in loco.* The sum of the matter is, that Christ in the command employed a term, whose obvious import is to *instruct*, to make a *disciple*, or *learner*, precisely such as was Joseph of Arimathea. But I can furnish in support of this view high authority for the learned, and paramount authority for the Reformers. In his Debate with Rice, p. 367, Mr. Campbell says—"The great Grotius, in his simplicity, distinguished *matheteuo*, the first word in the commission, as distinguished from *didasco* the last; both translated *teach* in this common version, thus: *Matheteuo*, says he, "means to communicate the first, or elementary principles; then after baptizing those who receive these rudimental views, teach or introduce them as persons initiated into the higher branches of Christian doctrine." "This," continues Mr. Campbell, "is my view of the passage; and, certainly, it is the etymological and well received meaning of the word, all the world over."

I am now prepared to apply the rule under discussion to the commission. "Go, *matheteusate*, communicate the first or elementary principles," of religion, to "all nations." How? The connected *active participle*, says Mr. Campbell, points out the *manner* of obeying the command—"*immersing* them into the name of the Father, Son, and Holy Spirit." Communicate elementary religious *instruction*, by *immersing the body in water*. Is it not absurd? But I have not yet reached the climax of this absurdity. The second, as well as the first, subjoined participle prescribes the mode of performing the command. Let us follow the rule. "Go—communicate the *first or elementary* principles" of the Gospel to all nations. How? *Mirabile dictu!*

By teaching, or introducing them, "as persons initiated, into the *higher branches of Christian doctrine.*" Communicate the *elementary principles* by teaching the *higher branches!* Is it necessary to say more to expose the fallacy of the rule? How incontrovertible then is the conclusion of that profound scholar, and eminent critic, Dr. G. Campbell, concerning the commission, Mat. 28 : 19-20.—"There are manifestly three things which our Lord here distinctly enjoins his apostles to execute with regard to the nations, to wit: *matheteuein, baptizien, disdaskein;* that is, to convert them to the faith—to initiate the converts into the church by baptism—and to instruct the baptized in all the duties of the Christian life."

I must furnish another testimony on this subject, though pointedly at variance with the testimony of the same witness elsewhere given. "In the commission which Messiah gave to his apostles for converting the nations, he commanded three things to be done, indicated by three very distinct and intelligible terms, viz: *matheteusate, baptizontes, didaskontes.*" Camp. on Bap., p. 116. This point is now settled.

I must briefly notice one more argument in support of the identity of conversion and baptism. It is founded on Acts 3 : 19. "*Repent ye, therefore, and be converted,*" &c. The argument is briefly this—Peter on the day of Pentecost preached repentance—immersion—and remission of sins—and in Solomon's portico, repentance—conversion—and the blotting out of sins. Mr. Campbell maintains that the latter was the same proclamation as the former, conversion being substituted for immersion This is a mere assumption. It is contrary to the plain and well understood import of the language used. The argument, if argument it may be called, is based on a fallacy. It is this—that the apostles in their addresses to sinners proclaimed, uniformly, the same truths, and duties, and in the same order. Nothing can be farther from the truth. We have but a brief outline of their discourses in the Acts of the Apostles; but they exhibit the greatest variety of topics and arrangement. Their addresses are all in harmony—all substantially containing the Gospel—but no two of them are precisely alike in language, method, or matter. To infer then that Peter preached baptism in Solomon's porch, contrary to the plain import of his language, because he did on the day of Pentecost, is not merely illogical, and opposed to the history of the apostolic preaching, but is to indulge in a license in biblical interpretation which may lead to the most pernicious consequences.

Before I quit this subject, I must offer a few remarks on another point. Mr. Campbell labors earnestly to prove that the early Christian Fathers called *baptism regeneration.* I shall not dispute this position. Their testimony seems to be entitled to but little credit. Their writings abound in peurile conceits, gross mistakes, and pernicious errors. None pays less deference to their testimony than Mr. Campbell, when it is not in harmony with his views. Baptism was early confounded with regeneration, of which it is, as he teaches us, the "emblem." Camp. on Bap., p. 430. The sign was mistaken for the thing signified. To this mischievous mistake there is among mankind a strong tendency. We see it in the monstrous doctrine of transubstantiation, and in the idolatrous worship of the host. It is displayed no less clearly in the unscriptural practice of infant baptism, the absurd dogma of baptismal regeneration, and many other errors with which the Christian world has been deluged. I only wonder that Mr. Campbell, the Reformer, the restorer of a "pure speech," should be found following this evil tendency.

PRAYER NOT A DUTY OF THE UNBAPTIZED.

We have the doctrine of Campbellism on this point in the following extract :—

"No man can have a holy spirit otherwise than as he possesses a spirit of love, of meekness, of humility ; but this he cannot have unless he feel himself pardoned and accepted. Therefore the promise of such a gift wisely makes the reception of it posterior to the forgiveness of sins. Hence in the moral fitness of things in the evangelical economy, baptism or immersion is made the first act of a Christian's life, or rather the regenerating act itself; in which the person is properly born again—'born of water and spirit'—without which into the kingdom of Jesus he cannot enter. No prayers, songs of praise, no acts of devotion in the new economy, are enjoined on the *unbaptized*." Chn. Bap., p. 439.

This passage abounds in errors; but I shall limit my remarks to one—a serious one—that the *unbaptized are not required to pray, or perform other acts of devotion.*

This is not a chief, nor a prominent, but, certainly, not an unimportant item in the "current Reformation." It is not directly expressed, but clearly implied in the language used. "No prayers, songs of praise, no acts of devotion in the new economy, are *enjoined on the unbaptized*." But if they are not enjoined, either by express command, authoritative example, or fair implication, they are not obligatory. "Where no law is there is no transgression," and, consequently, no obligation. Error is prolific, and always brings forth after its kind. The error under consideration was the natural offspring of Mr. Campbell's false views of regeneration. Conceiving, most erroneously, that immersion was "the *first* act of a Christian's life, or rather the *regenerating* act itself," he readily concluded that neither prayer, nor any other act which implied spiritual life, could be demanded of the *unimmersed*. This was an article of the primitive Campbellism, often and variously expressed. It has not, so far as I have observed, been repeated in the later writings of Mr. Campbell, nor has it been repudiated. It stands among the recorded and stereotyped items which compose the "ancient Gospel." It may have, it probably has, sunk into comparative forgetfulness; but I well remember that many of the primitive Reformers heartily embraced it, and deemed prayer before immersion as an invention of the "mystic doctors," a relic of the dark ages, and a grievous innovation on the "ancient order of things;" an error, in short, closely allied to "*experience before baptism.*"

I do not know that Mr. Campbell would now maintain, or that any of the Reformers now embrace, the doctrine clearly inculcated in the above extract; but I must, in justice to the system under examination, briefly expose its fallacy.

Prayer has been the duty of man under every dispensation of religion. The obligation to this service springs from the relation between the infinitely merciful God, and fallen, guilty, and dependent man, in a probationary state. It is an essential element in true piety. It is the very breath of spiritual life—a life which, I have already shown, does not depend on the act of immersion, but, in the evangelical order of things, precedes that act. It implies repentance faith, and Scriptural regeneration. No man can pray acceptably to God without renouncing his sins, believing in Christ, and having a new heart. And no man was ever a proper subject for Christian baptism who had not been taught to pray, sincerely, and fervently.

What say the Scriptures on this point? "And Jesus spake a parable unto them, (the disciples,) to this end, that men ought always to pray, and not to faint." Christ taught that *men*—not baptized men merely—but *men*, irrespective of their character, relations, or professions—*all* men, *ought*, are under obligation, to pray. Though the term *man* is not found in the Greek, and the language may be fairly rendered, *It is proper to pray always*, yet it is obvious that the common version gives its true sense. Prayer is proper for *all men*, at *all times*. Nay, but, says Mr. Campbell, "no prayers in the new economy are enjoined on the *unbaptized*." The publican prayed in the temple, and returned home justified, without baptism. The dying thief prayed on the cross, and was admitted into Paradise, without baptism. There is but one method, that even the ingenuity of Mr. Campbell can employ to evade the force of these Scriptures. It may be said, that Christ spake the parable of the unjust judge, and that the examples of the publican and of the thief occurred, before the new economy was fully set up. Well, I will furnish another, and unexceptionable example. When Saul of Tarsus was converted, the Lord directed

Ananias to go to him, "for, behold," said the Lord, "*he prayeth.*" Acts 9: 11. It is clear from this Scripture, beyond a question, not only that Saul prayed before his baptism, but that his prayer was acceptable to the Lord, and that Ananias was sent to instruct and baptize him in consequence of its acceptableness; and this example of acceptable prayer has all the weight, authority, and efficacy of an explicit command to the unbaptized to pray.

Baptism is the first positive rite in the new economy to which the believer is required to submit; and every believer should yield to it a submission as prompt as his circumstances will properly allow. But baptism is not the *unconditional* duty of a believer. His obligation to be baptized may depend on a thousand circumstances beyond his control. No properly authorized administrator may be willing to baptize him—he may be beyond the reach of one—the state of his health, or his want of personal freedom—and numerous other causes, may preclude the possibility of his baptism; and, consequently, the obligation to be baptized. But is he not required to pray, and engage in other acts of devotion, until he finds an opportunity of performing what Mr. Campbell calls "the regenerating act?" To ask the question, is to answer it. God has not made the duty of prayer or praise to depend on the act of baptism. The connection is wholly imaginary. It has no existence, and, so far as I am informed, never had an existence, except in the brain, whose fecundity has supplied such a variety and exuberance of speculations for the pages of the Christian Baptist, and Millennial Harbinger, and in the minds of those, whether many or few, who have, with unquestioning docility, derived their theological notions from these sources.

THE REMISSION OF SINS IN BAPTISM.

"Remission of sins" is equivalent to pardon or forgiveness, and does not differ essentially from justification. The phrase signifies deliverance from the obligation to suffer the punishment due to sins. The subject is one of manifest and transcendent importance. Its claims to our careful and devout attention are commensurate with the value of the soul, the malignity of sin, the preciousness of the blood of Christ, the depth of perdition, the height of glory, and the vastness of eternity. Our knowledge on this subject must be derived solely from Divine revelation. Whether God will forgive sins, and if he will, through what medium, and on what conditions, are questions which only He can decide, and of his decisions we can have no knowledge, except as he reveals them to us.

What do the Scriptures teach on this vital subject? The orthodox belief is—that, in virtue of the atonement of Christ, God, freely and fully, remits the sins of all those who heartily repent, and cordially believe in Christ. In no article of faith are those Christians, usually termed evangelical, more generally and firmly united than in this. It is the distinguishing tenet of Protestant Christendom. Mr. Campbell, on the other hand, maintains that penitent believers are forgiven, not before, but in the act of immersion. "Peter," he says, "to whom was committed the keys, opened the kingdom of heaven in this manner, and made *repentance*, or reformation, *and immersion, equally necessary to forgiveness*. . . . When a person is immersed for the remission of sins, it is just the same as if expressed, in order *to obtain the remission of sins*. . . . I am bold, therefore, to affirm, that every one of them who, in the belief of what the apostle spoke, was immersed, did, *in the very instant in which he was put under water, receive the forgiveness of his sins, and the gift of the Holy Spirit*." Chn. Bap., p. 416, 417. I have italicised some clauses in the above sentences to draw particular attention to their meaning. The believer in Christ, however sincere, and whatever may be his moral state, is condemned, exposed to all the dreadful consequences of disobedience, until the *very instant when he is put under water*. Mr. Campbell teaches that baptism is perfectly useless, "as empty as a blasted nut," to all who are pardoned. "If men," he says, "are conscious that their sins are forgiven, and that they are pardoned before they are immersed ; I advise them not to go into the water, for they have no need of it." Chn. Bap., *unexpurgated* edition, vol. 6, p. 160.

The doctrine of *Baptismal Remission* is the main pillar of Campbellism. It was slowly and gradually developed in the writings of Mr. Campbell, as it was, or was supposed to be, disinterred from the accumulated rubbish of past ages. It was, at length, fully revealed, strongly stated, and defended, at large, with all the learning, dialectic skill, and unwavering confidence of the redoubtable Reformer, in the famous *Millennial Harbinger Extra.* This precious relic was afterwards substantially embalmed in *Christianity Restored,* and in the *Christian System.* The *Extra* for a time spread dismay in the ranks of the "regulars." Such an array of learning, logic, and authority, few were bold enough to encounter. But time tries all things. We have grown familiar with the *Extra.* We have seen many of its positions successfully assailed. We have seen the Reformer himself modifying, or abandoning some of his points. The most timid have recovered from their alarms.

The system of *Baptismal Remission,* developed in the *Extra,* I now propose to examine, with as much particularity as my plan will allow.

Mr. Campbell, after some preliminary remarks, presents and discusses his views of "the Christian institution for the remission of sins," under *twelve propositions.*

The first *six* propositions he engrosses into one leading proposition, in the following words, viz.: "*The converts made to Jesus Christ by the apostles were taught to consider themselves pardoned, justified, sanctified, reconciled, adopted, and saved; and were addressed as pardoned, justified, sanctified, reconciled, adopted, and saved persons, by all who first preached the Gospel of Christ.*" Chn'ty Restored, p. 191.

To this engrossed proposition, I have no objection. I am only surprised that Mr. Campbell should have deemed it necessary to encumber his argument with an elaborate discussion, of seven pages, to prove what no respectable writer, Protestant or Romanist, orthodox or heterodox, so far as I have observed, has ever denied. Let the proposition then stand "as irrefragably proved."

But while I concur with the writer as to the truth of his proposition, I can by no means agree with him in his definition of its terms. "These terms," he says, "are expressive, not of any quality of mind, —not of any personal attribute of body, soul, or spirit—but each of them represents, and all of them together represent *a state*, or *condition*." Does not the word "*sanctified*" denote an attribute of the soul or spirit? Is it not expressive of moral quality? It is generally so understood by Christian writers. When Christ prayed for his disciples, "Sanctify them through thy truth," he desired that an effect might be produced on them, or in them, by divine influence, through the truth, and this could have been no other than a moral effect—the imparting or increasing of some quality of the soul or spirit. Does not Paul clearly distinguish it from *justified*, which means a legal state? "But ye are *sanctified*, ye are *justified*, in the name of the Lord Jesus," &c. 1 Cor. 6 : 11. I drop this subject. I readily concede that the term "*pardoned*," though not found in the common version of the New Testament, and the term *justified*, denote a state, and that the term *saved* refers to a state, as well as to moral character; and these are the only terms of importance in this discussion.

I pass over all that Mr. Campbell has advanced concerning his engrossed proposition, as having no material bearing on the question at issue, and proceed to notice—

"*Prop.* 7. *A change of views, though it necessarily precedes, is in no case equivalent to, and never to be identified with, a change of state.*" p. 194.

Very well! I concur in this proposition. I know no one who dissents from it. I dismiss the two or three pages devoted to its illustration without farther consideration, and proceed to record—

"*Prop.* 8. *That the Gospel has in it a command, and as such must be obeyed.*" p. 196.

Here the author falls into a grand fallacy. "The

Gospel," he says, "has in it a *command*." Where did he learn this? It is not so said in the Scriptures. Nor is any thing recorded from which it may be legitimately, or even plausibly inferred. The texts quoted by Mr. Campbell are far from sustaining his proposition. The Gospel is, in some sense, a law. It is called by the Apostle James, "the perfect law of liberty." Jas. 1 : 25. Wherever the Gospel comes it imposes on those who hear it an obligation to obey it. But his conceptions of obedience to the Gospel must be extremely contracted who supposes that it consists in a single act. To "*obey the Gospel*" is more than to be *immersed.* This act, though right in its proper place, is not obedience to the Gospel. Repentance, faith, love, baptism, prayer, praise, watchfulness, participation in the Lord's Supper, and perseverance in every good work, are all required by the Gospel, and comprehended in obeying it. It is most illogical to infer, that because the apostles speak of obedience to the Gospel, that it has in it a *command* that must be obeyed.

"*The obedience of the Gospel* is called *the obedience of faith*, compared with the obedience of law"—says Mr. Campbell. Very good! I endorse the sentence. But, by what authority, divine, or human, or according to what rule of logic, does he call the "obedience of the Gospel," an "*act* of obedience," and the "obedience of faith," "*the act* of faith?" Let us hear him—

"Whatever *the act of faith* may be, it necessarily becomes the line of discrimination between the two states before described. On this side, and on that, mankind are in quite different states. On the one side, they are pardoned, justified, sanctified, reconciled, adopted, and saved: on the other they are in a state of condemnation. This *act* is sometimes called *immersion, regeneration, conversion.*"

If the "obedience of faith" is an *act*, it is a mere assumption that that act is *immersion*. I will cut this matter short. I will prove by testimony, which in this discussion is next in authority to that of Holy Writ, that the phrase "obedience of faith," or "obey the Gospel," does not mean "a single act," and, consequently, does not mean *immersion*. I will quote Mr. Campbell against Mr. Campbell; or the matured and subtle opponent of Mr. Rice against the ardent and impetuous author of the *Extra*, resolved on establishing a favorite system. Hear the deponent—

"We neither believe nor teach that the phrase 'obedience of faith' means one single act; or that obeying the Gospel is one solitary deed. Certainly they do not '*obey the Gospel*,' who do not obey the first precept, any more than they who obey the first, and afterwards apostatize. The Gospel calls for perpetual obedience, or a life of conformity to its pure and elevated piety and humanity." Debate with Rice, p. 534.

Having, through the puissant aid of Mr. Campbell, demolished the *eighth* proposition, I will now proceed to examine—

"Prop. 9. *That it is not faith, but an act resulting from faith, which changes our state, we shall now attempt to prove.*" p. 198.

This proposition brings up the real question at issue. The previous propositions, with the sixteen pages devoted to their illustration, and proof, are of very little consequence in its decision. We are at last brought to the simple question, *What do the Scriptures teach concerning the means by which forgiveness, or justification must be obtained?* On this question I take issue with Mr. Campbell, and maintain *that it is faith, and not an act resulting from faith, that changes our state, or secures our justification.*

Let us endeavor to free from all encumbrance the question under discussion. Men are by nature sinful, alienated from God by wicked works, and are, consequently, condemned, or obnoxious to punishment. Between a state of condemnation and justification—a state of pardon and of guilt, there is no medium. The transition from the one state to the other must be instantaneous. I maintain, in common with evangelical Christians of every name, that the sinner passes from a state of condemnation to a state of justification at the precise moment when he truly *believes* in Christ, or, which is the same thing, *receives* him as a Deliverer. John 1: 12. This justifying faith is not the "bare belief of the bare truth." I will gladly permit Mr. Campbell to define it for me. "It is," he says, "a belief of testimony. It is a persuasion that God is true; that the Gospel is divine; that God is love; and that Christ's death is the sinner's life. It is trust in God. It is a reliance upon his truth, his faithfulness, his power. It is not merely a cold assent to truth, to testimony; but a cordial, joyful consent to it, and reception of it." Debate with Rice, p. 618. If this definition of faith does not harmonize with the views of faith elsewhere recorded by the same writer, that is no concern of mine. Now, this faith is the principle of a new, or spiritual life, involving reconciliation with God, and unfeigned submission to the authority of Christ. He who thus believes is, in the Scripture sense of the terms, converted, regenerated, a new creature. He was a rebel, but he is now a child, or, as Mr. Campbell says, "With it (faith) a man is a son of Abraham, a son of God; an heir apparent to eternal life—an everlasting kingdom." p. 618. This joyful convert now obediently inquires, "Lord, what wilt thou have me to do?" God sees the change, approves it, and freely and instantly forgives the penitent believer, for Christ's sake. But, according to Mr. Campbell's theory, this believer, who has given his "cordial, joyful consent to the" truth, this "son of God" is condemned—exposed to "everlasting destruction from the presence of the Lord," until he performs the "act of faith," or until "*the very instant when he is put under the water.*"

If Christ and the apostles do not teach that the remission of sins, or justification, is suspended on faith, and not any act resulting from faith, I do not comprehend in what terms this instruction could be conveyed. But "to the law, and to the testimony"—What saith the Scripture?

I answer,

1. *That throughout the New Testament, the remission of sins, or justification, is unequivocally and unconditionally, connected with faith, or with exercises which imply its existence.*

In confirmation of this position, I can furnish only specimens of the apposite declarations with which the Scriptures abound.

Listen then, in the first place, to the testimony of the "Teacher sent from God." In his memorable nocturnal conversation with the Jewish Rabbi, Nicodemus, he employed this significant language. "He that believeth on him (the Son of God) is not condemned, but he that believeth not, is condemned already, because he hath not believed in the name of the only begotten Son of God." John 3: 18.

The Saviour here points out two opposite conditions --a state of condemnation or guilt, and a state of freedom from condemnation, or justification. He testifies, and we are bound to receive his testimony, that the believer is in a state of justification, and the unbeliever in a state of condemnation.

Let us now turn to the "Acts of the Apostles," and examine the sermons dictated by the spirit of inspiration, and addressed both to the Jews and the Gentiles.

Peter shall be heard first. He healed a cripple at the gate of the Temple, called Beautiful. A multitude was quickly drawn together, in Solomon's porch, by the report of the miracle. Thus Peter addressed the assembly: "Repent ye therefore, and be converted, that your sins may be blotted out." Acts 3: 19. They were a company of sinners, needing to have their sins blotted out, or remitted. An inspired apostle stood before them, to guide them to the enjoyment of the ineffable blessing. "Repent," said he, change your minds, "and be converted," reform your lives, (and these exercises clearly imply faith,) "that your sins may be blotted out." I cannot for a moment suppose that if they had complied with Peter's exhortation they would have remained "unpardoned."

We will hear this witness again. Instructed by a vision from Heaven, the Apostle went from Joppa to Cesarea, to preach the Gospel to the Gentiles.

Arriving, he found Cornelius, the Centurian, with his kinsmen and near friends, convened to listen to his instructions. He preached to them Jesus—his resurrection, and his appointment to be "the Judge of quick and dead." "To him," said Peter, "give all the Prophets witness, that through his name whosoever believeth in him shall receive remission of sins." Acts x: 43. *Name* is frequently put in the Scriptures for *person.* "The *name* of the God of Jacob defend thee." Ps. xx: 1. "Thou hast a few names (persons) in Sardis which have not defiled their garments." Rev. iii: 4. By the "name of Christ" we are to understand the person of Christ, with his character, sufferings, and works. That the virtue of the name of Christ, to procure the remission of sins, is limited by baptism, is a mere conceit. Peter said to the cripple, "In the *name of Jesus Christ* of Nazareth, rise up and walk; and he leaping up, stood and walked." And to the multitude, who were astonished at the miracle of healing, he said, "And his name, *through faith in his name,* hath made this man strong, whom ye see." Acts iii: 6 and 12. If "*whosoever* believeth in him" (Christ) does not receive remission of sins, I do not perceive how "the Prophets" can be vindicated from the charge of bearing false witness. But they did not testify falsely. "WHOSOEVER," without regard to rank, character, clime, or outward condition, believeth in Christ, "SHALL RECEIVE *remission of sins.*"

It is now time that we should listen to the testimony of the "Apostle of the Gentiles." Paul was invited to address the Jews of Antioch in Pisidia, assembled in the Synagogue. "Christ crucified" was, of course, his theme. "Be it known unto you therefore," said the infallible teacher, "men and brethren, that through this man," the Holy One whom God had raised again, "is preached unto you the forgiveness of sins: and by him all that believe are justified from all things, from which ye could not be justified by the law of Moses." Acts xiii: 38, 39. Never was testimony more explicit. It seems designed to answer every inquiry, and solve every difficulty on the momentous subject of justification. If the inquiry is, Through what channel do we receive the remission of sins? the Apostle answers, "*Through this man* (Christ) is preached unto you the forgiveness of sins." Is the question, How is the privilege of justification enjoyed? the reply is, "They that *believe* are justified." Do we ask, Are all believers justified, or only such as change their state by an overt act? Paul answers emphatically, *all.* "By him ALL that believe are justified."

We will now direct our attention to the Apostolic epistles. Let us first open the letter "to all that be in Rome, beloved of God, called to be Saints." The chief design of Paul ir writing this epistle was to elucidate and establish the evangelic doctrine of justification by faith, without the deeds of the law. Here, if any where, we may expect to find an explicit and satisfactory exposition of this subject. The writer could not, I should think, guided as he was by the spirit of inspiration, have omitted to mention, in the discussion, baptism, if its performance were indispensable to justification. Such an omission would be unaccountable, if not unfaithful. The Apostle, having demonstrated that all men, both Jews and Gentiles, are guilty in the sight of God—that by the deeds of the law no flesh could be justified, proceeded to unfold, with great clearness and precision, the Gospel method of justification. "For if Abraham," these are Paul's words, "were justified by works, he hath whereof to glory; but not before God. For what saith the Scripture? Abraham believed God, and it," Abraham's faith, "was counted unto him for righteousness," or justification. "Now to him that worketh is the reward not reckoned of grace, but of debt, But to him that worketh not," with a view to justification, "but believeth on him that justifieth the ungodly, his faith," not his baptism, "is counted for righteousness." Rom. iv: 2, 5. I know of no passage of Scripture which, in so small a compass, developes, so clearly, God's plan of making sinners righteous, or of justifying the ungodly. Paul says to men, in effect, you are guilty—you deserve to perish in your sins—you cannot be justified by your own works—you cannot in any measure, expiate your guilt—but God has graciously devised and revealed a scheme for the salvation of men. If they believe in Christ—cordially embrace him as their Saviour—their faith shall be counted, or imputed to them for righteousness—they shall be treated as if they were righteous—not because their faith merits this privilege for them, but because God justifies them freely by his grace, "through the redemption that is in Christ Jesus."

Throughout this elaborate discussion of the subject of justification, the apostle does not pen a single syllable on the influence of the "act of faith," or immersion, in securing this privilege. The best proof of this omission is furnished by the fact that Mr. Campbell, ingenious as he is in the selection of proof texts, does not venture to quote one from this epistle in support of his theory. And the omission is utterly at war with the doctrine that faith and baptism are equally necessary to obtain remission of sins or justification.

I have barely time to cite a text from the epistle to the "churches of Galatia," in which the truth contended for is distinctly and emphatically stated. "We who are Jews by nature and not sinners of the Gentiles, knowing that a man is not justified by the works of the law, but by the faith of Jesus Christ, even we have believed in Jesus Christ, that we might be justified by the faith of Christ, and not by the works of the law." ii: 16. It would be easy to multiply quotations to prove that men are brought into a state of justification by faith in Christ; but these specimens from the epistles must suffice.

Perhaps it may be objected against the position under discussion, that the Apostle James affirms, "that by works a man is justified, and not by faith only." ii: 24. To this objection I reply, the Apostle Paul no less pointedly declares, "that a man is justified by faith, without the deeds of the law." Rom. iii: 28. If the language of these writers is to be understood without limitation, they, it seems to me, flatly contradict each other. But we must not charge the spirit of inspiration with folly. Paul manifestly writes of the evangelic scheme of justification. Works of every kind are excluded wholly from the merit of justification. Men are justified by faith, through the redemption which is in Christ, by free grace, without the meritorious influence of works. The design of James is, to show that men are justified not by a dead, but living and fruitful faith. "What does it profit, my brethren, though a man say he hath faith, and have not works? Can faith (such a faith) save him?" Certainly not "Faith, if it hath not works, is dead, (incapable of justifying,) being alone." It is no better than the faith of devils. "Was not Abraham, our father, justified by works when he had offered Isaac, his son, upon the altar?" But how did works justify Abraham? Why, "faith wrought with his works, and by works was faith made perfect"—exhibited as a living, fruitful faith. "And the Scripture was fulfilled, (verified) which saith, Abraham believed God, and (mark this,) *it was imputed unto him for righteousness.*"

Whether this be the correct solution of the difficulty, is not material in this discussion. The objection cannot avail the advocates of baptismal remission. "A man," says James, "is justified by *works*"—not by baptism, but by works—an obedient life. In whatever sense the language be understood, it effectually explodes the notion that the remission of sins, or justification, is obtained "in and through immersion."

II. *That in many places in the New Testament spiritual blessings, which imply the remission of sins, are positively promised to faith.*

In support of this position, I observe,

1. *That salvation is promised to faith.* The remission of sins is comprehended in salvation. Christ saves his people from their sins—from their guilt as well as their practice. A sinner *saved* and *unpardoned* is a manifest impossibility. If then salvation is enjoyed by faith, so is pardon. Hear what Paul says: "I am not ashamed of the Gospel of Christ: for it is the power of God unto salvation, to every one that believeth, to the Jew first, and also to the

Greek." Rom. 1: 16. The Gospel is the powerful and efficient means which God employs for saving men. But to whom does its saving efficacy reach? "To *every one* that believeth." Does its saving power extend to all nations? Yes, "to the Jew first, and also to the Greek."

Paul and Silas were committed to prison in the city of Philippi, for preaching the Gospel of Christ. God graciously and miraculously interposed for their rescue. A great earthquake shook the foundations of the prison, and all the doors were opened, and every one's bands were loosed. The jailor, seized with a conviction of his guilt and danger, fell down before Paul and Silas, and said, "Sirs, what must I do to be saved?" Never was a more important question propounded. Never was a more direct, explicit, and satisfactory answer given. "Believe on the Lord Jesus Christ, and thou shalt be saved." And is it possible that these inspired men directed the anxious prison keeper to do that which, being performed, would have left him still in an unpardoned, unsaved state? Did they promise salvation to an exercise with which it is not essentially connected? Surely not.

2. *Adoption into the family of God is the privilege of believers.* That the remission of sins is inseparably united with this honor, I need hardly attempt to prove. To suppose that the sons of God are still unpardoned is a gross absurdity. That be-

lievers enjoy this high honor the evangelist John testifies. " He (the Word) came unto his own, and his own received him not. But as many as received him, to them gave he power (right or privilege) to become the sons of God, even to them that believe on his name : which were born, not of blood, nor of the will of the flesh, nor of the will of man, but of God." 1 : 11, 13. Or, as the passage is rendered by Dr. Campbell, " But to as many as received him, believing in his name, he granted the privilege of *being children of God*, who derive their birth not from blood," &c. If God has graciously conferred on believers the privilege of being sons of God, who can disannul it ?

3. *Eternal life is distinctly promised to faith.* To bestow eternal life on men " dead in trespasses and sins," is the prime end of Messiah's mission on earth. "I am come," said he, " that they might have life, and that they might have it more abundantly." Every spiritual blessing is conferred in subservience to this benevolent design. Now listen to the teaching of Him who cannot lie. "As Moses lifted up the serpent in the wilderness, even so must the Son of man be lifted up ; that whosoever believeth on him should not perish, but have eternal life." Jno. 3 : 14, 15. Now just as certainly as the Israelites, bitten by the fiery serpents, were healed by looking at the brazen serpent, on the pole, will " whosoever believeth" in Christ, gain eternal life.

But you shall have testimony more explicit than this, if more explicit testimony can be. "Verily, verily, I say unto you," these are the words of Christ to the captious Jews, "he that believeth on me hath everlasting life"—not he may have, nor he shall have—but he HATH everlasting life—he has within him the embryo of immortal life—"being born again, not of corruptible seed, but of *incorruptible*, by the word of God which liveth and abideth forever." Jno. 6: 47—1 Pet. 1: 23.

III. *That privileges which are inseparable from the remission of sins are frequently promised, in the New Testament, to exercises or graces that imply the existence of faith.*

I will proceed at once to confirm this proposition.

1. *The kingdom of Heaven,* (which doubtless includes all the blessings of the kingdom—the remission of sins, among the rest,) *is promised to humility.* "Blessed," said Jesus, in his inimitable sermon on the mount, "are the poor in spirit: for theirs is"—not may be or shall be, but is already, "the kingdom of Heaven." Mat. 5: 3—see also to v. 11.

2. *Salvation is promised to prayer.* "For whosoever shall call on the name of the Lord shall be saved." Rom. 10: 13. Salvation includes, as has been already stated, the remission of sins. It is promised to him who "shall call on the name of the Lord." This promise is not made to a heartless, hypocritical calling on the Lord. "This people,"

said the Son of God, "draweth nigh to me with their mouth, and honoreth me with their lips; but their heart is far from me." But the promise is made to sincere, believing prayer—to such as "call on the Lord out of a pure heart"—to such as pray, "lifting up holy hands, without wrath and *doubting*." 1 Tim. 2 : 8. "For without *faith* it is impossible to please God." Heb. 11 : 6. "How then shall they call on him in whom they have not believed?"

3. *Adoption*, which supposes the remission of sins, *is declared to be the privilege of such persons as follow the guidance of the Spirit.* "For as many as are led by the Spirit of God," (and if those who repent and believe the Gospel are not led by the Spirit of God, by what spirit are they led?) "they *are the sons of God.*" Rom. 8 : 14. Perhaps it may be replied that the Spirit of the Lord will lead men to an observance of the Christian ordinances. I grant it. And he will lead those persons under his influence "all the length of the celestial road." But when do they become the sons of God? Not till they reach the end of their journey, or at the middle of it—or in the commencement of it? At the beginning surely. Otherwise it would not be true that "*as many* as are led by the Spirit of God,"—but such only as have traveled the prescribed distance—"are the sons of God."

IV. *That the remission of sins was, in various*

cases, possessed and enjoyed by faith, without, or before baptism. This we can clearly show.

Jesus was crucified between two malefactors. One of them railed on him. The other, touched with compunction at the remembrance of his crimes, said unto Jesus, (and this prayer implied faith,) "Lord, remember me when thou comest into thy kingdom." Jesus replied to him, long after he had said to Nicodemus, "Except a man be born of water and of the Spirit, he cannot enter into the kingdom of God," "To-day shalt thou be with me in Paradise;" and he certainly did not go to Paradise in his sins. Luke 23 : 39, 43. Perhaps it may be said that this was an extraordinary case. Then, let us examine another instance.

The publican went up to the temple to pray, and "standing afar off, would not lift up so much as his eyes unto heaven, but smote upon his breast, (conscious of his guilt,) saying, (and this prayer evidently was the "prayer of faith,") God be merciful to me a sinner." And did God hear the prayer of this penitent believer and remit his sins? Yes! "This man went down to his house (not baptized, but) *justified* rather than the other." Luke 18 : 10, 14. So true it is, that "a broken and contrite heart" God will not despise. Possibly it may be objected (though the objection is, in my view, of no validity,) that these cases occurred before the giving of the apostolic commission. Well, then, to silence the last objection, let us select another and an apposite case.

I have already adverted to the conversion of Cornelius and his friends; but I must again recur to the interesting subject. While Peter was uttering these memorable words, "To him (Jesus) give all the prophets witness, that through his name whosoever believeth in him shall receive remission of sins," "the Holy Ghost fell on all them which heard the words;" and they began to "speak with tongues and to magnify God." It is not affirmed by the historian that these Gentile converts were forgiven before their baptism; but consider carefully the facts of the case. Peter affirmed that whosoever believeth in Christ (the Gentile as well as the Jew,) shall receive remission of sins. In attestation of this truth the Holy Ghost was poured on all the hearers; that is, they were copiously endowed with the miraculous gifts of the Spirit. Now, I ask, can any man in his sober senses, and whose mind is not warped by theory, believe that these Gentile converts were "baptized with the Holy Ghost," Acts 11 : 16, while they were yet in their sins, with the wrath of God abiding on them? The Jewish converts censured Peter because he went in to men uncircumcised, and did eat with them. The apostle triumphantly vindicated his conduct. "Forasmuch," said he, "as God gave unto them the like gift as he did unto us who believed on the Lord

Jesus Christ, what was I, that I could withstand God?" Acts 11: 17. When he saw that God had received the Gentiles to his favor, his Jewish prejudices were slain, and he inquired, "Can any man forbid water, that these should not be baptized," not in order to receive, either the remission of their sins, or the gift of the Holy Ghost, but who "have received the Holy Ghost," and by fair inference the forgiveness of their sins? Acts 10: 43, 48. I know not what impression this case may make on other minds; but to my own mind it furnishes a conclusive refutation of the dogma, that we have the remission of "sins in and through immersion."

"Many blessings," says the Reformer, "are metonymically ascribed to faith, in the sacred writings." Metonymy is "a trope in which one word is put for another." But for what word is faith put? We know not, and he has not informed us. He continues—"We are said to be justified, sanctified, and purified by faith—to walk by faith, and to live by faith, &c., &c. But these sayings, as qualified by the apostles, mean no more than by believing the truth of God, *we have access* into all these blessings." Chn'ty Restored, p. 198. Is this all? When Christ asserts that, "He that believeth on the Son hath everlasting life," does he mean, not that he has the germ, or assurance of life, but merely access to it? When he affirms, that the believer "is not condemned," does he mean simply to teach, that he is condemned, but has access to a state of justification? When Paul declares that "faith is counted for righteousness," does he mean that faith is not counted for righteousness, but the believer is in a condition, in which, by performing an "overt act," he may have access to this blessing? Mr. Campbell asserts, but does not prove his position.

I must notice what he considers a conclusive refutation of all the arguments of his opponents in support of the doctrine of justification by faith, previously to baptism. "When they find," he says, "where remission of sins is mentioned without immersion, it is weak, it is unfair, in the extreme, to argue from that, that forgiveness can be enjoyed without immersion. *If their logic be worth any thing, it will prove, that a man may be forgiven without grace, the blood of Jesus, and without faith; for we can find passages, many passages, where remission, or justification, sanctification, or some similar term occurs, and no mention of either grace, faith, or the blood of Jesus.*" Chn'ty Restored, p. 217.

The italicised sentence above, on account of its supposed importance, is printed by its author in bold capitals. A few remarks will suffice to show the feebleness of this objection. *Faith is indissolubly united with grace and the blood of Christ* The blood of Christ is the object of saving faith "Whom (Christ) God hath set forth to be a propi tiation *through faith in his blood,* to declare his righteousness for the remission of sins," &c. Rom. 3 : 25. Faith is the product of grace, and through grace faith is imputed for righteousness. Rom. 4 : 3–5. Faith implies—is inseparable from—repentance, conversion, holiness. Now, suppose remission, or justification is, in many passages, promised, where no mention is made of "either grace, faith, or the blood of Jesus ;" *the blessing is promised to some holy exercise or quality which implies the existence of faith, and is inseparably united to grace and the blood of Christ. But, mark this! baptism is not essentially connected with faith, nor with any of the exercises which suppose the existence of faith.* A man must be a believer, in the full, Scriptural sense of the term, before he is a fit subject of baptism. A period longer or shorter, must elapse between the moment of believing and the moment of immersion. Nay, there is no certainty, there can be none, that immersion will ever follow the act of believing. The sum of the matter is this, when remission or justification is promised to faith, then repentance, conversion, the new birth, holiness, the spirit of obedience, the grace of God, and the blood of Christ, are implied—are all indissolubly united. *But neither baptism, nor a participation in the Lord's supper, is supposed in the promise, nor essentially connected with the blessing.*

The wisdom and grace of God are eminently

manifested in making faith, and not immersion, the line of discrimination between the states of condemnation and justification. It is a line invisible to us, but not to God. It marks the precise point at which the rebel becomes a child—It is the commencement of spiritual life—and is the source of all true obedience. "Indeed, true faith *necessarily works*; therefore, a working faith is the only true, real, and proper faith in Divine or human esteem." Campbell on Baptism, p. 282. It is inseparable from conversion, or regeneration, and an exercise acceptable to God. Let us hear the opinion of the Reformer on this point. "Now as faith in God is the first principle—the soul-renewing principle of religion; as it is the regenerating, justifying, sanctifying principle; without it, it is impossible to please God. With it," I must repeat this sentence, "*a man is a son of Abraham, a son of God; an heir apparent to eternal life.*" But on this subject I can furnish higher authority than that of Mr. Campbell. The Apostle John says, "*Whosoever believeth that Jesus is the Christ, is born of God.*" 1 John 5 : 1. Now, in view of the excellent nature, and momentous relations of faith, does it not seem most worthy of God, and most suitable to man, that it should be the exercise to which the remission of sins, and eternal life are promised? Can "a son of Abraham, a son of God," be still in a state of condemnation? Even Mr. Campbell, who once maintained so strenuously, that a man cannot be born of God, until he is born of water, is constrained to admit, "*that to be born of God, and born in sin, is inconceivable.* Remission of sins," he says, "is as certainly granted to the *born of God,* as life eternal, and deliverance from corruption, will be granted to the children of the resurrection, when born from the grave." Christianity Restored, p. 208. If then the believer is "a son of God," as Mr. Campbell in one place testifies, and as the Scriptures distinctly teach, it is a *monstrous supposition,* at war alike with our conceptions of the evangelical scheme of justification, and the character of the Supreme Ruler, that he is in his sins, until he can perform "an overt act," which he may never be able to do.

It must, however, be conceded that there is *a connexion between baptism and the remission of sins.* In some sense *baptism washes away sins.* I purpose to inquire what this connexion is?

Baptism must either be the *means,* or the *condition* of *obtaining* the remission of sins; or it is the *means* of *declaring,* or *confessing,* the remission of sins, previously obtained by faith. Either it sustains a relation to forgiveness like that which repentance and faith sustain; or its relation to forgiveness is that of a sign to the thing signified.

There is no medium between these schemes. The Rev. Mr. Meredith, the late estimable editor of the

Biblical Recorder, labored hard, ingeniously, but unsuccessfully, to establish an intermediate scheme. But in spite of the most subtle distinctions, we are forced to the conclusion, either that baptism is an act upon the proper performance of which God has promised that forgiveness shall ensue, and without such performance there is no promise of forgiveness; or that baptism is a sign or declaration of forgiveness actually received and enjoyed by faith in Christ.

Mr. Campbell without dispute embraces the former scheme. Baptism, according to the "ancient Gospel," is not the figure or formal acknowledgment of the remission of sins, but the indispensable, and, it would seem, the only condition of obtaining it. "I assert," he says, and truly, it is mere assertion, "that there is but one action ordained or commanded in the New Testament, to which God has promised, or testified, that he will forgive our sins. This action is Christian immersion." Chn. Bap., p. 520.

Is this scheme of forgiveness Scriptural? Is *baptism*, like repentance and faith, an *indispensable condition of the remission of sins?*

Let the reader notice—*First.* That this scheme of remission flatly contradicts plain and numerous Scripture testimonies. These testimonies, or specimens of them, I have already adduced. Now, it is a sound and admitted principle of Biblical interpretation, that the Scriptures should be construed in harmony with themselves. The obscure must be elucidated by the clear, and the figurative by the literal. It is impossible for words to express more clearly, pointedly, and emphatically, than do the Scriptures, that God has suspended the forgiveness of sins on the exercise of faith. Take for an illustration the words of Christ to the Jewish Rabbi—"He that believeth on him (the Son) *is not condemned*," and is consequently, pardoned, or justified. Now, "baptism for the remission of sins," a phrase susceptible of different interpretations, must be construed in harmony with this unambiguous language of the great Teacher. And the remark is true of all the texts under consideration.

Secondly. That the Scriptures manifestly make a distinction between the relation which faith, and that which baptism bears to the remission of sins. We read in the Scriptures, and many such passages may be found, "He that believeth not shall be damned." "Except ye repent, ye shall all likewise perish." "If any man love not the Lord Jesus Christ, let him be anathema maran-atha." Now, we do not read, nor is it intimated, nor is any thing recorded, from which it may be fairly inferred, that if a man is not immersed, he is condemned, doomed to perish—and to be anathematized at the coming of our Lord. But if Christ has made, as Mr. Campbell contends, repentance, faith, and immersion "*equally necessary* to forgiveness," how can it be accounted for, that neither Christ nor his apostles ever uttered a malediction against the unbaptized? How can their silence on this point be reconciled with their love and fidelity to the souls of men, and at the same time with the doctrine that the penitent believer, glowing with love to Jesus, is under the curse, until he is immersed?

Thirdly. There are consequences involved in the theory of baptismal remission which may well make us hesitate to adopt it. God has a perfect right to prescribe the conditions of forgiveness; and we are bound to receive, with readiness and gratitude, such as he may prescribe. But when any interpretation of the divinely prescribed terms of forgiveness leads to conclusions, absurd in themselves, at variance with the genius of the Gospel, and seemingly derogatory to God, we certainly should hesitate long, and examine carefully, before we adopt it. The conclusions, logically deducible from the doctrine of baptismal remission, are such as to make me believe that it is based on a misinterpretation of the Scriptures.

Let us now seriously notice some of the legitimate consequences of the dogma which I am combating.

If the remission of sins is enjoyed only through immersion; or, in other words, if "baptism is the *only medium* divinely appointed, through which the efficacy of the blood of Christ is communicated to the conscience," then, I remark,

1. That the salvation of men, even of penitent believers, is in the hands of the authorized baptizers. Popish priests have claimed the power of remitting sins ; but Protestants have ever considered the claim an arrogant assumption. I freely concede that those who maintain the sentiment which I am opposing may not have examined its bearing and consequences. I speak not of them, but of their doctrine. It is, however, as clear as that two and two make four, that the remission of the believer's sins, according to this theory, depends, not on the will of God, but on the will of man. He cannot baptize himself ; and if the qualified administrator does not choose, under no matter what plea, to baptize, (or regenerate) him, he must either be pardoned without immersion, be saved without pardon, or be lost. No sophistry can evade this consequence.

2. That salvation may be entirely beyond the reach of the most humble, obedient and faithful servants of Christ. Let me suppose a case. Fidelis, after a careful examination of the subject, became a convert to Christianity. Deeply conscious of his guilt and unworthiness, he cordially embraced Christ, as his prophet, priest, and king ; consecrating to him, in the unfeigned purpose of his heart, his body, soul, and spirit ; with all his time, and all his possessions. Enraptured with the Saviour's charms, he rejoiced in his word and worship from day to day. Having settled his views on the subject of baptism,

he designed, at the earliest opportunity, to take on him the badge of discipleship in baptism. But, by order of Tyrannus, an inveterate enemy to Christ, he was arrested and cast into prison, for his ardent zeal, and dauntless testimony in the Redeemer's cause. To him baptism is now impossible. And poor Fidelis cannot enjoy the remission of his sins. Perhaps, it may be replied, "That God is merciful —that he does not require impossibilities—and that he may accept the will for the deed." These are the very considerations which make me suspect that God has not suspended the remission of sins on that which to a good man may be impracticable—on something extraneous to the new creature. Besides the persecuted Fidelis needs something more solid than a "perhaps," a "may be," or a conjecture, to support him in his dark and solitary confinement; God has not withheld the stable ground of comfort, as I have clearly evinced.

3. That the enlightened and tender conscience can never be fully satisfied. Questions as to the validity, and sin-cleansing efficacy of baptism must arise. I can easily know when I have passed from Virginia into Ohio, because they are separated by water. I may certainly know that I have been immersed; but whether I have received valid, regenerating baptism, is another matter. Does its efficacy depend on the qualifications of the administrator? on his piety? on his baptism? on his church

connexion? on his ordination? on his intention? Is apostolical succession, either in the line of baptism or of ordination, essential to its validity? Is its sin pardoning virtue connected with the views entertained of it by the subject? If "baptism is the *only medium* divinely appointed, through which the efficacy of the blood of Christ is communicated to the conscience," then, it would seem to me, that the believer, tremblingly alive to his own salvation, must be filled with intense and ceaseless dread, lest the *channel*, through some defect, or leak, should permit the grace of pardon to escape before it reaches his sin-smitten conscience. Indeed, some have been goaded by this very apprehension to a repetition of the ordinance.

4. That repentance, the most sincere and lasting—faith, the most vigorous—love, the most self-sacrificing—the sanctifying influence of the Holy Spirit—the atoning blood of Christ—his intercession before the throne—and the abounding grace of the Father, are all, without baptism, unavailing for salvation. I do not affirm that all who adopt the sentiment which I am combating, push it to this extent, but I fearlessly aver that this is its plain, legitimate, and inevitable consequence. This gives to baptism an unscriptural prominence in the Christian system. It must tend, as the kindred dogma of transubstantiation has tended among Papists, to engender superstition. At first the water of bap-

tism is deemed of equal moment in the scheme of salvation with the cleansing blood of the Redeemer; and by degrees the sign will come to be substituted for the thing signified—the ceremonial to be preferred to the vital. What has occurred may occur again. Strange as it may appear, the error which I have been exposing, is the root of infant baptism. We learn from Salmasius, a learned historian and critic, quoted by Booth in his Pædobaptism Examined, that among the ancients, "an opinion prevailed that no one could be saved without being baptized; and for that reason, the custom arose of baptizing infants." This error had its origin, according to the testimony of Suiceras, a learned divine and professor of Greek and Hebrew at Zurich, (quoted by the same indefatigable inquirer after truth,) in a "wrong understanding of our Lord's words, *except a man be born of water and of the Spirit, he cannot enter into the kingdom of heaven.*"

"It (infant baptism) arose from false views of original sin, and of *the magical power of consecrated water.*" Prof. Hahn's Theology, p. 556.

"The immediate occasion of infant baptism, *it cannot be denied,* was extravagant ideas of its necessity to salvation." Dressler's Doctrine of the Sacrament of Baptism, p. 152. Chris. Review, June, 1838, p. 198, 199.

I can easily conceive the influence of this error on ignorant and superstitious people. If baptism be deemed essential to salvation, the motive to extend its efficacy to every individual who might, by possibility, be qualified to receive it, is irresistible. It would be administered first to the sick—then to persons of very tender age—then to children, whose capacity for the exercise of faith is very doubtful—and finally to unconscious infants. The consideration that none could be saved without baptism, and that its performance could do no serious injury, would lead from step to step in the path of error, till the design and spirit of the ordinance would be lost and forgotten. I inquire—

5. What will be the condition of a believer dying without baptism? I have already shown conclusively that the believer is "born of God"—that he possesses "everlasting life," and that he is a child of God; and yet, agreeably to the theory under consideration, "unpardoned, unjustified, unsaved," &c. In this condition he may unquestionably die. What would become of him? He could not be received into heaven without pardon, and consequently in his sins; nor would he be sent to perdition, with a regenerate heart, and possessing eternal life. There would be no place for him but purgatory. And yet, in the opinion of Protestants, there is no such place as purgatory. I leave him to be extricated from his dilemma by those whose unscriptural, I had almost said absurd, dogma has placed him in it.

Lastly. Mr Campbell recoils from the consequences of his own doctrine. If, as he maintains, Peter "made repentance, or reformation, and immersion *equally necessary to forgiveness*," then it is as clear as the noon-day sun, that no man can be a Christian, and no man who hears, or has an opportunity of hearing the Gospel, can be saved, in time or eternity, without immersion. Can a man be a Christian without repentance? Can a man, under the light of the Gospel, be saved without repentance? Mr. Campbell will hardly answer these questions in the affirmative. But if immersion and repentance are equally necessary to forgiveness, then no man can be a Christian, or be saved, without immersion, except, indeed, a man may be a Christian or be saved, without forgiveness. Mr. Campbell seems sometimes half inclined to look this consequence full in the face. "Infants," he says, "idiots, deaf and dumb persons, innocent Pagans, wherever they can be found, with all the *pious Pædobaptists*, we commend to the mercy of God." Chn. Sys., 233. As there is no promise of their salvation, he turns over all *pious* Pædobaptists, and, of course, all other unimmersed believers, with infants, idiots, &c., to the "uncovenanted mercies of God." At another time, when a milder spirit rules him, or, more probably, when his system is out of view, he writes, in a measure, like an *unreformed* Christian minister. "Amongst them all,' he says, alluding to the Christian sects, "we thank the grace of God, that there are many who believe in, and love the Saviour, and that, though we may not have Christian churches, we have many Christians." Camp. on Baptism, p. 16. Yes! thanks to "the grace of God," we have "*many Christians*," without immersion, without conversion, without regeneration, and without the remission of sins!! It is exceedingly difficult for error to be consistent with itself. Mr. Campbell shows in this admission that he does not fully believe his own doctrine. He is forced, in spite of his system, to concede that repentance and immersion, are not equally necessary to secure the remission of sins.

If baptism, as I have endeavored to show, is not a condition, or means of obtaining the remission of sin, then it follows that it is a symbolic declaration of the remission of sins already obtained through faith in Christ. In support of this conclusion, I remark,

First—That it is in perfect harmony with the teaching of the Scriptures. This point has been sufficiently elucidated, and the reader must judge of it for himself.

Secondly—That it is according to analogy. There are two New Testament institutions—baptism and the Lord's supper. The latter is unquestionably a symbolic ordinance. Bread and wine are used to symbolize the broken body, and sin-atoning blood of Jesus. May we not reasonably infer that both ordinances are of the same general nature—that as one is symbolic so is the other? If we do not literally, but only in a figure eat the Lord's body, and drink his blood, in the supper, does it not seem probable that our sins are not literally, but only in a figure, washed away in baptism? As we do not derogate from the importance of the Lord's supper, but assign to it its true position in the Christian system, as a means of promoting the edification and piety of believers, by insisting on its symbolic character; so neither do we derogate from the scriptural importance of baptism, by maintaining that sins are not literally but only in a figure remitted by it. The Papists interpret the language relating to the Christian ordinances with perfect consistency. They carry out the principle of a literal exposition. They maintain that in the eucharist the body of Christ is literally eaten, and his blood literally drunk, and that in baptism sins are literally washed away. But are they consistent expositors of Scripture who teach that in the eucharist we eat the body, and drink the blood of Christ in a figure, but that in baptism our sins are literally, really washed away? I think not. In the same sense in which the broken loaf in the Lord's supper is a sign of the crucified body of Jesus, is the water of baptism a sign of the cleansing efficacy of the blood, or atonement of Christ. In like manner as we eat the body of Christ in the supper, do we wash away our sins in baptism.

Thirdly—That it is in harmony with what Paul affirms of himself. 1 Cor. 1 : 17. "Christ sent me not to baptize, but to preach the Gospel." The apostle did not mean that he was unauthorized to perform the rite of baptism; for he baptized Crispus and Gaius, and the household of Stephanus, and perhaps some others; and he would not have baptized them without authority. The commission to preach is co-extensive with the commission to baptize. The apostle clearly meant, "Christ sent me not (mainly) to baptize, but to preach the Gospel." Baptism was not unimportant—it was a solemn duty—an impressive ordinance—a symbolic rite; but preaching the Gospel was the great, supreme business of Paul, as it should be of every Christian minister. If, however, baptism is the regenerating act, and as essential to forgiveness as repentance, I ask any candid and discerning man, whether Paul could have used such language? "I thank God," said he, "I baptized (regenerated) none of you but Crispus and Gaius." Thank God I did not do the very thing without which my preaching is vain—your faith is vain—and your sins cannot be forgiven! His language is most discordant with the theory of baptismal remission; but strikingly harmonizes with the conclusion I am aiming to establish. The blood of Christ—the publication of the Gospel—the influence of the Holy Spirit—repentance—faith—regeneration—are *indispensable to salvation ;* and baptism is an *open, solemn acknowledgment,* or declaration that salvation is received and enjoyed, through the blood of Christ, by repentance and faith, produced through the agency of the Holy Spirit.

I will now endeavor briefly to show that the passages of Scripture principally relied on by Mr. Campbell for the support of his doctrine, utterly fail of establishing it, and are in agreement with the theory of symbolic remission maintained in this chapter.

To begin with the commission, Mark 16 : 16. The assurance that "*He that believeth and is baptized shall be saved,*" does by no means warrant the conclusion that the remission of sins does not precede baptism. There is perfect accordance between this promise and the plain, literal declaration of Jesus, that "He that believeth on the Son is not condemned." Certainly, if he that believes on the Son is not condemned, he who not only believes in the Son, but, in submission to his authority, is baptized, is not condemned.

Let us next notice the famous passage in this controversy, Acts 2 : 38. "*Repent and be baptized* every one of you in the name of Jesus Christ, *for the remission of sins*, and ye shall receive the gift of the Holy Ghost." That baptism is *for* the remission of sins none will deny. But the import of the passage turns on the force of the term "*for.*" In the Greek the preposition εἰς is used. Every scholar knows, and every intelligent reader may learn from unquestionable authority, that it bears in the New Testament various meanings. It is sometimes, but rarely, rendered *for*, in the sense of, "*in order to.*" Its usual rendering is *into.* A regard to the context, the sense of the passage, and other considerations, must determine its import in any particular place. It is only necessary to show that on sound principles of hermeneutics, it may be fairly understood in harmony with what I have endeavored to prove is the plain doctrine of the Scriptures, and this can easily be done. In Mat. 3 : 11, we have these words—"I indeed baptize you with water *unto* (εἰς) repentance." Here the term cannot without gross impropriety be rendered *for*, or *in order to.* We know that John did not baptize his disciples in order that they might repent. He demanded of them not only repentance, but fruits meet for repentance, before he admitted them to baptism. He baptized them, not that they might obtain repentance, but as a sign, or acknowledgment that they had repented. Mat. 3 : 8–9. Now, in the very sense in which the Harbinger baptized his disciples (εἰς) *unto, for, into* repentance, did Peter command his pentecostal hearers to be baptized (εἰς) *for, unto, into* the remission of sins—

that is, not to procure, but as a sign, or acknowledgment of, this privilege, which God has graciously and inseparably united with repentance and faith. I could produce many similar examples, but this will suffice to show how fairly the passage harmonizes with the symbolic theory of baptism.

On Acts 22 : 16, it is needless to add any thing to the remarks which I have already made on the figurative import of the ordinance.

"Jesus answered, verily, verily, I say unto thee, *Except a man be born of water, and of the Spirit, he cannot enter into the kingdom of God.*" *John* 3 : 5.

The Reformers quote this text with great confidence in support of their views. Let us candidly examine it. The phrase *γεννηθὲ ῇξ ὕδατος*—"born of water," does not elsewhere occur in the Scriptures. Its import must be learned from the language itself, the context, and the current teaching of revelation. What is its meaning? Mr. Campbell maintains that it means baptism, and founds his argument for baptismal remission wholly on this interpretation. Concerning this opinion, I have several remarks to offer—

First. It is perfectly *gratuitous.* No argument has been presented, and none, it is presumed, can be, in its support. All that can be plausibly said in favor of it is, that if the phrase does not mean baptism, it is not easy to perceive what it does mean.

Now I protest against building so important a theory as baptismal remission on a *mere assumption.*

Secondly. Mr. Campbell relies on *authority* for the confirmation of his opinion. "This," he says, "is neither an interpretation of my own, nor of modern times; but if ever there was a Catholic interpretation—not Roman Catholic or Greek Catholic —but if ever there was a Catholic interpretation, it is the interpretation which I have given; for all agree to it, both ancient and modern." Debate with Rice, p. 481. It must be conceded that the preponderance of authority is in favor of this interpretation. This, however, is only a part of the truth. A majority of "ancient and modern" writers, especially of the "Greek and Latin Fathers," on whose concurrent judgment Mr. C. relies for the support of his interpretation, cast the weight of their authority not only in favor of baptismal remission, which he believes, but of *baptismal regeneration,* which he rejects. This text is the stronghold of the doctrine. A misconception of its meaning was the root of that most prevalent error, infant baptism. Besides, no man has less respect for human authority than Mr. Campbell, when it is in conflict with his own views.

Thirdly. It makes Christ's answer to Nicodemus *irrelevant.* The Saviour said to the Rabbi, "Verily, verily, I say unto thee, except a man be born again, he cannot see the kingdom of God." The Jewish ruler did not understand the language—attached a gross, sensual meaning to it—and demanded an explanation of it. "How," said he, "can these things be?" According to the popular interpretation, Christ, instead of answering the question, merely combined with the obscure proposition, another, which must have been perfectly unintelligible to Nicodemus. If the great Teacher employed a figurative phrase, well understood among the intelligent Jewish rulers, to elucidate the nature of the spiritual birth, his answer was in harmony with the question of Nicodemus, and the whole context; but if he used a phrase never before nor afterwards employed, by an inspired teacher, to denote baptism, his language was adapted to confound rather than instruct the neophyte.

Fourthly. It fully *justifies the ignorance* of the Jewish ruler. I take it for granted, that Christ intended to be understood by Nicodemus, and used such language as a suitably qualified ruler of the Jews could have comprehended. Christ reproved his pupil for his inexcusable ignorance—"Art thou a master of Israel, and knowest not these things?" But how could a teacher in Israel be censurable for not understanding phrases peculiar to Christianity—nay, a doctrine which had never before been enunciated? If Christ meant to teach Nicodemus that he must be baptized before he could enter into the kingdom of God, he employed language which it was impossible for the ruler to comprehend, and then reproved him for his official ignorance. But Christ did not reprove the master unjustly. He ought as a Jewish teacher, and as a student of the Scriptures, and of Rabbinical writings, to have understood the language used by the Redeemer for illustrating the nature of the new birth.

Fifthly. It makes the answer of Christ to Nicodemus *false.* The "*kingdom of God*" must mean the church of Christ—on earth, or the state of heavenly glory. This position, it is presumed, will not be called in question. Now it is not true that none enter into the visible church on earth, who are not born of the Spirit. In the purest churches there are members who are not regenerated. In the apostolic churches, there were some who were not properly of them. "They went out from us," said John, "but they were not of us; for if they had been of us, they would have continued with us." 1 Jno. 2: 19. The kingdom of heaven is like a net, which gathers both good and bad. Mat. 13: 47-48. Nor is it true, that none enter into the heavenly glory who are not baptized. From this conclusion, though it follows legitimately from his doctrine, Mr. Campbell himself recoils. The Saviour's declaration then, as interpreted by the Reformers, and many others, is not true. There is but one method of evading this conclusion. It is sometimes affirmed, for the purpose of avoiding it, that a man cannot *constitutionally* enter into the kingdom of God, except he is baptized, and born of the Spirit. But, by what authority is this long word foisted in the passage ? There is nothing in the context to justify its insertion. Christ affirms positively, and without limitation, "Except a man be born of water, and of the Spirit, he *cannot* enter into the kingdom of God."

Lastly.—If the phrase "born of water" means *immersion*, the passage in which it is found *yields no support to the doctrine of baptismal remission.* If the "kingdom of God" means, as Mr. Campbell understands it to mean, the reign of Messiah on earth—the visible church—then the text proves merely that a man cannot enter the church without baptism, and leaves the subject of the remission of sins, wholly untouched. So far as this passage teaches us, a man may be pardoned before, or after, as well as in the act of immersion. It has no relevancy to the subject under discussion.

But what does the text under discussion mean? It is not incumbent on me to show its meaning. I have proved that it does not refer to baptism, and that if it does, it fails to support the doctrine of baptismal remission—this is sufficient for my purpose. I will, however, perform a work of supererogation. I will quote on this subject a passage from a sermon of the Rev. James Saurin, formerly pastor of the French church at the Hague, celebrated alike for his learning, eloquence and piety. "The phrase," says this incomparable writer, "to be born of water and of the Spirit, is a Hebraical phraseology, importing to be born of spiritual water. By a similar expression, it is said in the 3d chapter of St. Matthew, 'I indeed (says John the Baptist) baptize you with water unto repentance, but there cometh after me one mightier than I; he shall baptize you with the Holy Ghost and with fire;' that is, with spiritual life"—(fire, I presume, is meant.) . . . "The Jews call the change which they presume their proselytes had experienced, *a spiritual birth; a new birth; a regeneration.* It was one of their maxims that the moment a man became a proselyte, he was regarded as a child, once born in sin, but now born in *holiness.* . . . Though it be not necessary to prove by numerous authorities the first remark we shall make on the words of Christ, 'To be born of spiritual water,' and to be 'born again,' it is proper at least to propose it; otherwise it would be difficult to account for our Saviour's reproving Nicodemus as being 'a master in Israel, and not knowing these things.' For a doctor in the law does not seem reprehensible for not understanding a language peculiar to Jesus Christ, and till then unheard of; whereas the blame naturally devolved on this Jew for exclaiming at expressions familiar to the Rabbins." Saurin's Sermons, translated from the French, by

Rev. Robert Robinson, and others. Vol. 2, pp. 419, 420.

"Christ also loved the church, and gave himself for it; *that he might sanctify and cleanse it with the washing of water by the word.*" Eph. 5 : 25, 26. This text is adduced by Mr. Campbell with great confidence in support of his cherished theory, that sins are remitted in the very act of immersion. Let us patiently examine it. Several remarks made in the investigation of John 3 : 5, are equally applicable to the passage in hand. That the phrase, καθαρίσας τῷ λουτρῷ τοῦ ὕδατος, that he might "cleanse it by the washing of water," which occurs nowhere else in the New Testament, means baptism, is simply an *assumption*, and cannot be proved. The weight of authority is in favor of this interpretation, but a large measure of it, both Romanist and Protestant, presses the text into the service of baptismal regeneration. But admitting, for the sake of argument, that the phrase means baptism, the passage cannot, with any fairness, be offered in support of baptismal remission. The reader must keep his eye on the question at issue, Are sins forgiven in baptism? Christ gave himself for the church that he might *sanctify* and *cleanse* it *with the washing of water—baptism* by the word. Christ does two things for the church, *sanctifies* and *cleanses* it, with the washing of water. Now, the first of these terms, in the *usus loquendi* of the New Testament, never refers to a change of state, or the remission of sins, but invariably to a moral change. The term ἁγίαση, from ἁγιάζω, to separate, consecrate, purify, "sanctify," *is never used by any inspired writer to denote pardon or justification.* It is, as has already been shown, distinguished from justification. 1 Cor. 6 : 11. It means to make holy. "The very God of peace *sanctify* you wholly." 1 Thess. 5 : 23. "He that is holy, *let* him *be holy* still." Rev. 22 : 11. If there is a respectable author in the English tongue, except those who use the Bethany dialect, who gives it any other meaning, I have yet to learn who he is. The word καθαρισας, from καθαρὶζω, to cleanse, render pure, to free from the influence of error and sin, is nearly as unfavorable to the argument of Mr. Campbell. It is used to denote the healing of the leper: "Lord, if thou wilt, thou canst make me *clean.*" Matt. 8 : 2. It is employed to signify the process of moral purification in the redeemed: "Let us *cleanse* ourselves from all filthiness of the flesh and spirit, perfecting holiness in the fear of God." 2 Cor. 7 : 1. "Who gave himself for us, that he might redeem us from all iniquity, and *purify* unto himself a peculiar people, zealous of good works." Tit. 2 : 14. In one place, the word probably refers to the removal of guilt from the conscience by the blood of Christ. Heb. 9 : 14. In every other passage, where it relates to the redemption of men, it denotes a moral renovation. That both sanctify and cleanse, have, in the text under consideration, reference to a moral purification, seems to be beyond reasonable dispute. The Apostle tells us distinctly for what *purpose* Christ sanctifies and cleanses the church, with the washing of water, by the word. It is that he may present it to himself "a *glorious church*, not having *spot*, or *wrinkle*, or *any such thing*, but that it should be *holy*, and *without blemish*." These are clearly moral effects—effects in harmony with the universal meaning of the word *sanctify*, and almost universal meaning of the word *cleanse*. Christ proposes to purify, adorn, and perfect his church "with the washing of water by the word." If the phrase "washing of water" means baptism, then the text teaches, not the remission of sins in the act of baptism, but rather baptismal regeneration and sanctification. At any rate it will be the business of those who contend for that meaning of the phrase, to free the passage from a consequence which is exceedingly plausible, if it is not legitimate. But are such moral effects as the Apostle so graphically describes attributable to baptism? This moral cleansing is ascribed to *faith*—"Purifying their hearts by faith." Acts 15 : 9; to the *word of God*—"Seeing ye have *purified* your souls in obeying the truth, through the Spirit;" 1 Peter 1 : 22, and to the *blood of Christ*—"The blood of Jesus Christ his Son, cleanseth us from all sin." 1 Jno. 1 : 7, but *never*, unless it be in the text under examination, to *baptism*. There is, indeed, a λουτρόν, or bath, which cleanses the soul, as the washing of water cleanses the body ; but this bath is not baptism. "In that day, there shall be a fountain opened to the house of David, and to the inhabitants of Jerusalem, for sin and for uncleanness." Zec. 13 : 1. He has a poor conception of this sin-cleansing fountain, who supposes that it is baptism. Multitudes have been baptized who have not been cleansed from sin and uncleanness ; and as many have been cleansed who have not been baptized. This soul-cleansing fountain is beautifully described by England's evangelic bard :—

> "There is a fountain filled with blood,
> Drawn from Immanuel's veins;
> And sinners, plunged beneath that flood,
> Lose all their guilty stains."

The same wondrous fountain is portrayed, with different imagery, by one less gifted in song, but not less fervent in spirit, or learned in the Scriptures, than was the gentle Cowper.

> "Here at Bethesda's pool, the poor,
> The withered, halt, and blind,
> With waiting hearts expect a cure,
> And free admittance find.
>
> Here streams of wondrous virtue flow,
> To heal a sin-sick soul;
> To wash the filthy white as snow,
> And make the wounded whole."

Whether the blood of Christ, or the Gospel which reveals the efficacy of that blood, be considered the fountain, is not material—for these things are inseparable—this is the true *loutron*—the soul-purifying bath. In this the church is sanctified and cleansed, and made "a glorious church, not having spot, or wrinkle, or any such thing."

I see but one method of attempting to evade the force of the above reasoning. It may be said that "Christ loved the church and gave himself for it," to deliver it from the guilt as well as the pollution of sin—to secure for it the remission of sins, as well as sanctification. This is readily granted. Some passages of Scripture, however, display the grace of God, and the efficacy of Christ's blood, in the remission of sins, without any allusion to sanctification. "Being justified freely by his grace through the redemption that is in Christ Jesus." Rom. 3 : 24. In other passages the purifying efficacy of Christ's blood is exhibited without any reference to justification—"Jesus also that he might sanctify the people with his own blood, suffered without the gate." Heb. 13 : 12. The text we are discussing belongs to the latter class of Scriptures. Christ gave himself for the church that he might sanctify and cleanse it—and by so doing make it holy, faultless and glorious—worthy of himself. Remission of sins is a blessing which believers derive from Christ--and this truth is plainly taught in many portions of the Bible; but this Scripture has no reference to the remission of sins, and consequently cannot prove that they are remitted in the moment of baptism.

"According to his mercy *he saved us, by the washing of regeneration* and renewing of the Holy Ghost." Titus 3 : 5.

"The like figure whereunto *even baptism doth also now save us* (not the putting away of the filth of the flesh, but the answer of a good conscience toward God,) by the resurrection of Jesus Christ." 1 Peter 3 : 21.

These two passages may be conveniently examined together.

The phrase "washing of regeneration" is found no where in the Scriptures but in the text cited from the epistle to Titus. It is generally, not universally supposed to signify baptism. That it does cannot be proved. My own opinion is, that it is exegetical of the following words, "renewing of the Holy Ghost." Regeneration is called a washing, because it is a moral cleansing; and this washing is precisely equivalent to the "renewing of the Holy Ghost." The text may be rendered "the washing of regeneration *even* (καὶ) the renewing of the Holy Ghost." The Greek participle καὶ is frequently rendered *even* in the New Testament, Mat. 8 : 27 25 : 29. Mark 6 : 12, &c. But, so far as this argument is concerned; I will admit that the words "washing of regeneration" mean baptism.

The text above cited from Peter is one of the most obscure in the apostolic epistles. Commentators have been greatly perplexed and divided concerning its import. As it is not necessary for my purpose, I shall not attempt to expound it.

Do these Scriptures teach that the sins of a believer are remitted in the act of baptism? This is the question under discussion. God *saves* us, "by *the washing of regeneration* (*baptism*) and renewing of the Holy Ghost." "*Baptism* doth also now *save* us."

The term *salvation* is of comprehensive import. It denotes the whole process by which we are delivered from sin, and fitted for the enjoyment of heaven. It includes a thorough moral renovation, the remission of sins, adoption into the family of God, and perseverance unto death in the way of holiness. It is commenced in repentance, carried forward in sanctification, and will be completed by the resurrection from the dead. The sincere believer in Christ, even before baptism, is in a state of salvation, but his salvation is incomplete. Now, God saves us by all the means which he employs to instruct, impress, purify, and preserve us. The written word, the ministry of the word, meditation, prayer, baptism, the Lord's Supper, afflictions, are all means by which God saves us. We are said to be saved by faith—saved by hope—to save ourselves and others, 1 Tim. 4 : 10—to work out our own salvation, Phil. 2 : 12. Salvation is promised to him that endureth to the end. Matt. 16 : 22. Christ is the author of eternal salvation to all them that obey him. Heb. 5 : 9. And we are saved by baptism. All these things have an influence in securing our salvation—are among the means by which God, in his mercy, carries on and completes the work. Baptism, which symbolizes the regenerating influence of the Spirit of God, and is a public and solemn acknowledgment of the remission of sins through faith in Christ, is designed and fitted to separate us from the world, impress on us our obligations to Christ, and aid us in the pathway to heaven. It certainly, however, does not follow from this position that the remission of sins is suspended on the act of baptism. This conclusion is drawn from the assumption, that whatever promotes our salvation is essential to the forgiveness of sins—an assumption manifestly false. "He that endureth to the end shall be saved"—but is the believer unpardoned until he finishes his race? or, is he not pardoned at the commencement of it? Christians are exhorted to *work out their own salvation*—but are not their sins forgiven before the completion of the work? We are saved by baptism—not as a condition of obtaining the remission of sins, but as one of the means which God employs to perfect the work of our salvation ; a means not indispensable to that result.

The remaining propositions of the *Extra*, I will very briefly dispose of.

The *tenth* sets forth that "*immersion and washing of regeneration are two Bible names for the same act.*" Chn'ty Restored, p. 223. Mr. Campbell's views on regeneration, having a very loose connexion with the subject of the remission of sins, I have pretty fully discussed in another place, and will dismiss without farther remarks.

Under the *eleventh proposition,* Mr. Campbell furnishes a long list of authorities to prove that the early Christian Fathers considered *immersion* as the "*regeneration*" and "*remission of sins,*" spoken of in the New Testament. If this was the testimony of the Fathers, it differs very widely, on one point, from Mr. Campbell's system. "All the Apostolic Fathers," says the *Extra,* "allude to, and speak of" *Christian immersion* as the "*remission of sins.*" Now, according to the Bethany Reformation, immersion is not the "remission of sins," but the means of obtaining it. Which is right, the Apostolic Fathers, or the father of the "current Reformation ?"

I deem these Fathers of very little importance in the controversy. That they early attached an undue importance to Christian ordinances is very clear That they called baptism "regeneration," confounding the symbol with the thing symbolized, and ascribed to the act a sin-cleansing efficacy, is quite as evident, and entitled to as much consideration, as that they employed in regard to the eucharist strong language which is confidently cited by the Papists in support of the dogma of transubstantiation. If Mr. Campbell can prove the identity of baptism and regeneration, if he can establish the doctrine of baptismal remission by the authority of the Fathers, the Romanists can by testimonies equally clear, pointed, and unexceptionable, support the doctrine of the real presence in the mass. That the early converts to Christianity from heathenism should have had a strong tendency to attach an excessive and superstitious importance to the ceremonials of religion, will surprise no one who carefully considers the character of their idolatrous training, and the natural bias of imperfectly educated minds. To this tendency, and the seemingly trivial mistakes that early sprang from it, we trace that stream of superstition, error and impiety, which has so long overflowed and desolated the larger portion of the so-called Christian world. We should be careful how we follow a leader, who, to overwhelm the opposers of a favorite theory, would open afresh this copious fountain of pollution and mischief.

Mr. Campbell's *twelfth* and last *proposition* in support of baptismal remission, maintains that "*the reformed creeds, Episcopalian, Presbyterian,*

Methodist and Baptist, substantially avow the same views of immersion, (as those developed in the *Extra,*) *though apparently afraid to carry them out in practice.*" Chn'ty Restored, p. 231.

I will leave the other denominations to vindicate their own creeds, if they deem it proper to do so. Some of them employ language on the subject of baptism which I do not approve, any more than I do that of Mr. Campbell on the same subject. But on behalf of the Baptists, I affirm that they have never taught, and never held any views substantially agreeing, or that could by any ingenuity be tortured into an agreement with, Mr. Campbell's notions on the identity of immersion and regeneration, and on the remission of sins in the very instant of being put under water. The assertion is a gross misrepresentation of the Baptist denomination and of every member of it ; and Mr. Campbell himself furnishes the proof of this misrepresentation. He quotes the Baptist creed as follows—

"Chap. XXX. Section 1. Baptism is an ordinance of the New Testament, ordained by Jesus Christ, to be unto the party baptized a sign of his fellowship with him in his death and resurrection ; and of his being engrafted into him.; of remission of sins, and of his giving up himself unto God, through Jesus Christ, to live and walk in newness of life." Chn'ty Restored, p. 234.

The Baptists have always maintained that baptism is a *sign* of the remission of sins; nor have they been ashamed, as Mr. Campbell insinuates, to carry out this view, so far as it could be, in practice. But is it possible that Mr. Campbell can think that the teaching of the Baptist creed is "*substantially*" the same as his theory of baptismal remission? If so, he is the most unfortunate writer that has ever put pen to paper. We might as well endeavor to understand the ravings of a bedlamite as the stereotyped writings of the Bethany Reformer. But let us read his remarks on the creed—

"The Baptist follows the Presbyterian church as servilely as the Methodist church follows the English hierarchy." We are willing to follow the Presbyterians, so far as they follow the Bible; and if this be servility, it were a pity but that the Reformer had possessed a good measure of it. It might have saved him from many profitless speculations, unseemly contradictions, and pernicious errors, and the world from a "Reformation," which, to speak charitably, has been of very questionable benefit. But let us hear more of the commentary. "But she (the Baptist church) avows her faith that immersion is a *sign* of remission." And then, as if to obscure the subject, he continues—"A sign of the past, the present, or the future! A sign accompanying!" Now, he knew perfectly that the Baptists, without a dissentient, understood baptism to be a sign, as the terms of their creed plainly import, of the remission of sins already received and enjoyed by faith in Christ; but whether it be "a sign of the past, the present, or the future," it differs as widely from Mr. Campbell's notions of the identity of immersion and regeneration, and of remission through the act of immersion, as the Lord's Supper of the New Testament differs from the Papal Mass.

WEEKLY COMMUNION.

One article of the Bethany Reformation is, that all the churches of Christ are *required to commune at the Lord's table every Lord's-day.* Mr. Campbell's views on this subject are expressed in the following condensed proposition, in his Millennial Harbinger Extra, No. II, p. 69.

"*The breaking of the one loaf, and the joint participation of the Lord, in commemoration of the Lord's death, usually called the 'Lord's Supper,' is an instituted part of the worship and edification of all Christian congregations in all their stated meetings.*"

The practice of weekly communion was not peculiar to the Reformers. It prevailed among several Christian sects in Scotland, where Mr. Campbell received his collegiate education, and early religious impressions. It was not seriously opposed among the Baptists, except as it was a part of a system, containing many objectionable principles, and usually advocated as the harbinger of other *reforms*, or changes, of far more questionable propriety.

It is not my purpose to follow the circuitous and prolix train of propositions and arguments by which the *extra* aims to establish the *divine authority* of weekly communion. What I have to say on the subject may be comprehended in a few plain positions, in the brief discussion of which the most important of these arguments will be noticed.

1. *Weekly communion is not commanded in the Scriptures, either by Christ or his apostles.* This point is conceded. Every commemorative institution, except the Lord's Supper, ordained by divine authority, had a fixed time for its observance. Mr. Campbell infers from analogy that the Lord's Supper—a commemorative institution—must have a stated time for its observance, and that time is every Lord's-day. Extra, No. II, p. 73. This reasoning is not legitimate. In every commemorative rite, except the Lord's Supper, divinely ordained, the *time* of its observance is a part of the law of the institution. The law of the Passover prescribes definitely the *time*, as well as the manner of keeping it. But the Saviour in the law of the Lord's Supper does not prescribe the times of its observance, bu uses most indefinite language on the subject. "This do ye, as *oft* as ye drink it, in remembrance of me. For as *often* as ye eat this bread, and drink this cup, ye do show the Lord's death till he come."

1 Cor. 11 : 25-26. Why was the Lord's Supper made an exception to this rule? Does not a difference in the form of the law establishing this rite, imply a difference in the rite itself?

The Lord's Supper is not, however, wholly anomalous. Fasting and prayer, the former, at least, a positive institution, are Christian duties, the times of whose observance are not divinely prescribed, but left to be decided by the circumstances and desires of the worshippers. Why may not the Lord's Supper belong to the same class of religious duties?

2. *It does not clearly appear from the Scriptures that weekly communion was practised by any of the apostolic churches.*

Three passages of Scripture are chiefly relied on by the advocates of the practice for its support.

The *first* text is Acts 2 : 42. "And they continued steadfastly in the apostles' doctrine, and fellowship, and in *breaking of bread,* (partaking of the Lord's Supper,) and in prayers." From this language Mr. Campbell infers that the first Christian congregation, which met in Jerusalem, "did as statedly attend upon the breaking of the loaf in their public meetings, as they did upon any other part of the Christian worship." Mill. Har. Extra, No. II, p. 69. All that can be logically deduced from this text is, that "breaking of bread" was a part of the instituted worship, steadily observed, by the first Christian church; but whether it was observed daily, weekly, or monthly, before or after prayer, or more or less frequently than prayer, does not appear. It may be affirmed of a church that communes monthly, as truly as of one that communes weekly, or daily, that it continues steadfastly "in breaking of bread."

The *second* passage relied on in support of the practice is Acts 20 : 7. "And upon the first day of the week when the *disciples came together to break bread,*" &c. From this passage it is inferred that it was the custom of the disciples to meet on the first day of the week, and that the primary object of their meeting was to break bread. The premises do not justify the conclusion. It is not logical to derive a general conclusion from a particular fact. The fact stated in the text is particular. When Paul, the founder of the church, was in Troas, the disciples came together to break bread. Suppose it had been a special appointment for communion, in view of the presence of the distinguished apostle, or the stated monthly communion of the church, might not the historian have said, nay, would he not have been compelled to say, in recording the event, "On the first day of the week *when the disciples came together to break bread?*" On that particular day the disciples in Troas came together to break bread, but whether they invariably came together on the first day of the week for the same purpose cannot be learned from the text, or its context. All that can be fairly affirmed is that the text is in harmony with weekly communion, and contributes, with other testimonies, to show the *probability* of its prevalence in the apostolic churches. See Mill. Har. Extra, No. 2, p. 70.

Another text quoted in proof of weekly communion is 1 Cor. 11 : 20. "When ye come together therefore into one place, this is not to eat the Lord's Supper." "To act thus," says Mr. Campbell, "is unworthy of the object of your meeting. To act thus is not to eat the Lord's Supper. It is not to show forth the Lord's death. Thereby declaring that this is the chief object of meeting." Mill. Har. Extra, No. 2, p. 72. As the Corinthians met weekly, and as eating the Lord's Supper was the chief object of their meeting, it is inferred that they communed weekly. From this reasoning I dissent. The Corinthian church sadly profaned the Lord's supper. They changed it into a bacchanalian feast, perverting it from its true design. The apostle reproved them for their impiety. "When ye come together therefore into one place," for receiving the communion, whether daily, weekly or monthly, "this is not to eat the Lord's Supper," but to desecrate it. Whether they came together for other purposes than to eat the Lord's Supper it was not the design of Paul to consider. Of their communion seasons, and only of their communion seasons, does he discourse ; and *when* they as sembled to "break bread" they profaned the institution. Of this text I must say, as of the preceding, it accords with the practice of weekly communion, but can only be logically urged in support of the *probability* of its observance in the primitive churches.

3. *Some of the arguments used in support of weekly, may with equal propriety be used in support of daily communion.* "Spiritual health as well as corporeal health, is dependent on food. It is requisite for corporeal health that food not only be salutary in its nature, and sufficient in its quantity, but that it be received at proper intervals, and these regular and fixed. Is it otherwise with moral health?" So reasons the Mill. Har. Extra, No. 2, p. 73. The writer might, quite as logically, have carried his analogy a little farther. As *daily* food is requisite for the health of the body, so *daily communion* is requisite for the health of the soul. Doctor Doddridge says—"We have great reason to believe that the eucharist was often celebrated among these primitive converts, perhaps much oftener than every Lord's day." Note on Acts 2 : 42. It would seem then that the probable practice of the first Christian church concurs with the logic of the Extra to lead the churches back, not to weekly, but to daily, or semi-weekly communion.

4. *Admitting that weekly communion was observed by the apostolic churches, does it follow that the prac-*

tice is obligatory on all churches? The soundness of this conclusion does not appear. If the law instituting the Lord's Supper, has left the times of its observance to be decided by the discretion of the churches, then the practice of the early churches, in the exercise of this discretion, is not obligatory on other churches. Let me illustrate this point by a similar case. The duty of Christians to contribute of their worldly substance for the support and spread of the Gospel is plainly revealed in the Scriptures; but the measure and manner of the contribution are to be determined by them in view of their resources, circumstances, and the exigency of the Redeemer's cause. Now, the first Christian church in Jerusalem "sold their possessions and their goods," "and had all things common." The law of Christ required that they should contribute, and they in their discretion and liberality contributed all they possessed. But is their example obligatory on churches in the present day? The advocates of weekly communion will scarcely maintain the affirmative. But if the example of the first church, under one indefinite law, is not obligatory on other churches, why should its example under another law, equally indefinite, be obligatory?

5. Conceding, as Mr. Campbell maintains, that the Lord's Supper "is an instituted part of the worship and edification of all Christian congregations *in all their stated meetings," it is grievously neg-*

lected not only by the religious sects generally, but by the churches of the current Reformation. These churches meet, particularly those in cities, twice every Lord's day, once on some week-day evening, and sometimes for many days and nights consecutively, and yet they break bread only once a week. If the Lord's Supper is an instituted part of the worship of *all Christian churches* in *all their stated meetings*, by what authority, in heaven or on earth, do the Reformed churches assemble, statedly and repeatedly, without breaking the loaf? If their principles are correct, they need another and an important reformation.

6. *There is no objection to weekly communion, provided it is not imposed on the churches as a term of communion.* The practise is not binding on the churches. But it is admitted that among the early churches, it is highly probable, that it did generally, if it did not universally prevail. I do not perceive any solid objection against returning to the practice. It may be well for the churches seriously and candidly to inquire, whether a more frequent celebration of the Lord's Supper—a rite so pregnant with instruction, and so eminently impressive—would not contribute to increase their piety and usefulness.

I cannot, perhaps, more appropriately, than at this point, introduce a few remarks on Mr. Campbell's views of what is usually termed "*Close Com-*

munion," No man was ever more clearly shut up by his principles to the necessity of insisting on restricted communion, than Mr. Campbell. Maintaining, as he does, that without immersion, there is neither regeneration, conversion, nor the remission of sins, he cannot, without gross inconsistency, receive the unbaptized to the Lord's table. Surely, those who are not "pardoned, justified, sanctified, reconciled, adopted and saved," as according to Mr. Campbell's theory, all unimmersed persons are not, are without Scriptural qualifications for communing at the Lord's table. The legitimate consequence of his principles he has very fully admitted.

In the year 1835, Mr. Campbell had a correspondence with William Jones, a distinguished Baptist minister of London. Mr. Jones proposed the following question. "*Do any of your churches admit unbaptized persons to communion ; a practice that is becoming very prevalent in this country ?*"

To this query Mr. Campbell replied—"Not one, as far as known to me. I am at a loss to understand on what principles—by what law, precedent, or license, any congregation founded upon the Apostles and Prophets, Jesus Christ being the chief cornerstone, could dispense with the practice of the Primitive church—with the commandment of the Lord, and the authority of his Apostles. Does not this look like making void the word or commandment of God, by human tradition ? I know not how I could exhort one professor to 'arise and be baptized,' as Ananias commanded Saul, and at the same time receive another into the congregation without it. Nay, why not dispense with it altogether, and be consistent?" Mill. Har., vol. 6, p. 18.

In 1843, in his debate with Rev. N. L. Rice, Mr. Campbell, to prove the liberality of the Reformers, spoke thus—"We, indeed, receive to our communion persons of other denominations, who will take upon them the responsibility of their participating with us. We do, indeed, in our affections, and in our practice, receive all Christians, all who give evidence of their faith in the Messiah, and of their attachment to his person, character, and will." Deb. with Rice, p. 785.

Mr. Campbell, in his debate with Rice, labored to show the perfect agreement of the above extracts; but labored unsuccessfully. If the passages are not contradictory, it will be hard to find a contradiction in the English language. To Mr. Jones he says, *We admit no unbaptized person to communion*—there is neither "law, precedent, nor license" for it. To Mr. Rice, he says, "*We receive to our communion persons of other denominations*," unbaptized persons, "who will take upon them the responsibility of participating with us."

Every man has a right to change his opinions; and for an honest and frank avowal of the change he deserves nc censure. Every man has a perfect right to explain the terms in which he expresses his opinions. But when, from inadvertence, obscurity of thought, or incorrectness of diction, he perpetrates a plain and palpable contradiction, he owes it to himself, to fairness, and to truth to acknowledge and correct the error.

CAMPBELLISM IN ITS DISCIPLINE.

One of the avowed objects, as has already been stated, of Mr. Campbell's Reformation was the union of all Christians on the apostolic foundation. Of the desirableness of the object there is no difference of opinion among the intelligent friends of the Redeemer. It is an end devoutly wished and prayed for by all who love Jesus Christ in sincerity The union so worthy to be sought by Christians, is not, however, a mere ecclesiastical union, cemented by worldly policy, and maintained by the ignorance, apathy and subservience of the laity, and the ghostly intolerance of the clergy; nor a mere nominal unity, in which men of all principles and all practices are held together by the utterance of a common "*Shibboleth;*" but a unity in faith and knowledge, cemented by love, and resulting in harmonious, cordial and effective exertions for the promotion of the Redeemer's kingdom.

What is the proper *foundation* of Christian Union? This is a very important question—a question which is clearly answered in the Scriptures

This foundation is "the truth"—that system of divine truth styled in the New Testament "the Gospel," "the faith," "the doctrine of Christ," &c. This truth, not merely as it is recorded in the Scriptures, but as it is understood, believed, loved and obeyed, becomes a bond of union among Christians. When Christ ascended up on high, "he gave some, apostles; and some, prophets; and some, evangelists; and some, pastors and teachers; for the perfecting of the saints, for the work of the ministry, for the edifying of the body of Christ: *Till we all come to the unity of the faith, and of the knowledge of the Son of God,* unto a perfect man," &c. Eph. 4: 8–14. The ascended Redeemer bestowed on his saints supernaturally qualified instructors, to secure their unity in "the faith," the "one faith" mentioned v. 5—the system of evangelical truth—and "the knowledge of the Son of God,"—of his person, character, work and offices—whom to know is life eternal. And one end which Christ proposed to secure by this enlightened union of the saints is their steadfast adherence to the truth. "That we henceforth be no more children, tossed to and fro, and carried about with every wind of doctrine, by the sleight of men, and cunning craftiness, whereby they lie in wait to deceive;" &c., verses 14 15. Christians are exhorted in the Scriptures to "continue in the faith grounded and settled," Col. 1: 23; to strive "together for the faith of the Gospel," Phil. 1 : 27 ; and "earnestly to contend for the faith once delivered to the saints." Jude 3. They are said to have "fellowship in the Gospel," Phil. 1 : 5. Christians love one another in the truth. "The elder unto the elect lady and her children, whom I love in the truth ; and not I only, but also all they that have known the truth ; for the truth's sake, which dwelleth in us, and shall be with us forever" 2 John, verses 1–2. If Christians "walk in the light," that is, in the knowledge of the truth, they "have fellowship one with another." 1 John 1 : 7. They are required to reject from their fellowship all who do not bring the "doctrine of Christ." "He that abideth in the doctrine of Christ, he hath both the Father and the Son. If there come any unto you, and bring not this doctrine, *receive him not* into your house, neither bid him God speed." 2 John, v. 10. The church in Pergamos were sharply reproved because they retained in their fellowship some who held the "doctrine of Balaam," and also some who held "the doctrine of the Nicolaitanes," which Christ hated. Rev. 2 : 14–15. From these Scriptures it is manifest that divine truth, or the Gospel, as it is believed, understood and loved, is the basis of Christian union. The saints love one another in the truth, and for the truth—in obeying the truth they have fellowship one with another—they are required to hold fast the truth, to contend earnestly for it, and to reject from their communion those who do not embrace it. Any union which is not founded on the knowledge and love of Divine truth is a union of ignorance, interest, policy or coercion; but not the union for which Christ prayed, and for which his people should labor.

It is by no means easy to define the measure of ignorance and unbelief compatible with the existence of genuine piety, and sincere Christian fellowship. There are, however, certain facts, doctrines and duties, fundamental to the Christian system; and the willful rejection of these, or any one of them, from whatever obliquity of intellect or of heart, precludes the possibility of enlightened, Scriptural, Christian union. The Gospel assumes the existence, and moral government of God—the depravity and guilt of man—and to deny either of these truths is to subvert the foundation of Christianity. The Gospel reveals the Divinity of Christ, the expiatory nature of his sufferings and death, his resurrection from the dead, and his investiture with regal authority at the right hand of the Father; and he that rejects either of these truths, rejects the Gospel itself. Repentance, faith, and a holy life, are plainly inculcated on men in the Gospel; and he that denies their necessity, perverts and destroys the system. The Gospel teaches a future state of rewards and punishments, from which it derives its strongest motives to piety; and he that denies or perverts this doctrine makes war upon, if he does not overthrow "the faith." It is not my purpose to furnish a summary of Christian doctrine, but only to point out some of the principles which are essential to the system, and the knowledge and admission of which are indispensable to the Scriptural union of Christians. I do not affirm that a perfect knowledge of all these principles is essential to Christian fellowship ; but I do most earnestly maintain that the persistent rejection of any one of them, under whatever plausible pretence, and with whatever show of argument, precludes the possibility of "fellowship in the Gospel." Fellowship, indeed, there may be, but it is the fellowship of error, pseudo charity, and worldly policy—a fellowship founded on a principle, which bids "God-speed" to him that brings not "the doctrine of Christ," and which retains in communion "them which hold the doctrine of the Nicolaitanes," that Christ hates.

On the subject of Christian Union, Mr. Campbell has written many things which deserve consideration. It is my purpose, however, to restrict my remarks at present, to the *foundation* on which he proposes to establish this union. It is laid down in his *Christianity Restored*, pp. 118, 119.

"But the grandeur, sublimity, and beauty of the foundation of hope, and of ecclesiastical or social union, established by the author and founder of Christianity, consisted in this, that THE BELIEF OF

ONE FACT, *and that upon the best evidence in the world*, is all *that is requisite, as far as faith goes, to salvation. The belief of this* ONE FACT, *and submission to* ONE INSTITUTION, *expressive of it, is all that is required of heaven to admission into the church.* A Christian, as defined, not by Dr. Johnson, nor any creed-maker, but by one taught from heaven, is one that believes this *one fact*, and has submitted to *one institution*, and whose deportment accords with the morality and virtue of the great Prophet. The one fact is expressed in a single proposition, *that Jesus, the Nazarene, is the Messiah.* The evidence upon which it is to be believed, is the testimony of *twelve men*, confirmed by prophecy, miracles, and spiritual gifts. The *one institution* is baptism into the name of the Father, and of the Son, and of the Holy Spirit."

The reader has now a full view of the platform, established, not by "the author and founder of Christianity," but by Mr. Alexander Campbell of Bethany, Virginia, for the joyful union of all the sects and parties in Christendom. Before we venture upon it, however, we must subject it to a careful examination.

"*The belief of one fact*," and "*submission to one institution*," constitute "the foundation of hope, and of ecclesiastical, or social union." So teaches Mr. Campbell.

"With us," these are his words, "Revelation has

nothing to do with opinions, or abstract reasonings; for it is founded wholly and entirely upon *facts*." Chn'ty Restored, p. 106 "All revealed religion is based upon facts." p. 113. I should suppose that Mr. Campbell uses the term "*fact*" in its secondary sense, as equivalent to "truth," if his own definition did not preclude that supposition. "Fact," he says, "means something done. That God exists is a truth, but not a fact; that he created the heavens and the earth is a fact and a truth." pp. 106, 107. I approve the definition. That facts occupy an important place in the evangelic economy must be conceded; but that the truths connected with them, and from which they derive their significance, are less important, must be denied. That God exists is a truth which lies at the foundation of all genuine religion, natural and revealed. "For he that cometh to God must believe that he is, and that he is a rewarder of them that diligently seek him." Heb. 11 : 6. That Jesus is the Son of God is a truth—that he wrought miracles is a fact; that he was put to death by Pontius Pilate, is a fact—that he died for our sins is a truth; that he rose from the dead, is a fact—that he rose "for our justification," is a truth; that he ascended up to heaven, is a fact—that he ever lives "to make intercession for us," is a truth; and it will scarcely be maintained that these facts are more important than the truths connected with them. Indeed, the Gospel facts, wonderful as they are, possess no value apart from the doctrine or truth, in which they had their origin, and by which their nature and uses are explained. The death of Jesus would be of no greater consequence to the world, than that of the two thieves who were crucified with him, were it not that the event is a part of a great system of truths, facts and duties, extending backwards to the creation of the world, and forwards through the ages of eternity. From the proposition, then, *that "all revealed religion is based on facts,"* I must beg leave to dissent.

But Mr. Campbell goes farther still. He narrows greatly the ground which he at first occupied. He sets aside all facts, as fundamental in religion, *except one.* "*The belief of one fact—is all that is requisite, so far as faith goes, to salvation.*" "This one fact," we are told, "is expressed in a single proposition—*that Jesus the Nazarene is the Messiah.* Now, according to Mr. Campbell's own definition, this proposition is clearly not a *fact,* but a *truth.* It is expressive not of something *done,* but of something that *exists.* In a note, Mr. Campbell writes —"The fundamental proposition is—*that Jesus is the Christ.* The *fact,* however, contained in this proposition is—that God has anointed Jesus of Nazareth as the only Saviour of sinners." p. 118. Now, I deny that the *fact,* as he terms it, is contained in the proposition. To affirm, as Mr. Campbell does, that the simple proposition, "*that Jesus is the Christ,*" contains the *fact,* "that *God* anointed Jesus of Nazareth, *the only Saviour of sinners,*" is to evince a strange obscurity of perception, or to presume very far on the credulity of his readers. And even if it were admitted, contrary to Mr. Campbell's own definition, that the proposition is expressive of *fact* rather than *truth,* why does he affirm that it expresses *one* fact, when it manifestly expresses *two?* That Jesus is the Nazarene, is one fact; and that this Nazarene is the Christ, is another, and totally different fact. "The evidence," Mr. Campbell continues, "upon which it (the '*fact,*' or, more properly the truth) is to be believed is the testimony of *twelve men,* confirmed by prophecy, miracles, and spiritual gifts." But why does he say on the testimony of *twelve men?* The apostles were divinely appointed, and important, but not the only oral witnesses of this truth. But we must believe it, if we believe it at all, not on oral but written testimony; and in the New Testament we have but *eight* witnesses, *three of* whom did not belong to the "*twelve men,*" the apostles. Thus loosely did this Reformer write on subjects fundamental in his system, and demanding the greatest clearness of thought, and accuracy of expression.

"*Jesus the Nazarene is the Messiah.*" This is an important proposition. But by what authority does Mr. Campbell make the belief of it "the foundation" of "ecclesiastical or social union?" There are other propositions contained in the Scriptures, expressing both facts and truths, equally fundamental in the evangelic system, and the belief of which is equally necessary to salvation. That "*Christ died for our sins,*" along with other important facts, is declared by Paul to be the Gospel which he preached to the Corinthians, and by which they were to be saved, if they would keep it "in memory." 1 Cor. 15: 1-3. It is through *faith in the blood of Christ,* that God declares "his righteousness for the remission of sins that are past." Rom. 3: 25. That *Jesus rose from the dead* is a fact of primary importance in the Christian system, and the belief of it is requisite to salvation. "If thou shalt confess with thy mouth the Lord Jesus, and *shalt believe in thine heart that God hath raised him from the dead,* thou shalt be saved." Rom. 10: 9. The "one fact," which is not a fact, seems to have been arbitrarily selected, by the Reformer, from many facts and truths equally important, and made the basis of "ecclesiastical union."

But, we must examine this foundation still more carefully. Does Mr. Campbell, by the proposition that "*Jesus the Nazarene is the Messiah,*" design to include those truths and facts, which are essentially connected with it, and which constitute the Gospel? I grant that a sincere and an intelligent belief that *Jesus is the Messiah,* supposes a belief in the whole system of which this truth is an important part. Salvation is promised to faith in the *blood of Christ*—in the *resurrection of Christ*—and in the *Gospel of Christ*, as well as to the belief of the "one fact" that "*Jesus is the Messiah*;" and this variety of language is accounted for by the simple, and well understood principle that the belief of one fact or truth is used to denote a belief in the system of which it is an essential part. Now, if by *the belief of one fact*, Mr. Campbell means the belief of all the truths and facts inseparably connected with it—in fine, the Gospel of Christ, I have, on this point, no controversy with him. But, then, it follows that Mr. Campbell has made no discovery on this subject—has proposed no new basis of ecclesiastical union. It is precisely that for which evangelical Christians have always contended. They maintain that the Gospel—the system of truth pertaining to human salvation—is the proper foundation for Christian union; and in this judgment Mr. Campbell concurs. Whether, in this aspect of the case, he can be vindicated from having made a great ado about nothing, and having written very vaguely and obscurely on a subject which called for clearness and precision, others may decide.

It can hardly be supposed, however, that the above is the proper interpretation of the language under discussion. It does not fairly admit of this construction. "*The belief of* ONE FACT—*is* ALL THAT IS REQUISITE, *as far as faith goes, to salvation.*

If a man believes the proposition, styled in the Bethany terminology "one fact," "that *Jesus the Nazarene is the Messiah*," it is not requisite to his salvation that he should believe anything else, whether fact or truth, in the universe. This is his simple, sole, all-comprehending creed, "*I believe that Jesus the Nazarene is the Messiah.*" In all the creeds, of all the sects, and in all the revelations of God, there is not a fact, truth or principle necessary to be believed in order to salvation, except this "one fact," which is to be believed on the "testimony of *twelve men*."

On this subject I join issue with Mr. Campbell. I cannot admit *that the belief of one fact is all that is requisite, as far as faith goes, to salvation.*

But let us hear the arguments in support of the position under discussion. "It is again and again asserted," says the writer, "in the clearest language, by the Lord himself, the apostles, Peter, Paul and John, that he that believes the testimony that Jesus is the Christ, is begotten of God," &c., p. 119. By this process of reasoning it can be proved with equal clearness, that the proposition that *Jesus is the Son of God*, or that *Jesus was raised from the dead*, is the "one fact," or truth, the belief of which "is all that is requisite, as far as faith goes, to salvation;" for to the belief of these propositions salvation is promised. The true principle of interpreting these passages has been already explained. But where, permit me to ask, is it stated, or intimated, or implied, in the Scriptures, that the "belief of one fact," "is *all that* is requisite, as far as faith goes?" To affirm that "whosoever believeth that Jesus is the Christ, is born of God," on the well understood principle, that he who believes that truth, also believes the facts and truths essentially connected with it, is widely different from affirming that the belief of *one fact is all the faith* requisite to salvation. But hear the Reformer again. "The Saviour expressly declared to Peter, that upon this fact, that he was the Messiah, the Son of God, he would *build his church.*" p. 119. Now, I must affirm that the Saviour expressly declared no such thing. Neither the word "fact," nor any term of corresponding import appears in the passage referred to. Mat. 16 : 18. The text is one, as to the proper interpretation of which, the most learned, pious, and distinguished Biblical critics have been greatly divided ; and to assume its meaning, and to employ that assumed meaning in support of a doubtful proposition, proves nothing so much as the paucity of the writer's arguments. But let us listen again. "And Paul has expressly declared that 'other foundation can no man lay (for ecclesiastical union) than that JESUS IS THE CHRIST.'" I do not remember ever to have met with a more glaring perversion of the Word of God than this Paul has expressly declared no such proposition. The passage has quotation marks, and yet no such passage is found in all the writings of Paul. The garbled text is recorded, 1 Cor. 3 : 11. It reads thus—"Other foundation can no man lay than that is laid, *which is Jesus Christ.*" The foundation, expressly declared by the apostle to be laid, is, not the "one fact," as the passage misquoted by Mr. Campbell would seem to import, *that Jesus* is *the Christ*, but *Jesus Christ, himself*. This apostolic declaration is in perfect harmony with other portions of Scripture. See Isaiah 28 : 16. Eph. 2 : 20. And, moreover, for Mr. Campbell's construction of the passage there is no authority in the common version, the New Translation, published by himself, nor the Greek text. On what ground he has made this most unwarrantable change in the text, I know not. He surely ought not to expect that it will be admitted on his mere declaration, in opposition to the plain import of the original, and its well established translation.

In consideration of the flimsy arguments which have been noticed, the writer proceeds to remark—"The point is proved that we have assumed ; and this proved, every thing is established requisite to the union of all Christians upon a proper basis." pp. 119–120. It is a striking peculiarity of Mr. Campbell's controversial writings that they abound in arguments to prove what nobody denies, and take for granted, or furnish very slight evidence of the main points at issue. Of the twenty-eight pages devoted to the discussion of the *Foundation of Christian Union*, not more than a page is occupied by the proofs, such as they are, that "the belief of one fact, is all that is requisite, so far as faith goes, to salvation." Whether these proofs are sufficient to establish the point, the intelligent reader must judge.

But I am not yet done with this foundation. It is quite too broad and comprehensive. It sustains, on its ample surface, not only all Christians, as defined "by one taught from heaven," but errorists of almost every class and grade. Arians, Socinians, Universalists, Materialists, Shakers, Mormons, together with many who are ignorant and superstitious, profess as firmly and consistently, as Mr. Campbell, himself to *believe that Jesus the Nazarene is the Messiah.* They put their own interpretation on the language, and conform their religious creed to that interpretation. If they submit to the "one institution," and their "deportment accords with the morality and virtue of the great Prophet," they are in the judgment of the Reformer, Christians, "as defined, not by Dr. Johnson, nor any creed-maker, but by one taught from heaven."

Just at this point the difference between the views held by the Reformers, and "Regulars," is clearly revealed We maintain that the belief of "one fact" is not all the faith that is requisite to salvation ; but that saving faith embraces the whole system of facts, truths, and duties, essentially connected with this "one fact." If, then, any person professing to believe that *Jesus, the Nazarene, is the Messiah*, is ignorant of the import of the proposition, or rejects any doctrine or fact, vitally connected with it, we consider it *prima-facie* evidence that he does not savingly believe the "one fact." He that denies the doctrine of human depravity and guilt—of the Divinity of Christ—of the vicarious and expiatory nature of his sufferings—or of a future state of rewards and punishments, furnishes decisive proof that he does not savingly believe the proposition that *Jesus is the Messiah* ; or, at any rate, that he does not bring the "doctrine of Christ," and should not be received into Christian fellowship. Such an errorist, whether baptized or unbaptized, our churches would promptly refuse to receive, and hold in fellowship. To do otherwise, would be to "bid him God-speed," and to efface the distinction between truth and error.

But the creed of the Reformation has but one article, viz. : *I believe that Jesus, the Nazarene, is the Messiah.* The belief of this proposition "is all that is requisite, as far as faith goes, to salvation." He that believes this "one fact," and submits to "one institution expressive of it," and whose morals are correct, is, according to the doctrine of the

Reformation, "a Christian," fit for "admission into the church." He is not required to believe any other fact or truth, contained within the whole compass of revelation. He may, along with the Rationalists, deny the inspiration of the Scriptures; he may, in company with the Pelagians, deny the doctrine of man's innate depravity; he may, in agreement with the various classes of Unitarians, pronounce "Jesus, the Nazarene," a creature—a man—a mere man—a fallible man; he may maintain, as do the Universalists, there is no punishment of sin, except in this life; he may, with the philosophic Priestley, insist that the soul of man is material, and perishes with his body; he may believe that Joe Smith was a prophet, and that the Book of Mormon is a new revelation from God; or he may be deplorably ignorant of the first principles of Christianity; but according to the fundamental doctrine of the Reformation, he is entitled to a place in the church of Christ. Let there be no evasion among the Reformers. This consequence is fairly and logically deduced from their boasted creed. And startling as it may seem to be, they may well be reconciled to it, as it establishes, what else it might be difficult to confirm, their claim to unusual liberality. A more liberal foundation for the union of all Christians, "as far as faith goes," without a total abandonment of evangelic truth, it would be difficult for human ingenuity to devise

But this boasted foundation is as inconsistent with itself, as it is with the Scriptures. It contains the elements of its own destruction. He who believes "one fact," is to submit to "one institution expressive of it." Now, is a man to be baptized without *believing* that Christ has commanded believers to be baptized? Why then is he to be baptized, and upon whose authority? But if he is to believe this, then something more is requisite, "*as far as faith goes*," even according to the Bethany platform, in order to the enjoyment of Christian Union.

These remarks on the foundation of Christian Union, might have been introduced with equal propriety under the head of *Campbellism in its organization*; but as I desired to discuss the doctrine in connexion with its practical results, I reserved the discussion for this place.

I now propose to examine the *actual working* of this scheme of Christian Union. Experience is a great teacher. Time tries all things. Many a fine theory has vanished at the touch of experiment. When Mr. Campbell's chief business was fault-finding, he had an easy, if not a grateful task. All churches, sects and parties, and all the instructions and labors of uninspired men, had their imperfections; and no great ability or research was required to discover, publish, and caricature them. We have now an opportunity of learning from observation, in a measure, the fruits of the Reformation. Mr. Campbell cannot reasonably object that churches built upon the Apostolic foundation, of "belief in one fact," and "submission to one institution," modeled after the "ancient order of things," and commended to the world by such confident and lofty pretensions of superior light, purity, and freedom, should be scrutinized with a careful and candid eye. What are the results of the *Discipline* adopted by the Reformers ?

It is discouraging to learn, as we do at the outset, "that the theory of the Reformation is far in advance of the practice." Mill. Har., vol. 4, p. 4. We have examined the theory, somewhat carefully, and have found it consistent neither with itself, nor the Scriptures ; and if "the theory *is far in advance of the practice*," the practice must be very unsatisfactory. It is due, however, to Mr. Campbell to observe, that his depreciation of the practice of the Reformation in comparison with its theory, was based on his views of the theory, and not on mine.

It has been shown that according to the fundamental principle of church organization maintained by the Reformers, no errorist, of correct morals, can be excluded from the church, provided he professes to believe that Jesus, the Nazarene, is the Messiah, and is immersed as an expression of this belief. I shall now proceed to show that the grossest errorists have been, knowingly and deliberately, received and retained in the churches of the so-called Reformation.

Of the withering influence of *Universalism* I need say nothing. In the year 1828, the Rev. Aylett Rains, a *Universalist* preacher, was baptized, in the Western Reserve, Ohio, for the remission of sins. In the same year he appeared at the Mahoning Association, with which Mr. Campbell was connected. Some of the brethren became alarmed at the introduction of a preacher among them holding such pernicious error. He publicly avowed that his peculiar views were unchanged; in other words, that he was still a Universalist. At the suggestion of Mr. Campbell, it was agreed, "that if these peculiar opinions were held as PRIVATE opinions, and not taught by this brother, he might be, and constitutionally ought to be retained." Mr. Rains declared that his views were, "in his judgment, matters of opinion, and not matters of faith," and "that he would not teach them," and was by "a majority of the brethren" sanctioned as a proclaimer of the Reformation. Mill. Har., vol. 1, 148.

Unitarianism, in all its phases, from high Arianism to low Socinianism, is, in the judgment of the Christian world, a far more serious error than Universalism. It divests the Gospel of its distinctive glory, and converts it into a lifeless, cold, and inefficient code of ethics. The atonement of Christ, deriving its efficacy from the essential and infinite dignity of his person, is the only foundation of a sinner's hope and consolation. The Reformers received Unitarians into their fellowship, and sanctioned their ministrations with a full knowledge of their errors. In the early part of the present century, a party of New Lights, headed by the Rev. Barton W. Stone, in the State of Kentucky, became Arians. In a letter to the Christian Baptist, published in the year 1827, he used this language: "If these observations be true, will it not follow undeniably, that the *Word* (*di' hou*) by whom all things were made, was not the only true God, but a person that existed with the only true God before creation began, not from eternity, else he must be the only true God; but long before the reign of Augustus Cæsar." p. 37. Mr. Stone's views of the atonement were in harmony with his conceptions of the person of Christ. He entirely rejected the vicarious and expiatory nature of Christ's sufferings; and maintained that they contributed to the salvation of men only as illustrating the Divine goodness, they constituted a strong motive to repentance and piety. The efficacy of Christ's death was resolved by him entirely into the power of *moral suasion*. Mill. Har., New Series, vol. 5, pp. 63, 64. The peculiar views of Mr. Stone were cordially embraced by the sect of which he was the leader. This party, without any change in their religious tenets, coalesced with the Reformers in the West. Mr. Campbell and Mr. Stone, the principal leaders of the Reformation, had a discussion on the points on which they so widely differed, and in his concluding article the former used the following language—" The discussion, on my part, was undertaken with a reference to two points: The first, the transcendent importance of the question itself—For what did Christ die? The second, a very general misconception, and consequent misrepresentation of our views of it. I did, I confess, expect that brother Stone would have more fully and satisfactorily relieved himself and the cause of the Reformation from the imputation of some of our opponents on the subject of Unitarianism in its sectarian acceptation." p. 538.

Of the extent to which the Arian notions of Mr. Stone did formerly, or do now, prevail among the Reformers, I have no means of ascertaining. In the year 1844, I made a tour in the West, of which notes were published on my return in the Religious Herald. From the notes I extract substantially the following paragraph, the statements in which, so far as I have seen, have never been called in question, and which, I presume, cannot be successfully contradicted.

" In the town of Columbia, Missouri, and its vicinity, the Disciples, better known as Campbellites, are somewhat numerous. They were formerly professedly Arians, but some years since they united with the followers of Mr. Alexander Campbell. I took much pains to learn whether their views of the divinity of Christ had undergone a satisfactory change. All, with whom I conversed on the subject, concurred in testifying that they reject the doctrine of Christ's divinity, and of his substitutional and piacular sufferings. One of the Professors of the University of Mo., (situated at this place,) informed me that in a conversation which he held with Mr. A., a distinguished preacher of the denomination in this State, he most distinctly repudiated these vital principles of the evangelic system. One thing is certain—the Disciples are not ignorant of the fact that they are generally believed to be Arians; and under this imputation they patiently lie. Unless there is a strange and prevalent misconception in the community, these Disciples stand in most urgent need of a thorough doctrinal reformation."

Mr. Campbell inquires, "Have they (creeds) not been the fruitful cause or occasion," not of some, or of most, but "of *all* the discords, schisms, and parties now existing in Christendom ?" Chn. Sys., p. 108. I presume, he would now cheerfully retract this assertion—for, though in the interrogatory form, it was intended to be an emphatic assertion. Certainly, some pretty well defined and serious errors have sprung up in the bosom of the Reformation, and have given rise to no little discord and party spirit. John Thomas, M. D., an Englishman, early, and with marked zeal, enlisted under the banner of the Reformation. He was the first Disciple who manifested any disposition to do his own thinking. All doctrines bearing the Bethany stamp were current among the Reformers, and were received, I will not say, without examination, but certainly with great readiness and cordiality. Dr. Thomas aspired to be, not a subordinate, but a co-ordinate Reformer. He admired, and extolled Mr. Campbell, approved of the Reformation, so far as it had been carried, but he was desirous to see it advanced to perfection, and he engaged with commendable ardor, in the effort to increase the light of the Reformation. New light he soon thought he discovered. He proposed to introduce new principles and practices into the Reformation. He maintained, with perfect consistency, that persons who had been baptized without proper views of the nature and design of baptism—ignorant of the new, or, as he deemed it, the old theory of baptismal remission—should be re-immersed, according to the true intent and spirit of the ordinance. Mr. Campbell agreed theoretically with the new Reformer on this point; for in his debate with Rice, he said, "Now if our baptism is for any other end or purpose than was that to which Paul submitted, it is another baptism, as much as bathing for health is different from a Jewish ablution for legal uncleanness or impurity. The action has a meaning and a design; *and it must be received in that meaning, and for that design, else it is another baptism.*" p. 439. Mr. Campbell and many of his disciples were baptized without any knowledge of the true import and design of the ordinance; but whether they did not perceive the logical consequence of their doctrine, or were unwilling to follow the guidance of the rising Reformer, is not apparent—but certainly they refused to receive baptism according to the meaning and design which they ascribed to it. Many, however, embraced Dr. T.'s doctrine, and with new light and fresh joy, were re-immersed into the name of the Father, Son, and Holy Spirit. I have not access to any authorized standard, if such there is, of Dr. Thomas' religious faith and opinions. Rev. N. L. Rice, in his Debate with Mr. Campbell, spoke of him and his doctrines, as follows, p. 793. "Dr. Thomas, of Virginia, a prominent preacher in the gentleman's church, contended that men have no souls—that they are constituted of body, blood, and breath—that the word *soul*, in the Scripture, means breath—and that infants, idiots, pagans, and Pædobaptists, are annihilated. My friend opposed his doctrines; but the Doctor insisted that he had received his training in Ireland and Scotland, where the people believe in ghosts and witches, and that, although a great reformer, he was not quite reformed. Mr. Campbell at length refused to hold Christian fellowship with him, and called on the church of which he was a member, to excommunicate him."

The fulminations of Bethany were not heeded by the Doctor's church. They had been initiated into the mysteries of a higher and more glorious Reformation; and they would not consent to sacrifice their new and gifted guide to appease the wrath of their early, and once honored, but now forsaken teacher. Owing to the intractable spirit of the new Reformers, Mr. Campbell found it necessary to change the voice of denunciation into that of argument, and finally of conciliation and compromise. The leaders met in Amelia County, Virginia, and after discussing the points at issue between them three days, without any change in the views of either, they, through the influence of common friends, became reconciled, and consented to coöperate in promoting the Reformation. The terms of their reconciliation, taken from Dr. Thomas' paper, are recorded in the Mill. Har., New Series, vol. 3, pp. 74, 75.

"We, the undersigned brethren, in free consultation, met at the house of brother John Tinsley Jeter, at Paineville; and after frankly comparing our views, unanimously agreed upon the resolution subjoined, and submitted the same for the consideration of brethren Campbell and Thomas; and brother Thomas agreeing to abide the same, all difficulties were adjusted, and perfect harmony and co-operation mutually agreed upon between them.

"*Resolved*, That whereas certain things believed and propagated by Dr. Thomas, in relation to the mortality of man, the resurrection of the dead, and the final destiny of the wicked, having given offence to many brethren, and being likely to produce a division amongst us ; and believing the said views to be of no practical benefit, we recommend to brother Thomas to discontinue the discussion of the same, unless in his defense when misrepresented.

"Signed by—Wm. A. Stone, Thomas E. Jeter, et als. The resolution being agreed upon by the brethren, brother Campbell and myself were requested to appear before them. The result of their deliberations was reported to us ; we acquiesced in the recommendation after a few words of mutual explanation ; and having recognized our Christian fraternity, the brethren gave in their names to brother Stone to be appended in the order affixed.

Paineville, Amelia, Va., Nov. 15th, 1838."

Dr. Thomas, whose monstrous errors had induced Mr. Campbell, in violation of his own principles of church organization, to denounce him as unworthy of Christian fellowship, was, as it appears from the above articles of agreement, not only retained in "Christian fraternity," but sanctioned as a co-operator in the Reformation ; on condition that he should abstain from the discussion of his peculiar articles of belief, "*unless in his defense when misrepresented.*"

It certainly can surprise no man acquainted with the condition and tendencies of the world, to learn that a community, rejecting and ridiculing "experience before baptism," and whose creed consisted in the simple and single article, "I believe that Jesus of Nazareth is the Christ," should gather into its capacious bosom a heterogeneous multitude of persons of almost every variety of creed. The unity which distinguished the early Reformers after a few years began to be broken. The language of Ashdod began to be mingled with the pure speech of Canaan. One principle of the Reformation is that every church member is an authorized preacher of the Gospel. "*He may,*" says Mr. Campbell, "*of right preach, baptize, and dispense the supper, as well as pray for all men, when circumstances demand it.*" Chn. Sys., p. 82. Under the stimulating influence of the Reformation ministers of the word were multiplied rather too rapidly, in the judgment of the Reformer. Some had the "vanity, self-esteem, or boldness to assume an office, and a character, which neither the church on earth nor in heaven" awarded to them. In his efforts to correct this growing evil, Mr. Campbell made the following frank, and, no doubt, truthful acknowledgment. Mill. Har., vol. 6, No. 2, p. 64.

"The cause of Reformation has suffered more

from this portion of its pretended friends than from all its enemies put together. This state of things is indeed generally attendant on the incipiency of all public and social institutions" (A very proper apology for the bitter fruits of the *Ancient Gospel*). "*But we have had a very large portion of this unhappy and mischievous influence to contend with. Every sort of doctrine has been proclaimed by almost all sorts of preachers, under the broad banners and with the supposed sanction of the begun Reformation.* We are glad to follow, rather than to lead public opinion amongst ourselves on this subject. Experience teaches with effect, what theory could not accomplish."

"*Every sort of doctrine has been proclaimed, by almost all sorts of preachers*"—these are precisely the effects which I should, *a priori*, expect to flow from the fundamental principle of church organization adopted by the Reformers ; and to the existence of which Mr. Campbell has borne an incidental and reluctant, but most explicit testimony. Persons, holding gross and mischievous errors, have crept into the purest and best governed churches of Christ ; but they enter them in violation of the principles of their organization, and remain in them, so long as they do remain, in spite of their system of discipline. Into the Reformed churches they enter constitutionally, and from them they cannot be excluded without an abandonment of their basis of union.

As the point under discussion .s of great importance, it is proper that we should attend to what Mr. Campbell has to say on it. I quote from his *Christianity Restored*, pp. 122, 123.

"I will now show how they cannot make a sect of us. We will acknowledge all as Christians who acknowledge the Gospel facts, and obey Jesus Christ. But, says one, will you receive a Unitarian? No; nor a Trinitarian. We will have neither Unitarians nor Trinitarians. How can this be! Systems make Unitarians and Trinitarians. Renounce the system, and you renounce its creatures.

"But the creatures of other systems now exist, and some of them will come in your way. How will you dispose of them? I answer, We will unmake them. Again I am asked, How will you unmake them? I answer, By laying no emphasis upon their opinions.

"What is a Unitarian? One who contends that Jesus Christ is not the Son of God. Such a one has denied the faith, and therefore we reject him. But, says a Trinitarian, many Unitarians acknowledge that Jesus Christ is the Son of God in a sense of their own. Admit it. Then I ask, How do you know they have a sense of their own? Intuitively, or by their words? Not intuitively, but by their words. And what are these words? Are they Bible words? If they are, we cannot object to them—if they are not, we will not hear them; or, what is the same thing, we will not discuss them at all. If he will ascribe to Jesus all Bible attributes, names, works, and worship, we will not fight with him about scholastic words: but if he will not ascribe to him every thing that the first Christians ascribed, and worship and adore him as the first Christians did, we will reject him, not because of his private opinions, but because he refuses to honor Jesus as the first converts did, and withholds from him the titles and honors which God and his apostles have bestowed upon him.

"In like manner we will deal with a Trinitarian. If he will ascribe to the Father, Son, and Holy Spirit, all that the first believers ascribed, and nothing more, we will receive him—but we will not allow him to apply scholastic and barbarous epithets to the Father, the Son, or the Holy Spirit. If he will dogmatize and become a factionist, we reject him—not because of his opinions, but because of his attempting to make a faction, or to lord it over God's heritage.

"And will you receive a Universalist too? No; not as a Universalist. If a man, professing Universalist opinions, should apply for admission, we will receive him, if he will consent to use and apply all the Bible phrases in their plain reference to the future state of men and angels. We will not hearken to those questions which gender strife, nor discuss them at all If a person say such is his private opinion, let him have it as his private opinion ; but lay no stress upon it : and if it be a wrong private opinion, it will die a natural death much sooner than if you attempt to kill it."

As this quotation contains the gist of the Campbellite discipline, I must be permitted to subject i to a careful examination.

Mr. Campbell teaches, in the above extract, that *Unitarians* and *Universalists* are to be received into the church, provided they will consent to hold their peculiar views as " private opinions." However erroneous and unscriptural may be their opinions, they have the full right to hold them in the church, if they will forbear to obtrude them on others. " We do not ask them," he says, " to give up their opinions ; we ask them only not to impose them on others." Chn'ty Restored, p. 121

It may seem strange to some that the Bethany Reformer, who is so zealous an advocate for the use of a "pure speech," and furnishes in the context of the extract under discussion, a long catalogue of words and phrases, condemned simply on the ground that they are not found in the Scriptures, should have made such frequent and important use of the term *opinions*—a term never employed by the writers of the New Testament. There is no valid objection to the use of this, or any other dignified term, in religious discussions, provided it is clearly defined, or well understood. What does he mean by this word? He has not made any attempt tc explain it—to inform us where faith ends and opinion begins.

Does he use the term *opinion* to denote speculations on subjects confessedly not included within the scope of revelation? This can hardly be the sense in which he uses it; for there is no person in Christendom who maintains that an agreement in such opinions is essential to church fellowship.

Does he by the term *opinion* mean the views which men entertain concerning the import of the Scriptures? I understand him to maintain that the persuasion of the Universalist, that the Bible teaches the final salvation of all men, and of the Unitarian, that Christ is not a divine being, but merely an exalted man, are *opinions*, which they are at liberty to hold privately.

This unscriptural and artificial distinction can be of no avail to the cause of the Reformer. Whatever he may call the peculiar views of the Unitarians and Universalists, they are clearly and avowedly matters of faith. The Unitarian *believes* that the Scriptures do most unequivocally teach, that Jesus, the Christ, the Son of God, is not the true God, but a creature. If this persuasion is with the Unitarian, not an article of faith, but a mere opinion; then it follows, that the persuasion of Mr. Campbell, that Christ is a divine being, is not a matter of faith, but a mere opinion. The Universalist *believes* that

God has clearly revealed the final salvation of all men—he receives the doctrine on what he deems divine testimony—and if this persuasion is not faith, it may be reasonably questioned whether there is any faith on earth. Now, allowing that unity of opinion is not necessary in order to church fellowship, the admission cannot help Mr. Campbell out of his difficulty. For the differences between Trinitarians and Unitarians are not mere differences of opinion—but are differences in faith—on fundamental principles of faith, if there be any such.

But call, if you please, the peculiar views of Unitarians, Universalists, &c., *opinions*, and not faith. I utterly object to Mr. Campbell's sweeping exclusion of all *opinions* from the basis of Christian Union. There are some opinions which entirely contravene the essential doctrine of the Bible. For example—it is a doctrine of the Bible, that Jesus of Nazareth is the Son of God. The Unitarian admits this doctrine, but entertains the *opinion* that the phrase "Son of God," imports, not his divinity, or essential Godhead, but his great elevation among creatures. Now, here the *opinion* of the Unitarian, and the *doctrine of the Bible* are at issue. Let us now see the effect of the great solvent by which Mr. Campbell proposes to melt into one all the discordant elements of Christendom. The Unitarian and Mr. Campbell use precisely the same words—"a pure speech," "Bible terms,"—but they attach widely different meanings to them—and know that they do ; and yet, because they use the same words, they profess to have unity of faith. They speak the same terms, with meanings as wide apart as the poles, and then boast of their harmony. What is this but sheer Jesuitism ?

But Mr. Campbell imposes a wholesome restriction on his Unitarian or Universalist brother. "If any person say such is his private opinion, *let him have it as his private opinion.*" Whence did Mr. Campbell derive this rule ? Why did he not furnish the chapter and verse, where it is recorded ? It is an important law : I should be glad to know its author. As Mr. Campbell does not pretend to claim for it divine authority, I must enquire into its propriety. If these private opinions are innoxious—do not unfit their holders for church fellowship—why may they not be propagated ? What evil can arise from the diffusion of such harmless opinions ? "If he (the Trinitarian) will dogmatize and become a factionist, we reject him,"—says Mr. Campbell. But suppose the Unitarian does not dogmatize, or become factious, but seeks, "not as lording it over God's heritage," but by kind and persuasive arguments to convince men that Christ is not God, and that his death was not vicarious, will he be tolerated ? It would seem not, from the quotation under consideration. But this conclusion draws after it another consequence. Mr. Campbell, of course, claims no preëminence over his Unitarian brother. Then, as the Unitarian must not proclaim his peculiar opinions of the person and work of Christ, so neither must Mr. Campbell. But what then is the moral value of the stereotyped proposition, *Jesus, the Nazarene, is the Messiah?* It means everything, and it means nothing; and what it does mean no man may say!

But Mr. Campbell has prepared a way of escape from this logical sequence. He has been careful not to doom himself and his brethren, Unitarians and Universalists, to absolute silence as to Scripture doctrine. They may use Scripture terms in a Scriptural sense. "If he (the Unitarian) will ascribe to Jesus all Bible attributes, names, works, and worship, we will not fight with him about scholastic words." "If a man professing Universalist opinions, should apply for admission, we will receive him, if he will consent to use and apply all the Bible phrases in their plain reference to the future state of men and angels." The law of Christian fellowship, prescribed by the Reformation, is that all shall use Bible terms, in the Bible sense, in speaking of Bible things. This is quite specious. I do not know who made this law, but I know who has broken it. Mr. Campbell has been a most flagrant transgressor of it. In his voluminous works, he has discussed almost every fact, doctrine, and duty of the Christian revelation, in a copious variety of unscriptural, and not unfrequently, most unwarrantable terms. But who is to decide what is the "plain reference" of "all the Bible phrases," and when a man ascribes to Jesus "every thing that the first Christians ascribed?" Is the professor himself? Then there is no restriction on church fellowship, except what each person may choose to impose on himself. Is Mr. Campbell, of Bethany? Then he is a pope, and ought to be infallible. Is the church to decide? Then an agreement, not merely in the belief of facts, or, properly of "*one fact*," but in opinions as to the meaning of the words and phrases in which the important facts and doctrines of revelation are expressed, is by implication clearly admitted as necessary to church union; and consequently there must be in every such decision, an expression, clearly indicated, of this agreement.

I am not yet done with this remarkable system of church discipline. The Trinitarian fares no better than the Unitarian or Universalist in the "current Reformation." "If he will ascribe," says Mr. Campbell, "to the Father, Son, and Holy Spirit, all that the first believers ascribed, and nothing more, we will receive him—*but we will not allow him to apply scholastic, and barbarous epithets to the Father, the Son, and the Holy Spirit.*" I have searched the lively oracles in vain for this restrictive law. It is not found in the creeds of the sects, the decrees of councils, nor the bulls of popes. It bears unmistakable marks of its Bethany origin. It hath "the image and superscription" of Mr. Alexander Campbell. But let us scrutinize it. "*Scholastic*" means pertaining to a scholar, or scholar like. A "*scholastic epithet*" is a term by which a scholar would express the quality of a person or thing. "*Barbarous*" is synonymous with unlettered, uncultivated. A "barbarous epithet" is such a word as an illiterate man would employ to denote the quality of a person or thing. The proscriptive rule is exceedingly comprehensive and rigorous. It permits neither learned nor unlearned terms to be applied to the Father, the Son, or the Holy Spirit. And the Reformer speaks, if not with pontifical, certainly with no hesitating authority—"*We will not allow him* to apply scholastic and barbarous epithets," &c. Having considered the import and authority of the law, let us inquire into its reasonableness. A *Unitarian* who believes that Christ was a mere man, or an imperfect man, and that he died only as a witness of the truth, if he will consent to call his belief an *opinion*, and keep it *private*, or use only Scriptural terms, which he knows are understood by those who hear him in a sense entirely opposite to that in which he employs them, must be received into Christian fellowship. He is worthy of all confidence, and fraternal love, though, according to Mr. Campbell's judgment, he errs on a fundamental point of the Christian system.

But if a *Trinitarian*, with sound views of the Gospel, and a heart glowing with its spirit, in his learning, applies an erudite, or, in his simplicity, applies an unrefined epithet "to the Father, the Son, or the Holy Spirit," to illustrate his perfections, or exalt his glory, *he must be rejected*. And what is this but to exalt words above truth, and to sacrifice "unity in the faith, and in the knowledge of the Son of God," on the altar of a barren, heartless, senseless agreement in words and phrases? And what, permit me farther to inquire, must be the moral influence of that church which virtually abolishes the distinction between truth and error? Nay, worse still, which gives to *covert Unitarianism* a marked preference over Trinitarianism, expressed, in epithets either "*barbarous*," or "*scholastic?*" And who is to execute this new and inflexible law? Every Reformed church. *We* will not allow the use of scholastic or barbarous epithets. No *Trinitarian*, who understands his duties or his rights, could consent to belong to a church claiming a power so unauthorized by revelation, and so abhorrent to reason.

I have not yet descended to the bottom of this pit. Every man who knows the truth is bound to publish it to others. This is a truth for the early and vigorous advocacy of which Mr. Campbell deserves praise. I honor the man who honestly, boldly and earnestly propagates the views, call them faith or opinions, which he deems true and important. I prefer a candid, out-spoken Unitarian, or Universalist, to a concealed one. Now, what does the Campbellite discipline do, but offer a reward for hypocrisy? It says to the candidate for church membership, if you honestly hold, and frankly proclaim, what we deem error, we cannot receive you; but if you will conceal your errors, we will embrace you with fraternal confidence and love. We have no objection to your errors—they are opinions—opinions are private property—"we do not ask" you "to give up" your "opinions"—but, whatever may be your sense of duty, you must hold your opinions "as private property," or if you express them at all, it must be in "Bible phrases, in plain reference" to these matters of opinion. Now, let any discerning man say, whether the hypocritical and unscrupulous errorist is not treated with a consideration and affection which are withheld from the honest and conscientious errorist, or even the orthodox Christian who expresses truth concerning the Father, the Son, and the Holy Spirit, in interdicted epithets.

I must notice another point in this remarkable extract. "If a person," observes the Reformer, "say such (Universalism) is his private opinion, let him have it as his private opinion; but lay no stress upon it: and if it be a wrong private opinion, *it will die a natural death much sooner than if you attempt to kill it.*" Whether Mr. Campbell intends this as a general or particular rule, I do not know. Whether this specified error, or all error, will die soonest by being let alone, Mr. Campbell does not inform us. Paul did not think the errors of the Judaizing teachers would perish sooner by neglect. Christ did not judge that the doctrine of the Nicolaitanes would die the sooner if there was no attempt to oppose it. The whole of Divine revelation is a vigorous combat with every system and species of error. What a pity it is that Mr. Campbell did not make an earlier discovery that error of opinion will die a natural death sooner than it can be killed. What a vast saving of ink, and paper, and toil, and anxiety, and exasperation, and alienation, it might have proved. But Mr. Campbell does not quite let error alone. He closes its mouth, or limits it to the use of Bible phrases, and gives it a home and countenance, and respectability in the church—that "it may die a natural death."

At this point, so far as the present discussion is concerned, the notable extract might be dropped. But for the purpose of showing the loose and inaccurate style in which Mr. Campbell treats the most important subjects, another sentence must be noticed. "What is a Unitarian?" To this question, he replies, "One who contends that *Jesus Christ is* NOT *the Son of God.*" Now, it may be safely affirmed, that no Unitarian has ever denied that

Jesus Christ is the Son of God. The Unitarians not only believe that Jesus is the Son of God, but maintain that they receive him as the Son of God, according to the scriptural and rational import of the phrase. To charge them, as Mr. Campbell has done, with denying that Jesus is the *Son of God*, is to do them gross injustice—springing, it is presumed, so far as he is concerned, not from *malice aforethought* but a culpable carelessness in the use of language.

True, in the same extract, he represents the Trinitarian as admitting, that "many Unitarians acknowledge that Jesus Christ is the Son of God in a sense of their own." But this can furnish no apology for the statement he makes that a Unitarian is one who *contends* that *Jesus Christ is not the Son of God.*"

If verbal criticism were composed of flesh and blood, it might grow fat on the food furnished for its nourishment in the obscurities, inaccuracies and mistakes, abounding on the pages of the Reformer.

We have seen that Universalists may be retained in the Reformed churches on the not very intelligible condition, that they will "consent to use and apply all the Bible phrases in their plain reference to the future state of men and *angels ;*" or, as it appears from the compromise with Dr. Thomas, "to discontinue the discussion of the same, *unless in their defense when misrepresented.*" But suppose they should deem it incompatible with their duty and independence, to keep silent, or act merely on the defensive, regarding their peculiar doctrines or points of faith? What then? Does the Reformation make any provision for the correction of the evil? A case calling for correction has recently presented itself. The "current Reformation" has been quite fruitful of heresies. First, Dr. Thomas led off a sect of *Materialists;* and lately Mr. J. B. Ferguson, pastor of the Reformed church in Nashville, having embraced *Universalist* views, is sustained by a majority of his church. The Millennial Harbinger, of January, copies from the Christian Age of December 22, as follows: p. 55.

"Mr. Clapp, of New Orleans, wrote to Mr. Gurley, of Cincinnati, alleging that Mr. Ferguson 'was with them fully;' that is, that he was a thorough Universalist, and that he would change the 'Campbellite church in the South.' I do not aim to give the exact words—I give the exact meaning."

On this subject Mr. Campbell says:—

"That Mr. Ferguson should seek to retain any position among us, is irreconcilable with any other view than that he intends to create a party in favor of Universalism. This is most unquestionably his design, if there be any truth in the documents, copied, in part, from the Christian Age, above. "Now, we award to every man what we claim for ourselves—liberty to preach and teach his own convictions. But we must hold it incompatible with candor and honesty, guilefully to hold a place amongst us, when he is no more of us than Messrs. Gurley and Quinby, whom he endorses and commends as worthy of the most ample success, in propagating bald and deformed Universalism ; and how any church amongst us can choose him as its pastor, unless they, too, are ultra-Universalists, demands an explanation, which is alike due to itself and to the Christian brotherhood."

Concerning the above statements and remarks, several things deserve to be noted—

1. The "current Reformation" seems likely to produce more than one schism for every generation, the number ascribed by Mr. Campbell to every "sectarian creed."

2. It is proper to recommend to the Reformers, a patient endurance of the evils for the removal of which their system has made no adequate provision. Mr. Ferguson occupies the foundation of Christian fellowship on which he was built. He believes *one fact*—has submitted to *one institution*—and his "*deportment accords with the morality and virtue of the great Prophet*," and is, therefore, "a Christian, as defined, not by Dr. Johnson, nor any creed-maker, but by one taught from heaven." He has violated no covenant. Surely the Reformers will not excommunicate and anathematize him ! Then he might write "What a dangerous matter it has

become, to think differently from" Mr. Campbell and his friends! "How perilous to view" the future state "differently from the 'keepers of the faith' of *Tennessee!* This alone exposes a person to the greatest anathema in the power of *Reformers.* They can do no more in *Tennessee,* as yet, than treat a dissentient as they would a murderer, or a vile adulterer!" It cannot be that the Disciples will knowingly subject themselves to such dreadful imputations.

3. Should Mr. Campbell succeed in persuading or shaming Mr. Ferguson and his party into an abandonment of their position in the ranks of the Disciples, he will be far more successful than the Baptists were in their early struggles with Mr. Campbell and his party. It was more than suspected that they intended "to create a party in favor of" the *Reformation.* The Baptists were willing to award to them what they claimed for themselves—liberty to preach and teach their own convictions—but they thought it incompatible "with candor and honesty," for men whose aim was to revolutionize the Baptist churches—who pronounced them a part of Babylon the Great—and whose labors were spreading discord and unhappiness among them—to hold a place in their churches. They would gladly have avoided the necessity of excluding the Reformers—of provoking the cry of persecution—but they could not. The Reformers

did not deem it proper to retire from a position which gave them a favorable opportunity for propagating their sentiments, and strengthening their party. The cup which they pressed to the lips of the Baptists, is now pressed to their own lips. It is bitter, but they must drink it. It may prove medicinal. If they retain the errorists, they cherish in their own bosom a faction whose aim is to "change the Campbellite church in the South," and if they exclude them, they sit in judgment on their religious faith, follow the spirit and example of the creed-making sects, and utterly repudiate their boasted foundation of church union. They are in a dilemma.

CAMPBELLISM IN ITS TENDENCIES.

When Mr. Campbell commenced his public career, serious apprehensions were entertained, by the most judicious observers, that it would terminate in wild speculations, fatal error, or, perhaps, downright infidelity. Several causes contributed to create and strengthen this apprehension. His religious views underwent early, various, and rapid changes. From ultra-Calvinism he quickly passed, through all the doctrinal stages, to low Arminianism—from being a Pædobaptist he became a Baptist, and soon left all his new brethren behind in his zeal for the ordinance of baptism. Other important changes were frequently occurring in his religious creed. No wonder that considerate Christians were prepared to see greater, and almost any, changes taking place in his views. It was supposed by many that he had a pretty strong leaning to Unitarianism. His rejection of the terms *Trinity*, and *Trinitarian*, some incautious and obscure remarks which he penned on this profound subject, and the early coalition of his party with Mr. Stone, and his Arian followers, gave birth and vigor to the supposition. Others, again, suspected that the tendency of the Reformation was towards the renunciation of all spiritual religion, and the adoption of a heartless formalism. This fear originated from the irreverent and sarcastic manner in which he treated religious experiences, and, indeed, the whole subject of earnest piety. These apprehensions of the evil tendencies of the Reformation were not confined to its opposers, but prevailed with many who viewed the labors of Mr. Campbell with more or less favor and interest. But Campbellism was not destined to realize, at any rate, in the first age of its existence, and to the full extent, these fears.

Several conservative influences conspired to check the evil tendencies of the system, if they really existed. It was a redeeming trait of the Reformation that it professed great reverence for the holy Scriptures. In common with other Protestant Christians, the Reformers maintained the supreme authority of revelation in matters of faith ; but they gave marked and unusual prominence to this point in their teaching. An unwillingness to tread the beaten track, and a desire to furnish original, striking and systematic expositions of the Scriptures, made them very unsafe religious guides ; yet the custom of referring all questions concerning faith and practice to the arbitrament of the Scriptures proved to be the sheet anchor of their preservation from the mælstrom of error into which they were drifting. They were mostly diligent and careful readers of the Bible; but they read it, with the glosses it received at Bethany. Their unavoidable association and intercourse with the Christian sects around them insensibly exerted over them a conservative influence. It was not easy, perhaps, not possible for them, to rise superior to the influences which by books, newspapers, sermons, and conversations, were constantly, though, for the most part, unintentionally, exerted to restrain their wanderings, correct their errors, modify their views, and assimilate them to the surrounding Christian denominations. The glory of being a discoverer of truth, and a reformer, may impel a man to endure, and even to glory in, reproach; but others, who do not aspire after this glory, will gradually seek, at any rate, as far as the love of truth will permit, to soften the asperities of an unpopular system, and conform it to the prevailing taste. He has been a careless observer of Campbellism who has not perceived its effort to get rid of the *odium theologicum* by conforming its teachings, more and more, to the popular views. The reader may find a striking exemplification of this remark in Mr. Campbell's debate with Rev. N. L. Rice. It was perfectly obvious throughout the discussion, that he was desirous of being accounted orthodox in his religious principles, and nothing so much annoyed him as the quotation of heterodox sentiments from his early writings.

Another cause, however, contributed more than both the above, to restrain the erring tendency of the Reformation, and, in a measure, to turn it into the paths of sobriety and moderation. This cause was *Thomasism*. The reader has already seen that Dr. Thomas embraced the principles of the Reformation, and proposed to follow them out to their legitimate results. His views and labors rendered him very unpopular, and brought upon the Reformation great reproach. Mr. Campbell, in opposing this new Reformation, was compelled to employ, in part, the very weapons which the Baptists, and other evangelical Christians, had used in their contests with him. In combating the errors of Dr. Thomas, he naturally sought sympathy and countenance ; and where could these be found except among the evangelical sects ? But if these were to be conciliated, they must be won, not by derision and contempt, but by candid and kind words, a return to evangelical principles, and the exemplification of the true Christian spirit. From the rise of Thomasism may be dated the decline of the vaunting, pugnacious spirit of the Reformation. Internal discussions and conflicts made the Reformers less intent on foreign conquests; and the bitter fruits of the Reformation, so early developed and matured, made them less confident of its excellence. Thus the tendencies of the system were checked, and its advocates were brought to reflection, under circumstances favorable to a correction of their early mistakes.

The means necessary for building are very different from those employed in tearing down. Mr. Campbell, in the commencement of his Reformation, was occupied in demolishing the "kingdom of the clergy," and all sectarian combinations. Every institution and every means, therefore, used in supporting and spreading the prevalent Christian organizations, was condemned as evil. But when he found himself at the head of a sect, he felt the necessity of resorting to the use of these condemned measures for the purpose of consolidating and increasing it. On this subject it will be proper to enter into details.

The reader has seen the utter contempt in which Mr. Campbell held the "hireling clergy." "Every man, who receives money for preaching the Gospel, or for sermons, by the day, month, or year, is a hireling in the language of truth and soberness." Such was the doctrine of the *early*, but it is not the doctrine of the *current Reformation*. Now, the Reformed churches have settled pastors, not reared up among them, but called from abroad to officiate in them, supported by regular salaries, and differing, in no material respect, from the ministers of other Christian denominations. They are "clergy," or "hirelings," according to the Bethany definition of these terms.

The extravagance, show, and pomp of city congregations was a popular theme for declamation with the Reformer of Brooke. Many simple minded and pious Christians wished him success in his efforts to correct the evil. Unfortunately, the Reformed churches are, in this respect, following in the wake of the sects. The writer was, not long since, in a large, beautiful and prosperous city, in the West, where the "Disciples' Meeting House" rose, in grand proportions, and towering turrets, above all the temples of the "Babylonians." Nor is this a solitary case. Every where the advocates of the "ancient Gospel," are vieing with the devotees of a so-called spurious Christianity, in the cost and adornment of their houses of worship.

Baptist *Associations*—the messengers of the churches met together for the purposes of fraternal consultation and advice—were pronounced by Mr. Campbell to be unauthorized of God. There was no "Thus saith the Lord" for them. Chn. Bap., p. 26. "I hope," said an early Reformer, who had fully imbibed the spirit of his master, "your paper will destroy *associations*, *State conventions*,—all of which are as assumed and as anti-scriptural as the infallibility and pontificate of the Pope of Rome." p. 144. But the Reformed churches soon felt the need of mutual intercourse and concert in efforts.

And Mr. Campbell, who could find no Scripture authority for Associations, thus lays down the law of Christian coöperation. "Whether the churches in a given district shall, by letter, messengers, or stated meetings, once or twice per annum, or oftener, communicate with one another; whether they shall send one, two, or twenty persons, or all go and communicate face to face, or send a letter; and whether they shall annually print, write, or publish their statistics, &c., &c., &c., are the mere circumstantials of the Christian institution. * * * Coöperation, as much as the intercommunion of Christians, is a part of the Christian institution." Chn. Sys., pp. 74-75. *Associations,* it seems, are unscriptural, but *Coöperation* meetings are "a part of the Christian institution." It amounts to this brief proposition, *What you do is wrong—if we do the same thing, and call it by another name, it is right.*

Bible Societies and *Sunday-Schools*—schemes of the clergy—were, in Mr. Campbell's early judgment, "fraught with mischief to the temporal and eternal interests of men." "I have for some time," said he, "viewed both Bible Societies and Sunday-Schools, as a sort of recruiting establishments, to fill up the ranks of those sects which take the lead in them." Chn. Bap., p. 80. No sooner, however, were the Reformed churches organized, than they found it necessary to resort to these "recruiting establishments" for the purpose of filling up their ranks;

and schemes of most pernicious tendency when cherished by the sects, became not only innoxious, but useful in the hands of their new advocates.

Colleges were, in the early period of the Reformation, placed among the marks of the beast. "The Baptists, too," he said, "have got their *schools*, their *colleges*, and their Gamaliels too—and by the magic of these *marks of the beast*, they claim homage and respect, and dispute the high places with those very Rabbis whose fathers were wont to grin at *their* fathers." Mill. Har., vol. 1, p. 15. In a few years after this passage was penned, we see its venerable author placed at the head of Bethany College, in Virginia, with the high-sounding title of President. And did he, *by the magic of this mark of the beast*, claim homage and respect, and dispute the high places with the Rabbis, who descended from the *grinning* fathers? Certainly not. He has no affinity with the beast. The seeming inconsistency is explained by this simple consideration. To overthrow the clergy and the sects, it was necessary to undermine the influence of colleges; the most effectual way of destroying their influence was to produce the impression that they were *marks of the beast*—appendages of the Romish hierarchy—but to give respect and influence to the Reformation, it was important to have a college, free, of course, from priestly rule, and who so worthy to preside over it as the father of the Reformation, to whom belonged the honor of the exhumation of the ancient Gospel?

To the *education of the rising ministry*, the Reformation, in its early stage, was most decidedly hostile. In reviewing a "Sermon on the duty of the church to prepare pious youth in her bosom, for the Gospel ministry," in the year 1826, the editor of the Christian Baptist wrote as follows: p. 221.

The "sermon is intended to proclaim that it is the duty of the church to prepare in her bosom pious youth for the Gospel ministry. Now, this is really a new message from the skies, for there is not one word, from Genesis to John, which says that it is the duty of the church to prepare pious youth for the Gospel ministry. This point could not be proved from the words of any previous ambassador, and it is unnecessary for any ambassador to prove his own communications to be true."

At what precise time it is not known, but before the beginning of the year 1854, the "new message from the skies" had been duly received and authenticated. The "Christian church" needed an educated ministry, and authority to raise up one was easily obtained. In the January No. of the Mill. Harbinger, of the present year, (1854) Mr. Campbell in a letter addressed to his wife, says: p. 40.

"Since I last wrote to you, I have been almost constantly on the wing, pleading the cause of man's redemption in the department of an educated ministry.

That this is one of the Lord's ordinances, cannot rationally be doubted by any student of nature and of the Bible. . . . We want not higher authority to teach or to constrain us to raise up—to educate and train men in human and Christian science, that they may be able to teach others also. . . . We are pleased to see that every form of Protestantism, Quakerism alone excepted, is intent on the proper education of its itinerant ministry."

Now, this is refreshing. It sounds so unlike the censorious, sterile, and hostile Campbellism with which our Noells, and Cloptons, and Semples, had to deal. It shows, conclusively, that reformatory, conservative influences have been modifying and improving the system. Every such indication of *genuine reformation* should be hailed with delight by the friends of evangelical piety.

The reader has already been informed, through the extracts transferred from the writings of Mr. Campbell to these pages, of his views on the subject of Christian missions; and will, doubtless, be surprised to learn that the Reformers, with Mr. Campbell at their head, have engaged in the missionary enterprise. Soon after their separate organization, they sent out, not *missionaries*, but *evangelists* —*paid* preachers—to proclaim the "ancient Gospel." For the appointment of *missionaries*, not endowed with miraculous power, there could, at that time, be found in the Scriptures, neither precept, example, or inferential authority; but the appointment and support of *evangelists* to itinerate and proclaim the "ancient Gospel," was plainly sanctioned by the "Living Oracles." But recently they have organized a *Foreign Mission Board*—and have sent forth, not a church, according to the original Bethany plan for evangelizing the world, but individual missionaries, "without the power of working miracles," of which, said Mr. Campbell, "the Bible gives us no idea." Chn. Bap., p. 15.

The above facts will suffice to show the favorable changes which have taken place among the Reformers. The Reformation has been gradually and greatly reformed. The present Millennial Harbinger is a far more respectable and dignified monthly than the old Christian Baptist. Though, it must be conceded, that its pages occasionally furnish proof that its veteran editor has not forgotten the art of vituperation. The Disciples generally are less opiniated, less eager for battle, and far more courteous and conciliatory, in their intercourse with other Christians, than they formerly were. In short, they seem to have taken the road back to Babylon, and have nearly completed their journey.

There is manifestly a growing desire among the Reformers to be accounted "evangelical," "orthodox," and "regular." A striking proof of this remark, was furnished, not long since, in the city of St. Louis, Mo. There was a Christian Association formed in that city. The members of the Association were required to be members of some "*evangelical* church." Applicants for admission from the Christian, or Reformed church, were rejected on the ground that they furnished no evidence of being "evangelical." To obviate the difficulty, a prominent member of the church, with, as it is stated, the concurrence of the pastor, and other leading members, drew up and presented a statement of the doctrines held by the church. Here follows the creed:

"The independent existence of one absolutely perfect Being, the Creator, Preserver, and Governor of all things: The divine inspiration, the authority, and sufficiency of the Holy Scriptures: The existence of three persons in the Godhead, the Father, the Son, and the Holy Spirit: the incarnation and Atonement of the Son for human salvation: The justification of the sinner by faith, without the deeds of the law, or meritorious works of righteousness, of any kind whatever, and the necessity of the Spirit's influence to regenerate the souls of men." Western Watchman, vol. 6, p. 126.

Concerning the above article several remarks are worthy to be made.

1. It is a *creed*. It is a brief summary of the doctrine in the belief of which the church is united. Though not formally sanctioned by the church, it

may be presumed to contain the truths deemed by them fundamental.

2. It is a *sound* creed. Its orthodoxy, so far as it goes, will be readily admitted by all evangelical Christians. It contains, expressed in plain, and well understood, but not exclusively scriptural terms, the truths which are, by the Spirit of inspiration, placed as the principal parts of the Gospel system. It is the "far famed tree of evangelical orthodoxy," whose bitter fruits Mr. Campbell so eloquently described. It was drawn up and presented for a worthy purpose—to furnish proof that those who were united in the belief and maintenance of its doctrines—were entitled to Christian confidence and affection.

3. Its adoption is a *virtual renunciation of Campbellism.* This will appear from several considerations. It applies certain "scholastic" terms, as "three persons," and "incarnation" to the Father, the Son, and the Holy Spirit, contrary to the express and imperative law of the Reformation. "We will not allow him, (the Trinitarian,) to apply scholastic epithets to the Father," &c. It sets at naught the foundation of Christian union laid by Mr. Campbell, and the Reformed builders generally —that the belief of *one fact,* and submission to *one institution* expressive of it, "*is all that is required of Heaven to admission into the church.*" And, lastly, it is a concession, in the face of all Mr

Campbell's teaching, that a profession of belief in the Scriptures is insufficient to indicate a man's faith.

4. It is a matter of *just and sincere gratulation* that these St. Louis Christians have given a clear and manly exhibition of their religious belief. They owed it to themselves, to the Christian Association, to the public, and, above all, to the truth, and to the God of truth, not to conceal their faith under loose and indefinite expressions, but to give it a free and honest utterance. If in doing so they have renounced the distinctive principles of the Bethany Reformation, they may have the consolation to reflect that they have followed the oracles of God.

5. If the Reformers generally are prepared to adopt this creed, with a few additions, to which, it is presumed, they have no serious objection, to complete the system, there seems to be no good reason why they should keep themselves, or be kept by others, in estrangement from their brethren of the evangelical sects. True, their Reformation would utterly vanish, except in dim and shadowy remembrance. But what of that? It was commenced, and prosecuted, most unsuccessfully, to promote Christian union—let it perish, with a fairer prospect of securing the same glorious result.

We have seen the vaunting pretensions of Campbellism to be the "ancient Gospel." All the worldliness, contentions, schisms and apostasies among the sects were ascribed by its advocates to ***creeds***, *evangelical orthodoxy*, *metaphysical speculations*, &c. It was confidently predicted that the fruits of the ancient Gospel would be as far superior to the fruits of the popular exhibitions of Christianity, as the grapes of Eshcol were to the apples of Sodom. The experiment has been made on a somewhat extended scale. What is the result?

The most enthusiastic admirer of the system must admit that its fair promises have not been fulfilled. The Reformation has proved a failure. Its converts have been considerably increased; but according to Mr. Campbell's concession, they are a heterogenious multitude, among whom "*every sort of doctrine has been proclaimed, by almost all sorts of preachers.*" It will hardly be maintained that the rapid increase of the Reformers is a proof of the truth of their system. Campbellism has been far outstripped in its conquests by Mormonism. If success in winning converts is the test of truth, the Bethany Reformer must confess the inspiration of the prophet of Nauvoo. But what has been the moral influence of Campbellism? Have the converts made by the "ancient Gospel" been preëminent for modesty, humility, disinterestedness, sobriety of deportment, good works, stability, and usefulness? Comparisons are invidious. They would not now be made, if they were not necessary to expose the fallacy of the liberal professions of the early Reformation. *It may be confidently affirmed, that experience has falsified them.* The fruits of Campbellism are not better than were the fruits of the Gospel preached by Noell and Semple, and their worthy compeers.

If the Reformation has accomplished any good, it is attributable, not to its peculiarities, but the great principles which it has inculcated, sometimes with strange inconsistency, in common with "evangelical orthodoxy." Just in proportion as it becomes assimilated to evangelical Christianity, and renounces, or ignores, its distinctive principles, we may hope for an increase of its usefulness.

CONCLUSION.

The rise, progress and variations—the principles, discipline and tendencies of Campbellism have been, somewhat carefully, examined. Many important points have been passed without notice. To attempt the correction of all the errors into which Mr. Campbell has fallen, would involve the necessity of a minute review of all the ponderous volumes which he has written. Scarcely a page of his writings is free from false logic, false philosophy, or false theology, to say nothing of philological, grammatical and rhetorical blemishes. But the writer has deemed it proper, so far as he has discussed the evils of Campbellism, to confine his remarks to its graver errors. It is suitable, in conclusion, to offer a few general remarks on the whole system.

The examination of the subject must tend greatly to strengthen the conviction that the system of truth, generally designated among Protestant Christians, *the "evangelical," or "orthodox faith," is Scriptural.* When Mr. Campbell was attacking it, with so much learning, ingenuity, and diligence, many feared that it would be overthrown. The fear was idle. To suppose that the essential principles of the Gospel had been for ages concealed, until they were brought to light, "in the year of grace, one thousand eight hundred and twenty-three," was a grand absurdity. Under a spiritual despotism, where wealth, learning, ambition, and interest are enlisted to maintain the existing hierarchy, and to repress and crush the spirit of inquiry and innovation, ignorance and error may be perpetuated. This remark explains the uniformity of error prevailing under the unbroken reign of "the man of sin." But where men enjoy freedom to read and study, to teach and practice, the Word of God, with ample means to investigate its import, it seems incredible that its fundamental principles should remain unknown. That the Protestant Reformation, in a good degree, freed the human mind from spiritual bondage, and stimulated it to vigorous and persevering efforts after truth, will scarcely be denied. Though some Protestant governments have imposed needless and injurious restrictions on religious inquiry, others have tolerated, protected and encouraged it. Many men, eminent for their piety, genius, learning, candor, and industry—men as good, and as great as the world has seen, or is likely to see—availing themselves of this liberty, have devoted their lives, under circumstances favorable to success, to the study of the Bible, and have been willing to peril and sacrifice all worldly advantages in the maintenance of its truths. That not one of them should have discovered the essential principles of the Gospel, until it was disinterred by Mr. Campbell of Bethany, is preposterous. Whence arose the difficulty of understanding the system? From its obscurity? This will scarcely be pretended. From want of candor, learning and industry in the inquirers? This, surely, will not be affirmed by one who has been so deeply indebted as Mr. Campbell, to his predecessors for his parade of learning and criticisms. It is pleasing to the pious mind to reflect, how the good and great, in every age and land, who have made the Scriptures their study and guide, have harmonized in their views of the essential facts, doctrines, and duties of Christianity. Divided they have been concerning ordinances, church polity, and various speculations, but united in all that pertains to the vital principles—the soul-saving truths—of the system. That any man should imagine, after so many gifted minds had carefully, laboriously, and with much prayer, studied the Bible, that *he* should be the *first*, in many generations, to discern its hidden import, and open it, in all its beauty, fulness and glory, to the admiring gaze of mankind, savors more of vanity than of a sound judgment—resembles more the hallucination of a distempered mind, than the dictate of sound Christian philosophy. The system of faith, held by evangelical Christians, is impregnable. It has withstood, and it is destined to withstand, the assaults of the most powerful, and the machinations of the most subtle, minds. All hope of any new and important discoveries in the system is visionary. Christianity does not belong to the progressive sciences. Its primary facts, principles, and duties were plainly revealed, and fully confirmed in the beginning ; and could be understood just as easily and clearly before the first number of the Christian Baptist appeared, as they can be now. It would be difficult for the most devoted admirer of Mr. Campbell to point to a single essential principle or duty of the Christian system, which he has disinterred, or on which he has shed any fresh light. If all his criticisms, arguments, illustrations, and declamations were struck from existence, there would not be one particle less of religious light in the world. The Bible would shine with undiminished lustre. The host of evangelical authors, who shone in the religious firmament, before the dawn of the Bethany Reformation, have retained their places, and their brilliance. After having pronounced the fruits of the "far famed tree of evangelical orthodoxy" to be spurious and pernicious, and having labored, with all his powers, and with untiring diligence, for almost thirty years, to uproot and destroy it, Mr. Campbell is, at length, constrained to come forward and claim the honor o' being orthodox. He has become, it seems, a "regular." The history of this Reformation furnishes a most illustrious proof of the truth, stability and excellence of "evangelical orthodoxy." It has undergone a fiery ordeal. Learning, ingenuity, wit and zeal, with all the weapons that proud rationalism, and scoffing infidelity, could furnish, have been employed for its overthrow, and employed with a signal want of success. Every distinctive principle of the popular evangelical system, as maintained by the Presbyterian, Methodist, Baptist and other orthodox Christian denominations, has been unscathed. The doctrines of hereditary human depravity—(denied by some of the Reformers)—of the necessity of the influence of the Spirit to renovate the soul of man—and of justification by faith, without any necessary connexion with the act of baptism—(which have been denied, or understood to be denied, by all the Reformers)— have firmly maintained their ground. Like some tall and hoary cliff, against which the mighty waves of the ocean have dashed, and foamed, and raged for a time, and to whose strength they have at last rendered homage, by subsiding into a comparative calm at its base, the evangelical faith, "the popular exhibition of Christianity," has received and resisted the threatening surges of the "current Reformation," until their force is spent, and their receding fury proclaims its stability. Commencing its assaults on all Christian denominations with dauntless intrepidity, and giving strong assurances of their early overthrow, and the speedy dawn of the Millennium, the Reformation has been frittered away to nothing, or has ended in a huge mass of inconsistencies and contradictions.

The course which the Baptists should pursue relative to the Reformers, is worthy of the gravest and most candid consideration. The propriety of their action in separating the Campbellites from their communion has been already discussed. Much as the necessity of the measure was deplored, by the conservative portion of the Baptist churches, time has clearly demonstrated its wisdom. There is now far greater harmony of views, and far less alienation of feeling, between the Baptists and Reformers, than there was previously to their separation. But still the question comes up, with augmented interest and importance, How shall we act towards the Reformers?

The union of all Christians, so far as it can be secured without sacrificing the claims of an enlightened conscience, or giving countenance to pernicious error, is greatly to be desired. It is the duty of every believer in Christ, not only to pray for this consummation, but by the cultivation of a candid, kind and forbearing spirit, to endeavor to promote it. The Reformers belong to the Baptist family, though, in our view, they are an erring branch of it. They agree with us on the action and subjects of

Christian baptism, however widely they may differ from us on other points ; and it is to be regretted that those who substantially concur in regard to church organization and ordinances should be divided in their affections and efforts. The principles which we hold in common have sufficient opposition to encounter from without, to make it exceedingly important not to weaken their influence, and retard their progress by discord and strife among ourselves. Union, however, valuable as it is, may be purchased at too high a price. A professional union, founded on a common use of words and phrases, to which we attach no meaning, or widely different meanings, or on a mutual agreement to conceal the truth, is neither Scriptural, reasonable, nor desirable. Fellowship in the Gospel—the only intelligent, hearty and efficient union of Christians—implies an agreement in the essential facts, principles and duties of the system. And this fellowship cannot be secured by unscrupulous compromises, and Jesuitical professions, but only by unity of views concerning Christian doctrine.

How far error may be tolerated by a church of Christ for the sake of union, it is not easy to decide. The Bible furnishes no direct and explicit answer to the question. Error may be so palpable and gross, call it faith or opinion, as to preclude the possibility of its toleration by a church, without a dereliction of duty, and a virtual abandonment of the cause of truth. Whether the Reformers hold religious views incompatible with their reception into evangelical Baptist churches, is the practical question. So far as the Disciples are affiliated with the Stonites, or Arians of the West, their reception into the fellowship of our churches would be, on our part, base unfaithfulness to the cause of Christ, and of truth. Nor would the evil be, in any degree, mitigated by their hypocritical consent to conceal their errors, or express them in Scriptural phrases, to which they have attached, and are understood to attach a false meaning. Without condemning and renouncing their error, they can have no Scriptural fellowship with those who understand and love the Gospel. How far this heterodoxy now prevails among the Reformers, the writer does not possess the means of deciding.

It would not be difficult from the writings of Mr. Campbell to draw up a creed, which in all essential points would be acceptable to evangelical Christendom. In this chiefly lies the danger of Campbellism. Thousands of persons have been seduced into the belief that the Reformers differ nothing from the Baptists, except in weekly communion, and other unimportant points.

But the reader has seen that Campbellism has two sides—an orthodox and a heterodox—an evangelical, and, for lack of a better term, it must be said, a Reformed side. It would be quite easy to select from Mr. Campbell's books, without any perversion of the quotations, a system of doctrine so utterly at variance with the Scriptures, and so repugnant to the feelings of pious people, that it would receive the undivided condemnation of every evangelical denomination.

Now, if the Reformers would secure the confidence and affection of orthodox Christians, it will not be sufficient that they should proclaim their own orthodoxy—as Mr. Campbell has recently proclaimed his—nor even to put forth, in some intelligible form, the orthodox articles of their belief; but they must explicitly repudiate the doctrines which they have been supposed to hold, at variance with the evangelical syetem. They may have been misunderstood, or misrepresented, or partly misunderstood, and partly misrepresented; but the effect in preventing Christian union is precisely the same, as if they had been rightly understood, and rightly represented. But while it may be conceded, that their views and intentions may have been misconceived, it must be maintained that their language has been candidly and fairly interpreted. But if they have been misunderstood or misrepresented, from no matter what motives, they owe it to themselves, their Christian brethren, and their Redeemer, to place themselves *rectus in curia*; and this cannot be done, either to the confusion of their foes, or the satisfaction of intelligent, inquiring Christians, but by a distinct and formal repudiation of the heterodox sentiments which they are charged with having published.

It is proper to descend to particulars. If the Reformers would secure for themselves the confidence and affection of the great evangelical family of Christians, let them explicitly disavow—

First. That all the converting power of the Spirit is in the Word—in the sense in which ninety-nine persons out of every one hundred understand the language, and, indeed, in the only sense of which it is fairly susceptible.

Secondly. That regeneration, the new birth, and conversion,are identical with baptism,in the language of Scripture, or common sense, or any other except that of superstition. And let them unequivocally maintain—

Thirdly. That prayer is the plain and imperative duty of believers, whether baptized or not.

Fourthly. That repentance, faith, and baptism, are not equally essential to the remission of sins ; but that this blessing is virtually, really obtained by faith in Christ, and only formally and declaratively in baptism. And,

Fifthly. That the belief of one fact, and performance of one act, with a moral life, is not a sufficient foundation for Christian union ; but that this union, to be Scriptural and valuable, must be based on the belief of the fundamental facts and doctrines of the Gospel.

It may be necessary for the Reformers to disavow other sentiments which they have maintained, or which, from their associations, they have been suspected of holding ; but the above principles having been clearly and repeatedly proclaimed, and made the very ground-work of the Reformation, must be repudiated, before they can reasonably hope to be admitted into the evangelical family.

This renunciation of the errors of Campbellism, in order to secure the proposed end, must be made, not in a fugitive essay, nor in equivocal terms, nor on individual responsibility, but in some explicit, formal, solemn, and authorized manner—like the "declaration of belief" presented by the Brush Run church to the Redstone Association, or the summary of doctrine drawn up by the *Christian church*, in St. Louis, to convince the Christian Association of the validity of their claim to be considered "evangelical."

For his indiscriminate, violent, and bitter attack on their cherished principles, on their institutions for diffusing the light of the Gospel, and on their well-meant efforts to meliorate the condition of men, and display the glory of Christ, Mr. Campbell owes an apology to the Christian world. Especially is this due, as he found it expedient, in building up the "*Christian church*," that is, his own party, to employ the same institutions, and the same means, for the use of which he so freely censured them. Though this apology may not be essential to the restoration of harmony between the Baptists and Reformers, it is indispensable to the restoration of Christian confidence in the leader of the Reformation.

Some concessions, too, may be due on the part of the Baptists, to secure the desired union. They have occasionally evinced, in their contests with the Reformers, an acrimony, seeming to spring from personal dislike, rather than zeal for the truth and honor of God, which they should readily admit, and, in future, carefully avoid.

The regular meeting of all the churches, in their respective places of worship, on every Lord's-day, which the Baptists have never opposed, they should more earnestly insist on, and more faithfully practice. Weekly communion they should not contend about, but let it be introduced into the churches wherever, and whenever it is deemed obligatory or expedient. They should not yield to the Reformers, as in truth they do not, in their reverence for, their submission to, and their diligent study of, the holy Scriptures.

As to the name by which they shall be called, neither the Baptists nor the Reformers should be much concerned. The Disciples of Christ were not called *Christians* until eleven years after his ascension; and then, whether the name was given by the Spirit of inspiration, assumed by them in honor of their Master, as a matter of expediency, or adopted by their enemies as a term of reproach, the sacred historian has not informed us, and we can only conjecture. We should be solicitous about truth and piety, not names. The name *Baptist*, it is presumed, was not assumed by those who bear it, after deliberation, and of choice, nor would it be practicable for them, at their option, to lay it aside. The appellation *Christian*, can never, in the present divided state of the religious world, be employed to designate, without a qualifying epithet, any particular party of Christians. But if we see eye to eye, speak the same things, and are animated by the same spirit, whether we are called Baptists, Reformers, or Christians, or are distinguished by some other name, is of little consequence. The primitive Christians were equally pious, happy, and useful, whether they were called Galileans, Disciples, or Christians. Our fathers ecclesiastic, were not less worthy when they were known as "Ana-baptists," than their descendants to whom has been accorded the name of Baptists.

Is there any prospect of the consummation of such a union as has been briefly sketched? None, it is to be feared, during the life-time of Mr. Campbell. The frequent changes of his religious views, have induced a general lack of confidence in his stability. His manifold inconsistencies, and contradictions, have awakened, in many minds, a suspicion as to the integrity of his purposes. In the course of the thirty years' conflict between the Reformers and Baptists, many distinguished combatants, whether justly or unjustly, is not material, have deemed themselves unfairly, unkindly, or rudely treated by Mr. Campbell; while he, doubtless, has against them a list of grievances, equally long and grave, to be redressed. Beside all these things, having for more than a quarter of a century, been *the man* of his party, it is not reasonable to expect that he would consent to unite himself with a denomination in which, though he might occupy a prominent place, he could not occupy the position of leader. In addition to these obstacles, it will require no small measure of humility and moral heroism in him, to acknowledge that his Reformation has proved a failure, and that his views are in substantial agreement with those of the sects against whom he has so long and fiercely warred. All these matters considered, there is very little ground to hope that, in the life-time of the Reformer, and with his approbation, such a union between the Reformers and Baptists will be effected, as truth, piety, and Christian coöperation demand.

Still there is ground to hope for the ultimate scriptural and cordial union of these parties. The work of assimilation between them is going on, and it will go on, with increasing rapidity, as the original causes of irritation are left behind and forgotten, and the veterans in the strife, gradually quit the battle-field. In many places Campbellism has lost its pugnacity, and is fast losing its distinctive elements, and receiving a new impression from the religious principles with which it is ceaselessly coming in contact. The Baptists, too, it must be admitted, are not precisely what they would have been, had there been no Reformation. They have not been uninterested spectators of the religious convulsions and changes around them. While they have seen no cause to abandon any of their distinctive principles, or practices, they have corrected many of their mistakes, burnished their armor, and learning wisdom alike from the successes and failures of their opponents, have prepared themselves for concerted, vigorous and determined efforts in support of what they deem the cause of truth, and of Christ. Let the process of assimilation go on. Good men should earnestly pray for its progress. All should aim to promote it by an honest, earnest adherence to the teaching of the Scriptures, by diffusing the light of truth, and, above all, by cultivating the spirit of the Redeemer—the spirit of love, gentleness, meekness, and candor.

But until this union can be scripturally, and with the concurrence of the churches, consummated, it becomes the Baptists to pursue a firm, straightforward, but conciliating course, receiving no Reformer into their fellowship without a distinct renunciation on his part of the peculiar principles of Campbellism, and a clear assent to the fundamental doctrines of the evangelical system, for which we have so long and faithfully contended.

CAMPBELLISM RE-EXAMINED.

SOON after my work, Campbellism Examined, was published, Mr. Campbell commenced a review of it in the Millennial Harbinger. He was thankful to the "*ten* worthy brethren," who had called me out to examine "something nicknamed Campbellism," as it would afford him an opportunity of extending the empire of this *something* "over myriads of new readers, thinkers and actors, in the grand ecclesiastic drama of the nineteenth century." But thankful as he was to them, he could be thankful to them no more, if, after reading his review of the book, they should "yet sanction or commend it, or print and circulate it through this community." Such was the boasting with which he began his review. Soon, however, seemingly dissatisfied with the results of his labor, he proposed to engage, in an oral or newspaper discussion, of the points at issue between us. As I declined this proposal, he resolved, with increased earnestness, to concentrate his attention on my book, and to continue his "expositions of its errors and misrepresentations," until he should do me "ample justice."

It is now time to inquire in what manner Mr. C. has redeemed his pledge. He has published nine pretty long numbers of the review, with other articles designed, either directly or indirectly, to expose the alleged errors of Campbellism Examined. These pieces are made up of a few petty, verbal criticisms, many offensive personalities, a huge mass of irrelevant matter, much empty declamation, frequent repetitions, and a most desultory discussion of some of the positions maintained in my book. No statement has been invalidated, no quotation shown to be unfair, and no argument manfully and logically met. The work remains intact. Allowing all the reviewer's arguments to be valid, which I am very far from doing, the force and importance of the volume would be but little diminished, the greater portion of it having received little or no attention. The most devoted friends of the reformation, and the warmest admirers of Mr. C., must admit that the review, and its kindred articles, are not a satisfactory reply to my book. They furnish its conclusive defence. Mr. C. himself must have a painful consciousness that he has utterly failed to meet its statements and reasonings. His conviction finds utterance in the last number of the review. "But the half of the sophistry and of the *ad captandum* rhetoric of this ill-fated book, has not yet been developed. Indeed, the broken and desultory manner in which we have hitherto noticed it, interru ted, as we always are, and have been, in making provision for numerous and various topics, (always on hand for a monthly periodical,) to say nothing of all the other duties of life incumbent upon us in our various relations to society, is by no means propitious to a luminous, connected, compact, and vigorous exposition of its leading perversions, misconceptions, and consequent misrepresentations of not only the special subjects on which it treats, but of all related to them. We cannot do the subject justice in our present method of reviewing it."—Page 553. A pretty candid confession this, that the review, begun with such high hopes and vaunting promises, has proved a failure. For aught that has yet appeared, the "ten worthy brethren" at whose request the book was written, should not forfeit all claim to Mr. Campbell's gratitude, if they still continue to " sanction or commend it, or print and circulate it through this community."

What will Mr. C. next do? With the laurels, won in many a well-contested field, still fresh on his brow, he cannot be expected to retire thus from the combat. Something must be done to meet the exigency. In the eighth number of the review, he writes—" But I cannot waste time in reasoning against positions so palpably false and so suicidal, as not a few of my friend Jeter's assumptions and positions are. Some are demanding of me a book on the subject, but really I do not think it worthy of a book."—p. 456. This was the deliberate and recorded judgment of Mr. C. In the next No., he says, "I purpose to suspend my review for some two or three months, and, in pursuance of the requests on hand, I will give a book for a book, and a line for a line; at the same price at which Dr. Jeter's book is sold and circulated by the anti-revisionist Baptists."—pp 553–4. So it seems that my work, though unworthy of such an honor, is to have a reply from the pen of Mr. C., in the form of a book, corresponding with itself in cost and size.

I should postpone any notice of the review until the appearance of the promised book, but for two reasons: *First*—I much doubt whether it will ever be published. As my work is unworthy of an extended reply, Mr. C. is not likely, amid his multiplied and important engagements, to find time to prepare it. *Secondly*—If he should write a book, I am desirous that it may be as free as possible from errors; and I wish, by pointing out some of the mistakes of the review, to afford him an opportunity of correcting them. I shall do little more than furnish hints for his guidance.

PERSONALITIES.

It is a great pity that religious controversy, in itself adapted to promote the interests of truth and righteousness, should so frequently degenerate into bitter personal invective. Mr. C. commenced his review with the seeming intention of treating me courtiously. "We shall," he says, "with all candor, and with all attention, concentrate our mind upon the efforts of our respectable, and I presume to say, very estimable friend, Elder J. B. Jeter." He had not, however, proceeded far before he began to depreciate my abilities and my book. "There are not a few things," he says, "in science, in learning, and in religion, which Mr. Jeter will not understand till he get another head or heart. We are, indeed, sorry for his sake, that we cannot create the one or the other." "He has too recklessly dealt in assertions, and even criticisms, for which he is not qualified, either by nature, by grace, or by education." The review, in every part, contains intimations that Campbellism Examined is a very feeble production, and unworthy, except for its endorsement, of a serious reply.

With me it is a small matter that my abilities should be disparaged by Mr. Campbell. If I entertained a high estimate of his judgment, I should know that in this instance it is exercised under circumstances not propitious to a correct decision. It demands a rare measure of candor and self-control to do full justice to the abilities of an opponent; and these are qualities in which the intelligent readers of Mr. Campbell's works will perceive that he does not abound. One, however, of two conclusions is perfectly clear. Either Mr. C. has a consciousness that my work is not so feeble as he represents it, or, he has a painful conviction of the weakness of the cause which he advocates. Why so labored a defence against so feeble an attack? Why a long review, many other extended articles, and then a book, to counteract the influence of mere "assumptions and presumptions," however respectably endorsed? Actions speak more loudly, and I may add, more truly than words. How tottering must be that cause which needs to be so carefully and strongly propped under so slight a pressure. It would seem that the taunt of Tobiah, the Ammonite, however unjust in its original application, is appropriate in the present case. "Were a jackal," according to Mr. Campbell's version—a feeble assailant—"to go against the stone walls which they are building"—the incongruous, unconnected doctrines of the reformation—"he would break them down."—p. 264.

Not confining himself to the disparagement of my intellect and labors, Mr. C. distinctly charges me with misrepresentation, garbling, slander, calumny, and such practices. I will furnish the reader with specimens of his accusations—"garbled and distorted quotations"—"in this calumny, Mr. Jeter is a false accuser, *unintentional*, we hope, in charity; but unquestionably a false accuser"—"Having been, and now being misrepresented by Elder Jeter of

Richmond"—"None of my traducers, not even Elder Jeter himself"—"judge of the fidelity, honesty, or capacity of Mr. Jeter"—"Mr. Jeter is, knowingly or unknowingly, willing it or not willing it, one of the most disingenuous and sophistical writers or reasoners that I have noticed in the Baptist church"—"We are much slandered in this book." Such are some of the epithets by which I am honored in Mr. Campbell's review. These are very grave charges; and by what code of morals the reviewer judges, who can pronounce the author, against whom they are all justly preferred, his "very estimable friend," (p. 65,) and "*brother*," (p. 71,) I know not. It may be jesuitical or pagan, it certainly is not Christian. To these accusations, I plead, *Not guilty*. I honestly and carefully endeavored to furnish in Campbellism Examined a fair and faithful representation of Mr. Campbell's peculiar views. That I may have mistaken his meaning on some points is possible; but no misconceptions have been pointed out. In making quotations from his works, I extracted only what was pertinent to my purpose, and, by the rules of discussion, I was required to do nothing more. I now affirm, that not one quotation in my book bears a different meaning from what the passage does in his works. If his positions and arguments are contradictory, it is no fault of mine; nor should I be blamed for placing ungarbled and fair extracts from his writings in juxtaposition. In Campbellism Examined, p. 45, at the end of the 8th line from the top, the clause, "until Christians are united," was omitted, whether by myself in transcribing, or the compositor in type-setting, I cannot tell. This omission has been held up, not by Mr. C., but by a writer in the *Ch'n Intelligencer*, as a specimen of the accuracy of my quotations. The slightest glance at the passage must satisfy the discerning reader that the omission does Mr. C. no injustice, but weakens my own argument. It is the very clause that I should have italicised.

The charges of the reviewer are mostly vague and general. I have slandered him, but in what he is not careful to show. There is, however, one exception to this remark.—pp. 182, 183.

"Mr. Jeter is not, perhaps, altogether a *responsible* writer." Perhaps not! I am very reluctant to be held responsible for Mr. Campbell's definitions of my words. "I would prefer to inculpate his *head* rather than his *heart*." This is very kind in Mr. C. "To explain myself: While condemning my opposition to creeds, he uses the following language—'The term creed, in its ecclesiastic sense, denotes a summary of Christian doctrine. There is in Christendom a great variety of creeds, from the so-called "Apostles' creed," down to the "Christian system," composed by Mr. Campbell as an exhibition of the principles of his Reformation.'"

The term "creed," from the Latin "credo," I believe is of very general signification. We have political and philosophical, as well as religious creeds. I defined its ecclesiastic sense to be "a summary of Christian doctrine." It is defined by Webster—"A brief summary of the articles of Christian faith—a symbol." With this definition agrees that of the Ency. of Rel. Knowledge—"A form of words in which the articles of faith are comprehended." Right or wrong, and whether I am responsible or irresponsible, this was my definition of the word "*creed.*" And to preclude the possibility of mistake, I affirmed, that "every intelligent Christian has a creed, written or unwritten." In this clearly, and, I think, correctly defined sense of the term, creed, I affirmed that the Christian system is Mr. Campbell's creed, composed, not for adoption in order to church fellowship, but as "an exhibition of the principles of his Reformation." But, continues Mr. C., "*It is not a historic fact*, that a summary of Christian *doctrine* is, in the *ecclesiastic* sense, a '*creed.*' * * * To make any summary of doctrine a *creed*, in the ecclesiastic sense, it must be submitted to a person, or to a community, for adoption, in order to church fellowship, or church organization." Mr. C. deliberately sets aside my definition of the word "*creed*," and dogmatically substitutes his own, and holds me responsible for it. "We never wrote, published, printed, or proposed for adoption, such a book written by myself or by any one else." And who affirmed, or insinuated, that he did? I asserted that the Christian System is Mr. Campbell's creed, *composed as an exhibition of the principles of his Reformation;* and I use the term *creed* in a sense which I defined —a sense in which it is clearly used by, at least, one respectable ecclesiastical writer, the editor of the Ency. of Religious Knowledge. And says the Reviewer, "In this calumny Mr. Jeter is a *false accuser, unintentional,* (unintentionally,) we hope, in charity; but unquestionably a *false accuser.*"—*Calumny* is a strong word. It means "*false accusation of a crime, or offences maliciously made or reported.*" True, Mr. C. softens the accusation by the charitable hope that my sin was *unintentional* —as if calumny could be unintentional—and by the insinuation that, perhaps, my stupidity renders me *irresponsible.* Allowing that Mr. Campbell's definition is right, and mine is wrong, candor could find in the passage nothing but the misapplication of a term—and one so carefully explained as to preclude the slightest possibility of injury to him, or his cause. His readiness to employ one of the harshest terms of the language in censure of my statement, proves quite clearly that he needs something more than fair criticism and sound argument to arrest the influence of my book. I am sorry for Mr. Campbell's sake that he has deemed it necessary to resort to such epithets in his review. My book speaks for itself. Dr. Lynd, whom Mr. C. thanks for his brief review of it, says—" The writer has treated the whole subject with great candor, and in a truly Christian spirit."

VERBAL CRITICISM.

The criticism of words, which is very proper in a merely literary production, seems to be entirely out of place in a grave theological discussion, except so far as it may be required to elucidate the points in debate ; but as Mr. C. has deemed it necessary to criticise my style in several places, for no other apparent purpose than to display the superiority of his philological knowledge, I must, reluctantly, reply to him.

I stated that the " religious education of children, the proper observance of the Lord's day, &c., were too much neglected." On which passage the critic remarks—" There is but one word in this exhibition that is of doubtful expediency, and that is the word '*too*,' prefixed to 'much.' He would seem to indicate that these duties might be much neglected with impunity, but they were *too* much neglected. This is a grammatical and logical inference. But in all candor, I do not think that Elder Jeter intended to say what his words indicate. He did not mean that these six sacred duties might, with impunity, be much neglected, and in this case they were only 'too much' neglected."—p. 71. So important did this criticism appear to the reviewer that he recurred to it frequently. This use of the word *too* is sanctioned by very respectable writers. I recently saw it used in this manner in an article copied from the *London Times.* Coleridge, one of the profoundest thinkers, and most polished writers of the present century, says, "I must concede to you that *too* many of the Pedobaptists have erred." Does he mean that error is harmless in many, and only hurtful when embraced by *too* many? But on this point I can introduce authority that must have weight with Mr. C. A writer of some distinction, whose critical acumen he will readily admit, has furnished examples of this use of the term, as if for the very purpose of neutralizing the above criticism. Let the reader turn over two leaves in the review, and read, p. 75—"He (Mr. Jeter) is, however, a very estimable man. But he has, *perhaps, too* recklessly, at the instigation of some over-excited *mere Baptists,* undertaken a work for which he is by no means pre-eminently qualified; and, *too* willing to do them service, has *too* recklessly dealt in assertions, and even criticisms, for which he is not qualified, either by nature, by grace, or by education." I have italicised the word too in this extract. The reviewer "would seem to indicate that" Mr. Jeter might have "*recklessly* dealt in assertions, and *even* criticisms, for which he was not qualified either by nature, by grace, or by education," with propriety; but unfortunately, "instigated by over-excited *mere Baptists*," he dealt in these things "*too* recklessly." "This a grammatical and logical inference. But in all candor, I do not think that Elder" Campbell "intended to say what his words indicate;" though my candor does not forbid me to think that he was more intent to correct errors in my style, than to avoid them in his own.

The reviewer quotes from Campbellism Examined. "The reformation demanded by the times was in *spirit* and *practice*, rather than *doctrine*." "*In doctrine*, I presume he means," adds the critic. Yes, *in* doctrine—the sentence is elliptical —any well-taught school boy would readily supply the ellipsis.—p. 71.

We shall now notice a more important criticism, pp. 550, 551.

"There are some sentences in Mr. Jeter's book, and not a few of them, of such ambiguity, that lest I should offend against propriety, I will merely quote them, or pass them; such as,

"'Mr. Campbell and his friends maintained the Association, in its action, not only transgressed the law of Christ, infringed the religious liberty of individuals, and were guilty of flagrant persecution, but plainly transcended its constitutional authority.' —p. 103.

"This sentence," continues the critic, "not being English, nor any living or dead tongue known to me, I pass without criticism. It is one of Mr. Jeter's solecisms. Who these '*its*' and '*were*' may indicate, I presume not to affirm."

I admit the fault of the sentence, but not the justice of the criticism. *Association* is a noun of multitude, and may, according to the rules of grammar, have verbs and pronouns agreeing with it, in the singular or plural number. But the number having been decided on should be retained throughout the sentence. I admit the error—either *its* should have been *they*, or *were* should have been *was*. It is a trivial mistake—a mere over-sight—not affecting, in the view of sound criticism, the perspicuity or the force of the sentence. When the reviewer affirms that the sentence is not "English, nor any living tongue" known to him, he excites the suspicion that something has disturbed the equilibrium of his mind, and hurried him beyond the bounds of fair criticism. Let me quote a passage from high authority, Review, p. 65. "But *we* shall, with all candor and with all attention, concentrate *our* mind upon the efforts of *our* respectable, and, *I* presume to say, very estimable friend, Elder J. B. Jeter." I have ventured to italicise the important words in the above sentence. Who are indicated by "*we*," "*our*" and "*I*" in it? According to editorial license, the reviewer might write in the singular or plural number—might say either *we* or *I*—but having selected his number it was inaccurate to depart from it in the sentence—yet, he did depart from it, speaking of himself first in the plural, and next in the singular number. Now, I will not, in the extravagance of criticism, affirm, that the sentence is not English—every child would know better—but I do affirm that it is clearly obnoxious to the same criticism with the sentence so unfairly censured by Mr. C. Still, I thank the critic for his slight correction ; and receive his petty verbal criticisms as an illustrious proof of the general accuracy of my style.

I am sorry I cannot reciprocate the favor which Mr. Campbell has conferred on me in criticising my book. The task of correcting the diction of his review would be entirely too onerous, as he will be convinced by a brief specimen of the labor. I will examine, with some care, the first eleven lines.

"We thank Elder Jeter, and the ten worthy brethren that called him out to examine something nicknamed 'Campbellism,' for the opportunity afforded us to extend its empire over myriads of new readers, thinkers and actors, in the grand ecclesiastic drama of the 19th century." Why does the reviewer say "*ten* worthy brethren?" There were *twelve*, and their names are printed in the front of the book. This is, however, a small mistake, indicating merely the carelessness of the writer. Was the "*something*, nicknamed Campbellism," which Elder Jeter was called out to examine, the genuine Bethany Reformation, or not? I cannot decide. I should conclude from the contemptuous manner in which the reviewer speaks of it, that it is not—but from his desire to extend its empire, that it is. Perhaps, he means that my examination of the spurious article will increase the spread of the genuine. Hear the critic again—"But we cannot thank him for the uncandid and partial examination of the matter which he has given; nor could we thank them if they, after reading our review of it, will yet sustain or commend it, or print and circulate it through this community." Of circulating a book through a community, I have a distinct conception; but how it can be *printed through* a community I do not comprehend. And the learned reviewer informs us that he shall have no respect for the ten brethren, if they, after reading his review, should continue to "print it (my book) *through this community*." He means, doubtless: *print it*, and circulate it through the community—*the* community, and not "*this* community." Attend to the reviewer once more—"If I were not reluctant to utter a surmize, I should suppose and affirm the hypothesis, that the call for this review grows, directly or indirectly, from opposition to the Bible Union." Was there ever such a jumble of incoherent words from the pen of a renowned critic! What authority has Mr. C. for his orthography of the word "*surmize?*" There is none in its derivation, nor, so far as I know, in respectable usage. It is not so spelt by Webster, nor Richardson, nor any of the writers quoted by the latter. I should conclude that the error was typographical, if it had not been repeated on p. 185. Let us now notice the structure of the sentence. We may conceive, assume, or state a "*hypothesis;*" but to *suppose a hypothesis* is precisely equivalent to *supposing a supposition.* The expression "*affirm a hypothesis,*" is a solecism. What is hypothetical cannot be affirmed—and what is affirmed is not hypothetical. And yet the learned reviewer says, "I should *suppose and affirm the hypothesis.*" He does not do either; and he tells us why—"If I were not *reluctant to utter a surmize,* (then) I should (both) *suppose* and *affirm* the *hypothesis.*" How his reluctance to utter a *surmise* could prevent him from *affirming* anything which he might have to affirm, I cannot explain, but, perhaps, he can.

Mr. Campbell will perceive that an attempt to criticise the language of his extended review would involve very serious labor. He may, by this time, be reminded of the old adage, *A man who lives in a glass house should be careful not to throw stones at his neighbor's windows.* I cannot close my remarks on this topic, without expressing the firm persuasion that the critical acumen of the reviewer may be very profitably employed in *revising* his own works.

THE REVISION OF THE ENGLISH SCRIPTURES.

Mr. Campbell has been exceedingly anxious to trace "Campbellism Examined" to the anti-revision influence. We have already seen that, but for reluctance "to utter a surmize," he would have supposed and affirmed "the hypothesis that the call for this (my) review grows, directly or indirectly, from opposition to the Bible Union." This hypothesis, and truly it is nothing but a hypothesis, obtrudes itself into almost every No. of Mr. Campbell's Review. It is, however, quite at variance with another hypothesis published in the *Christian Intelligencer*, that I had been thirty years in preparing Campbellism Examined—a period that carries us back far beyond the revision movement. But, why is Mr. C. so solicitous to identify my book with the anti-revision movement? If it had its origin in this influence, is it the less true, the less important, or the less entitled to consideration? I understand clearly the policy of the reviewer. His aim is, by attributing the book to anti-revision influence, to enlist in his favor that large, and highly respectable portion of the Baptists who are zealously seeking to procure a corrected version of the English Scriptures. But he will be disappointed: they perceive the artifice.

Of the designs of the respected brethren, at whose request I wrote Campbellism Examined, I know nothing, except what I have learned from their note to me, published in the work. Most of them are anti-Bible Union men ; but whether their opposition to this society had any influence in dictating their request, I know not. One thing I do know—I was not influenced by opposition to revision in complying with the request. I am in *principle* a revisionist—have been made so by the arguments of those whose measures I have disapproved. Though I do not co-operate with the Bible Union, I am not prevented from doing so by the connexion of the Reformers with the Society. Mr. Campbell ought certainly to feel gratified, that if the "worthy brethren," who requested me to write the book, were actuated by hostility to the revision enterprise, they were so utterly defeated in their scheme. In composing the book, I most sedulously endeavored to keep clear of that subject. There is no mention of it, no allusion to it, nothing to remind one of it, in the whole work. It may, indeed, lead some to call in question the thoroughness of Mr. Campbell's scholarship—his fitness for revising the common version of the Scriptures—but what has this doubt to do with the merits of the revision cause? One may surely believe, most honestly, that the Scriptures should be revised, and that he is not qualified, by the ripeness of his scholarship, and the soundness of his judgment to revise them.

I have not quite disposed of this matter. The May No. of the *Mill. Har.* copies from the *Religious Herald*, the publishers' notice of Campbellism Examined. After some remarks on the notice, which I pass, Mr. Campbell says :

"There is but one thing wanting, and that is the *names* and *standing, moral* and *religious*, of the '*several brethren*' of Mr. Jeter, '*at whose request*' it was written.

It is said that this is the most prudential act in the whole affair—*the concealment of their names.*" p. 279.

Why should the names of those brethren be concealed? They are all intelligent, respectable Christian gentlemen—most of them are ministers, filling prominent and important positions—and some of them are distinguished for their learning, abilities and influence. No cause needs to blush at having such friends. Their "*standing, moral* and *religious*," will compare favorably with that of any men, in any denomination of Christians, or enlisted in any cause. But what does Mr. Campbell mean by the *concealment of their names?* Does he intend to affirm that the mere omission of Sheldon, Lamport & Co., to publish their names in this advertisement, was a *concealment* of them? As reasonably might the President be charged with *concealing the names of his cabinet* because he failed to mention them in his late message to Congress. Mr. C. is too well acquainted with the meaning of words not to know that the mere neglect to publish is not concealment. Besides, the passage seems clearly to import that their names and standing, moral and religious, are prudently withheld from the public. Those whose information on this subject is derived wholly from the pages of the *Mill. Harbinger*, no doubt, believe, not only that their names are concealed, but that a revelation of their moral and religious standing would greatly weaken the influence of the book written at their request. And now what will they, and what will the reader think, when informed that *their names are published, in capitals, in the most conspicuous position, in the front of the book?* And yet, "it is said that this is the most prudential act in the whole affair—*the concealment of their names.*" By whom this was said, Mr. C. does not inform us. Perhaps, it was deemed "*most prudential*" to *conceal their names.* If their "*standing, moral* and *religious,*" were known, it might weaken the influence of their suspicion. I am not surprised that men should have been found weak enough, and bad enough, to say that the names of the worthy brethren had been concealed from "prudential" motives; by why Mr. Campbell should have publised their surmise, I cannot tell. He certainly knew that their names had not been concealed—though he miscounted them—and that the book composed at their request could receive no injury from a full revelation of their "standing, moral and religious."

THE BAPTIST MINISTERS OF THE PAST GENERATION VINDICATED.

It seems to have been the aim of Mr. Campbell, from the commencement of his Reformation, to depreciate the talents, labors and usefulness of the Baptist ministers of the past age. Of the continuance of this aim his review furnishes abundant evidence. On p. 72, we read—

"There were not a few laymen that knew more than their good old orthodox preachers. These preachers disparaged the more learned ministry of the Presbyterians and Episcopalians, and claimed a species of inspiration and a special descent upon them, or an immediate influence of the Holy Spirit, and abstract from, independent of, and paramount to, the written word. They did not go for '*book religion*,' but for 'Holy Ghost religion,' as they were wont to say. Servants uneducated and in the corn fields, and their masters in their carriages, with their diplomas in their secretaries, were equally the subjects of special visits, special grace, and special conversion. They went to church once a month, and told their experience at some big meeting. It was voted to be orthodox; they were immersed, and had a joyful season for a few days. Is this exaggeration, a fancy sketch, or a solemn reality? Deny it who can! So I found them in Kentucky in 1823, and in Virginia in 1825." The review contains much more in the same strain.

What motive can Mr. C. have in thus seeking to derogate from the reputation of the early Baptist preachers? The cause of truth and piety does not demand such invidious labor. Does he suppose that the more darkly he can paint the back ground, the more bright, beautiful and prominent will be the picture of his Reformation? Does he desire to exhibit by contrast with the old Baptist preachers the superior attainments and efficiency of the proclaimers of the "ancient gospel?" These Baptist worthies have, with few exceptions, descended to the tomb. Their voices, once so earnest and effective in beseeching sinners to be reconciled to God, they cannot now employ in vindicating their principles, labors and reputation.

It is not easy to refute such locse generalities as those contained in the above extract. Nothing is more common, and, I may add, more unfair, than to censure classes for the defects or errors of individuals belonging to them. The practice is, unfortunately, not confined to Mr. Campbell; but is to be the more deplored on this account. That there were faults among the early Baptist ministers no candid man acquainted with their history will deny.

They were mostly uneducated, in the technical sense of the word ; some of them were, doubtless, enthusiastic and visionary ; and others entertained very imperfect views of the system of divine truth. But the great majority of them were intelligent, evangelical preachers. They were men of faith, prayer and righteousness—plain, earnest, faithful, fearless ministers of the gospel—whose labors God delighted to honor—and who left a blessed impression on their generation. Many of them I knew, loved and venerated. Ministers more learned, and of higher pretensions, I have known ; but ministers, more self-sacrificing, laborious, devout and useful, I do not hope to see. Now, I do, in the name of these departed worthies, most solemnly protest against the indiscriminate censure of Mr. C. found in the foregoing quotation. Had he affirmed that there were *some* Baptist ministers of that time obnoxious to these censures, though I should have deemed them extravagant, I should, perhaps, have remained silent ; but when he charges these evils on the "good old orthodox preachers," without exception, or discrimination, I must deny the correctness of the accusations. As applied to the prominent ministers of the Dover Association, and of the Baptist denomination generally, they are an exaggeration—a caricature—I will not say a "slander," for that is an odious term, and, I trust, Mr. C. did not intend to do them injustice. They did not disparage learned ministers ; but were making liberal contributions for the establishment of the Columbian College, and other Institutions, for the education of young preachers. Their views of the nature of religion, and of spiritual influence, were those which now prevail among the Baptists. "Holy Ghost religion" is a phrase which I do not remember ever to have heard. For the correctness of these remarks, I appeal to the writings of Elder A. Broaddus, contained in the Christian Baptist, to the early pages of the Religious Herald, and other publications of that time.

The preaching of Elder John Kerr is singled out by Mr. Campbell as a special subject of animadversion. I quote from p. 130.

"Just at this point, I congratulate myself, that Elder Jeter will remember, with me, what an excitement and tumult of feeling Elder Carr (Kerr) got up at the Dover Association, to which he has alluded in the commencement of our acquaintance, after I had set down from a calm and deliberate address on the first principles of the gospel. It is only thirty years since on the 7th of October next, (1855.) It was equal to Wesleyan Methodism in its palmiest days. What a shaking there was in the camp! What a hugging of men with men! What weeping of females! What screaming of negroes! I thought I had got into a Methodist Camp-meeting, and began to apprehend that it would find its way into the preacher's tent. * * * But apart from the *action*, the *vociferation*, and the *intonations* of he ascending and descending climax of passion, I could not hear one word, or appreciate one idea, as the worthy parent of what I saw and heard in the great congregation. I confess it awakened more painful than pleasurable associations, because indicating a condition of the pulpit, and of the public taste, that depressed my spirit, and saddened my heart with many a painful association and anticipation as likely to arise from my new connexion."

I then heard Elder Kerr preach for the first time, and was somewhat disappointed in his sermon. It was more declamatory, and less instructive than I had expected. Of its effects my recollections are less vivid than are those of Mr. C. I had afterwards frequently the opportunity of hearing Kerr preach, and I deem it due to his memory, in view of the above disparaging extract, to state my impressions of his abilities and influence. God has endowed his ministers with a diversity of gifts. On Elder Kerr was bestowed the gift of exhortation. His doctrinal views were evangelical, and his piety sincere and ardent. He taught the way of salvation clearly. I have heard many preachers, of different denominations, and many distinguished public speakers, of various kinds ; but I must say that for beautiful, impassioned, and effective declamation, I have never heard him equalled. He was one of the most powerful of natural orators. Thousands now living can bear testimony to the efficiency of his labors Had he been as highly gifted in the instruction of the disciples as he was in the conversion of sinners, the history of the Bethany Reformation in Eastern Virginia would be widely different from what it is.

On page 69, we read—"In the year 1825, the Virginia Baptists immersed the candidates *into their own experience.* Yes, their *Christian* experience!! Thousands of them had as much *Christian* experience before baptism as after it. A few added that they had the additional experience of 'having obeyed a command'! I saw some strange sights, and heard some strange utterances, at the Baptist *Camp-meetings* in Old Virginia, in those days."

I do not comprehend what Mr. Campbell means by baptizing "candidates *into their own experience.*" The Baptists have always required an experience in order to baptism—an experience comprehending the various exercises which result in conversion. No man is fit for baptism who has not an experience of the depravity of his heart, the sinfulness of sin, his guilt in the sight of God, sorrow for sin, a sense of his own insufficiency, trust in Christ, love to him, and his people, in fine, all those convictions, conflicts, sorrows and joys which attend the new birth; and this may be called *Christian* experience—because it is the experience, not of a pagan or infidel, but of a young convert—an unbaptized Christian. If this is what Mr. C. means by being *baptized into experience*, then the Baptists, not only in the year 1825, but in all times have baptized the "candidates *into their own experience*," as John baptized his disciples *into* repentance. Mat. 3 : 11. If this is not what he means, what does he mean?

But says Mr. C., "I saw some strange sights, and heard some strange utterances, at the Baptist *Camp-meetings* in Old Virginia, in those days"—"in the year 1825," as the context shows. I confess this language surprises me. By "Old Virginia," he must mean Eastern Va.; for, not only is that the usual import of the appellation, but the Baptists in Western Va., so far as I am informed, have never held camp-meetings. Now, from all that I can learn, and I think my information is accurate, the Baptists of Old Virginia had no camp-meetings "in those days." The first Baptist camp-meetings of Old Va., within the present century, except a few feeble attempts, the dates of which I do not recollect, at a point which Mr. C. I presume has not visited, occurred in the year 1831. Since that time they have had but few. And can I be mistaken in supposing that, if Mr. C. attended any of them, he did so *incognito?* My curiosity is much excited. Is it possible that in disguise, he has been attending Baptist camp-meetings in Old

Virginia, and seeing "*strange sights*," and hearing "*strange utterances?*" Or does he draw upon his imagination, or the dim recollections of a departed dream, for these wonderful statements? I hope that in his promised book, he will not only reveal these strange sights and utterances, but also the *times* and *places* of the "Baptist Camp-meetings," at which his knowledge was obtained. He may thus dispel the mystery which otherwise must forever rest upon his astounding disclosures.

TRUE AND SPURIOUS REFORMATION.

I admitted in Campbellism Examined, the necessity of a reformation among the Baptists at the time Mr. Campbell first appeared in Eastern Virginia. It required no great stretch of candor to make the concession. They have made some progress since that time in knowledge and efficiency, but, unfortunately, they still need reformation. In nothing are they perfect; in many things their defects are obvious. But of what sect, or church, or class of Christians, are not these admissions true? The Disciples, Mr. Campbell himself being judge, stand in need of farther reformation. The reviser seized hold of these concessions to justify the reformation for which he pleaded. Referring to an extract from Campbellism Examined, he says, "This concedes all we ask, and all that our position before the living age requires." p. 67. "That a reformation was needed," he says in another place, quoting from the same work, "by the Christian sects of that time, none who possess a tolerable acquaintance with the (their) condition, and the claims of the gospel, will deny." p. 25. To which he adds, "Well, have we not done the work? If so, why complain?" p. 144.

Now, this reasoning seems to be very plausible—a reformation was admitted to be necessary—we wrought a reformation—"and this is all that our position before the living age requires"—but it is merely plausible. The argument resembles that of a surgeon who justifies the amputation of a limb on the ground that the patient had a diseased eye. I concede the necessity of a reformation in the Baptist churches—a reformation "in *spirit* and *practice,* rather than *doctrine,*" or *in* doctrine, as Mr. C. would express it. But, having disinterred what he termed the "ancient gospel," he engaged zealously in the propagation of certain speculations—such as —"*truth alone* is all that is necessary to the conversion of men"—that men are justified by an act of faith—"and this act is sometimes called immersion, regeneration, conversion"—that Peter has "made *repentance,* or reformation, *and immersion, equally necessary to forgiveness*"—"*The belief of this one fact*"—that Jesus is the Messiah—"*and submission to one institution, expressive of it, is all that is requir'd of heaven to admission into the church.*" With equal zeal he opposed certain measures and practices deemed by the Baptists important for the prosperity of the churches and the extension of the Redeemer's kingdom. But this subject demands a more careful examination.

One of the concessions by which Mr. Campbell seeks to justify his reformation is the following:

"Among the Baptist churches there were some sad evils. In parts of the country, the churches were infected with an antinomian spirit, and blighted by a heartless, speculative, hair-splitting orthodoxy. These churches were mostly penurious, opposed to Christian missions, and all enlarged plans and self-denying efforts, for promoting the cause of Christ." Camp. Ex. pp. 25, 26.

The class of Baptists described in the above extract, were called in some places "Old School," and in others, from the name of the place at which they held their seceding Convention, "Black-rock" Baptists. They separated themselves from the regular Baptists about the time of the rise of Mr. Campbell's reformation. This class of Baptists prevailed considerably in the region of Bethany. That the reviewer should have adduced the conceded evils among this small fragment of Baptists to vindicate his efforts at reformation fills me with surprise. I wonder that when he did so his cheeks had not been tinged with a blush.

Now, it is fully conceded that these antinomian

Baptists greatly needed reformation; but, unfortunately, Mr. C. has *done little, or nothing, tc eradicate* the evils among them. A few of them adopted his doctrinal peculiarities, because he concurred with them in certain cherished opinions; but the mass of them are as ignorant, bigoted and fruitless, as they were at the dawn of the Bethany Reformation. But this is not all. Mr. Campbell, far from endeavoring to correct the evils prevalent among them, catered to their corrupt taste, defended their erroneous views, and confirmed them in their opposition to "all enlarged plans and self-denying efforts for promoting the cause of Christ." But, I must notice particulars.

"*These churches were mostly penurious.*"—Their covetousness was a great evil, and much needed correction. How did Mr. Campbell propose to remove it? Let any one read the pages of the Christian Baptist, and he will learn. By insinuating that the clergy—ministers of Christ, not enlisted under the banner of his reformation—not some of them merely, but the cla s—were selfish and mercenary; and that all benevolent schemes for promoting the interests of religion were ingenious priestly devices to fleece the flock of Christ. "Look," said he, "again at the sums of money squandered at home and abroad under the pretext of converting the world; and again, wherein is the heathen world benefited by such conversions?"—Chris. Bap., p. 72.

These antinomian Baptist churches "*were opposed to Christian missions.*" This was a sore evil, which many of our brethren lamented, and endeavored by their faithful instruction, and by their consistent example, to correct. But by what method did Mr. Campbell aim to remove it? By proclaiming that Christian missions—which distinguished the age—were unauthorized—sectarian-rebellion against the throne and government of Messiah—like the Catholic missions—and in many instances "a system of iniquitous peculation and speculation." For condensed proof on these points the reader may consult Campbellism Examined, pp. 42–59. The success of this method Mr. Campbell triumphantly published from a Kentucky correspondent, in the Christian Baptist, p. 144. "Your paper has well nigh stopped missionary operations in this state."

These hair-splitting Baptist churches, self-styled "orthodox," *were opposed to "all enlarged plans and self-denying efforts for promoting the cause of Christ."*

They were opposed to all plans for the education of young ministers. They looked upon them as tending to corrupt the ministry, to destroy the best interests of souls, and to dishonor Christ. This evil, though not confined to antinomian Baptists, was, through the faithful labors, and benign influence of our fathers, beginning, at the period of Mr. Campbell's coming among us, to disappear in the regular Baptist churches. How did the reformer propose to aid in the correction of the evil? Not by condemning the education of *ungodly young men* for the Christian ministry—as he now would have the world to believe—a practice which has never received the slightest countenance among Baptists—but by publishing concerning a discourse by the Rev. Gideon Blackburn, D. D., as follows—"His sermon is intended to proclaim that it is the duty of the church to prepare in her bosom pious youth"—note this, *pious youth*—"for the gospel ministry. Now this is really a new message from the skies, for there is not one word from Genesis to John, which says that it is the duty of the church to prepare pious youth for the gospel ministry."---Christian Baptist, p. 221. By such instruction did Mr. C. endeavor to reform the antinomian Baptists; and, truly, it was most refreshing to their spirits, and, deeply averse as they were to progress, it was the means of bringing a few of them to embrace the "ancient gospel."

These churches were opposed to the "*reasonable support of pastors.*" This evil was not confined to this class of Baptists, but was "*too* much neglected" in all the churches. Before Mr. Campbell made his debut in Eastern Virginia, many Baptist ministers had perceived the evil, and made vigorous efforts to arrest it The Rev. Abner W. Clopton is worthy of a monument for his fearless, earnest, and successful labors in correcting it. Then the Bethany Reformer, learned, eloquent and distinguished, came to his aid, not proclaiming with Christ, "the workman is worthy of his hire"—but in his own peculiar style, "that every man who receives money for preaching the gospel, or for sermons, by the day, month, or year, is a hireling in the language of truth and soberness."---Chn. Bap. p. 233. And then he urged on the churches the duty of supporting their pastors, in the following manner: "The modern clergy say they do not preach for money. Very well; let the people pay them none, and they will have as much of their preaching still."---Chn. Bap. p. 43.

By such efforts did Mr. Campbell seek to promote the reformation, the necessity of which I conceded, and which concession, he says, is "all that we ask, and all that our position before the living age requires." He is welcome to the concession!

THE INFLUENCE OF THE HOLY SPIRIT IN CONVERSION.

The larger part of Mr. Campbell's review is devoted to the discussion of this important topic. Begin where he might, he was sure to glide into this subject. It is no easy matter to answer his arguments, because they are without arrangement, frequently on collateral issues, and not always perspicuous. Confusion, which in an army makes defeat.

easy, in an argument renders it difficult. I will briefly notice the most important points in the discussion.

In Campbellism Examined, I attempted to show that Mr. Campbell's teaching on the subject of the Spirit's agency, in the conversion of sinners, is inconsistent and contradictory. I admitted that he had put forth orthodox views on this subject—that he had maintained the popular doctrine that the Spirit and the Word *co-operate* in conversion. I also stated that, he taught, with equal clearness, that the Spirit in conversion does nothing more than persuade the sinner, by words or other signs, addressed to the understanding, to turn to God. Numerous quotations were furnished from his writings to confirm these statements. I was not alone in this interpretation of his language. It was so understood by the Rev. A. Broaddus, distinguished for his intelligence and candor. Dr. Lynd, whose "scholar-like epistle" reminds Mr. Campbell "so much in matter, manner and spirit, of the learned, and liberal, and gentlemanly Dr. Staughton," says, in his brief notice of Campbellism Examined, "It is clearly shown by the quotations that Mr. Campbell's views certainly destroyed the *agency* of the Holy Spirit in regeneration."---*Mill. Har.* 141. Indeed, I do not remember to have found an intelligent Christian, not a Reformer, who has paid attention to the subject, that does not concur in this view;

and many of the Reformers not only admit that it was taught by Mr. Campbell, but most heartily embrace and defend it. As I regarded this doctrine as erroneous and of injurious tendency, it was discussed at considerable length.

I had no wish to convict Mr. Campbell of heterodoxy; but sincerely hoped that he would endeavor to set himself right on this vital principle of Christianity. If his views on this point are in harmony with those of evangelical Christians generally, nothing can be easier than to make it appear. He owes it to himself, and the cause of truth, to say nothing of those who have been *perplexed* by his apparently conflicting positions, not merely to state his views on this momentous subject without ambiguity, but to show, if it can be shown, how these views can be harmonized with teaching, which in the estimation of everybody, except Mr. Campbell, and his peculiar friends, is flatly contradictory; and if this cannot be shown, to acknowledge that he has put forth indefensible statements. How easy it would be for him to evince that he holds substantially the views that have been generally entertained on this subject by intelligent, evangelical Christians, such as those recorded in Campbellism Examined, pp. 183–185,—and that he repudiates whatever he may have written not in agreement with this teaching.

I will now fully illustrate my meaning. In the

Debate with Mr. Rice, Mr. Campbell says, "There is the *Word alone* system, and there is the *Spirit alone* system. I believe in neither." In *Christianity Restored*, he says, "All the power of God or man is exhibited in the truth which they propose. Therefore, we may say, that if the light, or the truth, contain all the moral power of God, then truth alone is all that is necessary to the conversion of men, for we have before argued and proved, that the converting power is moral power."---p. 362. Now, Mr. Campbell may blame my head or my heart, but I am not alone in my infirmity ; there are many who are convinced that when he says, in one place, I do not believe in "*the Word alone system*," and, in another place, that "*truth alone is all that is necessary to the conversion of men*," he puts forth contradictory statements. I cannot reconcile them ; if Mr. Campbell can, does he not owe it to the Reformation for which he pleads, and to the weakness, or prejudice of its opponents, to do so? But *if he cannot*, does he not owe it to the cause of truth and piety, to confess his error, and to inform the world by which position he is resolved to abide? "There lies the rub." It may be unpleasant and humiliating to him to admit that he has contradicted himself; but in no other way, can he so highly elevate himself in the estimation of the Christian public, as by a frank and manly confession of his error.

Mr. Campbell has his own method of treating this subject, and I must attend to it. He has observed no order in the discussion, but I will reduce it to the best form I can.

First, then, *Mr. C. substantially concurs with me in my main position on this subject.* He writes, "He (I) propose to prove 'that there is an influence of the Spirit, *internal, mighty, and efficacious, differing from moral suasion, but ordinarily exerted through the inspired Word in the conversion of sinners.*' Ordinarily, yes, *ordinarily.* We say *always ;* he (I) says *ordinarily;* therefore the controversy is narrowed down to the *extraordinary* cases."---pp. 131, 132.

These *extraordinary* cases shall be considered in due time. I understand Mr. Campbell as agreeing with me that the conversion of sinners is effected not by moral suasion alone—not merely by arguments addressed to the eye or ear—but by an *internal, mighty, efficacious influence of the Spirit through the written Word.* This is the orthodox belief. But it was not for maintaining this truth that Mr. Campbell was censured and opposed by the Baptists. They did not call in question this doctrine. He cannot find in all their controversies with him, a single sentence in condemnation of it. But he, and his adherents were condemned for teaching that nothing but truth addressed to the understanding is necessary in conversion—indeed, that there is no influence of the Holy Spirit until after baptism. When Mr. Campbell establishes his orthodoxy on this point, he abandons his Reformation. All that he has written against the speculations, theories and mysticism of the "populars"—and he has written volumes on these subjects—must be understood as directed against the crudities of a few visionaries, the extravagancies of a still smaller number of ultra-Calvinists, or men of straw of his own creation. But he does not stop at the admission that my chief proposition, with the exception of a single word, is sound, and I must follow his devious course.

Secondly—Mr. Campbell *utterly misconceives the design of my argument on the influence of the Spirit.* He says, "To gather out of one hundred and fifty pages of his work any issue at all, it must be expressed in this formula—*The Holy Spirit works upon the human spirit, by actual contact, or impact, without and independent of either law or gospel.* I repeat it, if there be either sense or reason, argument or point, in his book, it is this."---pp. 258, 259.

This may do well enough for those whose information on this subject is derived solely from the pages of the Millennial Harbinger; but I am quite persuaded that of all the readers of my book he is the only one who has fallen into this strange misapprehension. Nothing can be more explicit than my statements on this subject. "It is fully admitted," I say, "that the Spirit operates through the

Word in the conversion and sanctification of men. But I understand Mr. Campbell to maintain that the influence of the Spirit in the work of conversion is limited, and of necessity, to the simple presentation of arguments, motives, truth, to the minds of men, by means of words, and other signs—that all the power of the Spirit in the conversion of men is *moral suasion*."---Camp. Ex., p. 123. On the position above ascribed to Mr. Campbell—a position which he did maintain, if language can express it—I took issue ; and I do not think that he can find a sentence in the seventy-seven pages devoted to the discussion inconsistent with my chief aim. True, I did maintain that the Spirit operates in conversion *ordinarily* through the Word ; but as the exceptional cases were not material in the discussion, I did not dwell on them. To preclude any misconception of my views on this subject, however, I penned the following passage—" On one merely speculative point"—supposing that Mr. Campbell admitted 'that conversion is effected by the personal agency of the Spirit'—" he differs from most or all of his brethren. They believe that this is God's ordinary, or usual way of converting sinners ; *the only way in which we should hope, labor and pray for their conversion;* but that He is not limited to this way." Now, mark the extraordinary instances contended for. " In the case of *dying infants or idiots, they believe that a moral change, equivalent to regeneration, is effected by the direct, personal agency of the Holy Spirit, without the Word.*"--Camp. Ex. p. 186. How Mr. Campbell could have so egregiously misapprehended my aim and argument, I cannot comprehend.

Thirdly—Mr. Campbell, not only misstates my position in the discussion, but *insists that I offered no argument in support of my true position.* He quotes from Campbellism Examined, " Mr. Campbell maintains, *or did maintain, that all the converting power of the Holy Spirit is in the arguments or motives which he presents to the mind in the written Word.* On this point I take issue with him. I maintain that *there is an influence of the Spirit, internal, mighty, and efficacious, differing from moral suasion, but ordinarily exerted through the inspired Word, in the conversion of sinners.*"---p. 125. Mr. Campbell having furnished this extract, proceeds to remark, "Now, with what argument does he (Mr. Jeter) assail or refute what he assumes and affirms I *did*, or I *do* maintain, concerning the *converting power ?* He makes an issue, but what does he prove ? What arguments ? What is the first, the second, the third ? I ask what is the *first ?* I cannot find it, unless it be the quotation of " the wind bloweth where it pleases ;" and " *so is every one that is born of the Spirit.*" *So* what ? Like the wind blowing ?—! I again ask—How is every one *so like the wind blowing ? &c.* If Mr.

Jeter's salvation depended on it, I question if he could explain the word *so* in this case. How is he so as the wind ?—! He had better send this question to Boston."---*Mill. Har.* p. 131.

The above passage from the pen of Mr. Campbell is an enigma, explicable only on the supposition that he had not read my book. He fairly states the issues which I made with him. Having endeavored to show that his chief argument against my position—*the inability of the Spirit to do more in conversion than present arguments to the mind*—was fallacious ; I proceeded to present at considerable length, five arguments against Mr. Campbell's theory of conversion. Concerning this theory, I endeavored to prove—

1. *That it overlooks, or at least, under-estimates the inveteracy of human depravity.* 2. *That it is incompatible with prayer for the conversion of sinners.* 3. *That it is inconsistent with the introduction of the Millennium.* 4. *That it is contradicted by the plain teaching of the Scriptures. And* 5. *That it is inconsistent with the plainly revealed, and, by Mr. Campbell, fairly conceded influence of the Holy Spirit in believers after baptism.* These positions the reader will, I think, find fully confirmed in my book.—pp. 125–174. Now, That the reviewer should have pronounced these arguments illogical, inconclusive, weak, absurd, or obscure would not have surprised me—such an estimate of my

labors I was prepared to expect from him—but I confess, that, after all the strange things which he has affirmed in this discussion, I was surprised to read this language, "He (Mr. Jeter) makes an issue, but what does he prove? What arguments? What is the first, the second, the third? I ask what is the *first? I cannot find it*, unless it be the quotation of 'the wind bloweth where it pleases,' and 'so is every one that is born of the Spirit.'" The reader will perceive by referring to Campbellism Examined, p. 126, that the quotation, which Mr. Campbell considers my only argument, was incidentally introduced, without comment, in reply to an assumption of his. And yet he can find no argument but this in favor of my position. I will only say, the arguments are visible. A well taught school boy may be convinced of their existence. But *Mr. Campbell cannot see them.* I will not affirm of him as he does of me, "There are not a few things in science, in learning, and in religion, which Mr. Jeter will not understand till he get another head or heart. We are, indeed, sorry for his sake, that we cannot create the one or the other."—pp. 73, 74. But I will affirm that some influence has obscured the mental vision of the reviewer. He does not display in this matter his usual perspicacity. And, I will also state that multitudes have seen the arguments, invisible to him, and have the full conviction that they have not been answered. It is to be hoped that before Mr. Campbell shall write his promised book, he will put on his spectacles, and make diligent search for them, that he may not only find, but refute them, if they are fallacious, lest some suspicious persons should surmise that the difficulty of finding a reply to the arguments was the real cause of their obscuration.

But suppose I offered no argument to sustain my position—"*that there is an influence of the Spirit, internal, mighty, and efficacious, differing from moral suasion, but ordinarily exerted through the inspired Word, in the conversion of sinners*—does not Mr. Campbell concur with me in it, except as to the extraordinary cases, which I deemed of little importance in the controversy? Why, then, does he seek to conceal or disparage the arguments by which I aimed to establish, not the exceptional cases about which we differ, but the main proposition in which he asserts that we agree? True, he has ignored, rather than refuted these arguments; but by censuring a sentence here and there—by carrying on a mere logomachy—he has betrayed a willingness to refute them, though that refutation would be, as he concedes, at the expense of a vital doctrine of Christianity.

Fourthly.—I will now notice *the extraordinary cases of conversion* to which Mr. Campbell takes exception. He agrees with me that there is *an influence of the Spirit, internal, mighty, and efficacious, exerted through the inspired Word, in the conversion of sinners.* I maintain, however, that the Spirit *ordinarily*, and Mr. Campbell that the Spirit *always* operates in this manner.

Before I enter on the discussion of this point, I will premise two things—

1. The exceptions to God's usual method of conversion are distinctly stated in my book. "In the case of dying infants, or idiots, they (evangelical Christians,) believe that a moral change, equivalent to regeneration, is effected by the direct, personal agency of the Holy Spirit, without the Word." Camp. Ex., p. 186. This point I did not discuss, deeming it of no practical importance, as we are called to labor and pray for the conversion of sinners only in the ordinary way. A more careful consideration of the matter, however, has convinced me that it is more important than I formerly thought. Truth is a unit. Speculative, may readily lead to practical error. A mistake on this point under examination must tend to Pelagianism on the one hand, or the denial of spiritual influence on the other; and both these extremes are subversive of Christianity.

2. Mr. Campbell, who was anxious to turn to his advantage my position that the Spirit *ordinarily* converts sinners through the inspired Word, was very careful to keep out of sight that the plainly stated exceptions were "dying infants or idiots."

I do not charge Mr. Campbell with intentional misrepresentation; but no reader of the Harbinger could learn my views on this subject. He would certainly suppose, contrary to the explicit statements of my book, that I teach that adults in a probationary state, are converted by the Spirit, sometimes through the Word, and sometimes without the Word. If the reviewer had informed his readers of the exceptional cases for which I pleaded, much that he wrote of "a purely *physical*, or *metaphysical* regeneration" would have appeared to be worse than useless.

I shall now proceed to show that *in the case of dying infants and idiots, regeneration takes place by the agency of the Spirit without the Word.*

I use the term "*regeneration*" in its well understood moral sense—as equivalent to conversion—or a spiritual renovation—that change by which the depraved soul of man is fitted for the heavenly kingdom.

In support of my position, I remark—

1. *That whatever may be legitimately inferred from the Scriptures is a part of divine revelation, and worthy of our belief.* For illustration—We are expressly informed that when the angel announced the birth of John the Baptist to Zacharias, he was struck dumb; Lu. 1: 20; we infer from the fact that at the birth of the promised child, the family made signs to the father "how he would have him called," that Zacharias was deaf—Lu. 1: 62; and his

deafness and dumbness are equally matters of revelation, and equally entitled to our credence. If, therefore, it can be fairly inferred from the teaching of the Scriptures that dying infants and idiots need a moral change to fit them for heaven, and that this change is effected by the Holy Spirit, without the Word, these truths are a part of revelation, and worthy of our belief.

2. *That infants are born with depraved natures.* This is the orthodox belief; and on this point Mr. Campbell is orthodox. In the *Christian System*, we read, "True, indeed, it is; our nature was corrupted by the fall of Adam before it was transmitted to us; and hence that hereditary imbecility to do good, and that proneness to do evil, so universally apparent in all human beings. * * * All inherit a *fallen*, consequently a *sinful* nature, though all are not equally depraved."---pp. 28, 29. Every child of Adam enters the world with a nature, *fallen—sinful—impotent to do good*, and *prone to do evil*.

3. *That dying infants and idiots are saved.* This is the popular doctrine; and, whether true or false, is held by Mr. Campbell. I quote from the *Christian System*, p. 29. "Condemned to natural death, and greatly fallen and depraved in our whole moral constitution though we certainly are, in consequence of the sin of Adam; still, because of the interposition of the second Adam, none are punished with everlasting destruction from the presence

of the Lord, but those who actually and voluntarily sin against a dispensation of mercy under which they are placed."

Take another quotation from the Debate with Rice, p. 655. "The atonement of the Messiah has made it compatible with God, with the honor of his throne and government, *to save all those infants who die in Adam.* He has made an ample provision for extending salvation from all the consequences of Adam's sin to whomsoever he will." I have italicized the important clause in the extract.

These passages, though they do not directly affirm, plainly imply the salvation of infants, dying in infancy; an inference, to which, if I understand Mr. Campbell, he will fully assent.

4. *That the salvation of dying infants, and by a parity of reason, of dying idiots, implies regeneration or a spiritual change.* The salvation by Christ is deliverance from sin. In the case of an adult, it is deliverance from liability to punishment, by the remission of sins; and from moral corruption, by regeneration, and sanctification. In the case of an infant, dying before the commission of sin, it is deliverance from depravity, or what Mr. Campbell terms "*fallen—sinful* nature." Less than this it cannot imply. Heaven is a holy place, and none but the holy are admitted to its enjoyments, or can appreciate them. Without holiness "no man shall see the Lord." Infants, dying in infancy,

must by some process, known or unknown, be freed from depravity—morally renewed—regenerated, or they can never be saved—never participate in the joys of heaven. This point is so generally admitted—so clear—so accordant with all that is revealed of the heavenly state, and the moral condition of humanity, that, I presume, Mr. Campbell will not dispute it. If, however, he does, the proof of it is at hand. Jesus said to Nicodemus, "Verily, verily, I say unto thee, Except a man be born again, he cannot see the kingdom of God." John 3: 3. The term "man," in this place, is used in its generic sense, to denote any one possessing human nature—any man, woman, or child. No human being, of any sex, age, or condition, can discern the nature, or enjoy the blessings of Messiah's reign, without this new, or divine birth; and this is true of his future as well as of his present reign—true of his celestial as well as of his earthly reign. A spiritual change—a holy nature—is indispensable to our entrance into the kingdom of God. If any doubt existed as to the correctness of the interpretation, it would vanish on a careful examination of the sixth verse, "That which is born of the flesh is flesh; and that which is born of the Spirit is spirit." Jesus here explains the nature of that change, which he had affirmed was a pre-requisite to admission into the kingdom of God. It is not a fleshly birth. "*That which is born of the flesh is flesh*"—is carnal, depraved, sinful. This sense of the text is so obvious that it will not, I am sure, be denied. Every child that has been born, except the adorable Jesus, has inherited, and every child that shall hereafter be born will inherit this fleshly, depraved nature ; and this corrupt nature cannot, without a spiritual renovation, participate in the blessings of Messiah's reign. Are infants, idiots, or any other class of human beings exempt from this necessity—a necessity which has its foundation, not in an arbitrary appointment, but in the depravity of human nature, and the essential principles of the divine government ? Let the intelligent and candid answer.

Having shown that the salvation of infants clearly implies their regeneration, or moral renovation, I remark,

5. *That this change is effected in the case of dying infants and idiots by the agency of the Holy Spirit without the Word.* If these classes of human beings are saved, which Mr. Campbell admits, they are converted—morally renovated. If they are renewed, it is neither by human nor angelic agency. The atonement of Christ, though it may procure, is not the agency which effects this change. In the scheme of human salvation revealed in the Scriptures, the Spirit is the agent, through whose power and grace, depraved man is renewed—made meet for the inheritance of the saints in light. There is a "renewing of the Holy Ghost," by which men

are saved, but I know of no other renewing agency adequate to such a result. This saving renewal, in the case of dying infants and idiots, must take place without the influence of the written Word, for of this Word they are ignorant. Of the process of this renewal, I know nothing ; but its reality seems to be plainly inferable from the acknowledged and fundamental doctrines of Christianity ; and so have reasoned and taught the enlightened guides of the church. Mr. Campbell will, I presume, admit that if the class of persons under consideration are regenerated, they are regenerated by the Spirit, without the Word.

I will now furnish an instance of the regeneration of an infant. It was predicted, by the angel, of John the Baptist, that he should "be filled with the Holy Ghost, even from his mother's womb."—Lu. 1: 15. To "be filled with the Spirit" is a high Christian privilege, (Ep. 5: 18.) implying, among other things, a *pure heart.* "*The infant Baptist was filled with the Holy Ghost.*" For what purpose was the Spirit richly bestowed on him? Obviously, to fit him for his mission ; and this fitness included moral purity, and this moral purity supposed regeneration. It cannot be imagined, without irreverence, that the Holy Spirit dwelt in an unregenerate, sinful heart. Where he dwells there must be holiness. The influence of the Spirit on the infant, John the Baptist, was not, in all respects, what it is on believers. On believers, the Spirit operates through the Word; on the infant harbinger, He operated without the Word; but in both cases the result was the same—moral purity. Will Mr. Campbell deny that the Baptist was made holy from his birth? Will he maintain that he was filled with the Spirit by means of the written Word? The fact that this unconscious babe was richly imbued with the Holy Spirit, scatters to the winds a whole volume of Mr. Campbell's sophistries on spiritual influence. The Spirit, that by an extraordinary method, fitted the infant John for his mission, can, in the same manner, fit dying infants for heaven.

On the subject of infant regeneration Mr. Campbell holds peculiar views—they constitute an important part of the "Ancient Gospel" disinterred at Bethany—and they shall receive special attention.

I quote from the Review, p. 123. "Regeneration without knowledge, faith or repentance," in the case of infants, dying in infancy, he should, in fairness have said, "is the confessed doctrine of the Baptist Confession of Faith, and of all the 'orthodox Baptists' in the United States. * * * To such a purely *physical* or metaphysical regeneration, we do, indeed, object." * * * "It amounts to neither more nor less than the impact of Spirit upon spirit—of the naked Spirit of God upon the naked spirit of man, without argument, reason, or motive." Such are Mr. Campbell's views of the Baptist doctrine of the regeneration of infants, dying in infancy.

Let us now attend to his arguments against infant regeneration. I continue the extract from the Review—"Need we assume, that whatever constitutes *regeneration* in any case—infant or adult, Jew or Gentile—constitutes it in all cases? Are not conception and birth the same in all ages of the world, and in all cases?" I will give him a fuller statement of the argument from the Debate with Rice---p. 620. "*Whatever is essential to regeneration in any case, is essential to it in all cases.* The change, called regeneration, is a specific change. It consists of certain elements, and is effected by a specific agency. If it be a new heart given, a new life communicated, it is accomplished in all cases, as generation is, by the same agency and instrumentality. If, then, the Spirit of God, without faith, without the knowledge of the Gospel, in any case regenerates an individual, he does so in all cases."

As Mr. Campbell frequently introduces this argument, and lays great stress on it, it is proper to test its strength. There is a manifest sophism lurking in the language of the argument. "Whatever is *essential* to regeneration in any case, is *essential to it in all cases.*" This is a mere truism—

equivalent to saying, "*Whatever is essential* to regeneration, is *essential to it*. Now, nothing is essential to regeneration, except that, without which, if there be any such thing, God cannot effect it. We must distinguish between an ordinary and an essential instrumentality. The products of the earth are the ordinary, the almost universal means of human sustenance; but God, when it suited him to do so, fed the Israelites with manna from heaven. A human father is the ordinary, and so far as we know, with a single exception, the universal, but not the essential means of generation—Mr. Campbell's assumption to the contrary notwithstanding—for that holy thing which was born of the virgin Mary was conceived of the Holy Ghost. Lu. 1: 35. Generation is the universal means of rearing up a family; but God is able of the 'stones to raise up children unto Abraham.'" Mat. 3: 9. The argument under consideration assumes the very point in debate—that the Word is *essential* to regeneration. That the Word—the preaching of the Word—the ordinances of Christ—the example and prayers of Christians—and the providences of God, both merciful and severe, are the ordinary, and, so far as we can judge, the only means of regeneration, except in the case of dying infants, and individuals in a similar condition, I concede and fully teach; but that these important means are indispensable to conversion, I deny, and Mr. Campbell cannot prove.

The fallacy of the reasoning under consideration may be shown by the application of the *argumentum ad hominem*. Mr. Campbell maintains the doctrine of the salvation of infants, dying in infancy—if he does not, let him say so, and I will suspend him on the other horn of the dilemma. To this doctrine we will apply his logic. "Whatever is essential to" *salvation* "in any case, is essential to it in all cases." But faith, repentance, and baptism, as he teaches, are essential to salvation in some cases. Therefore, faith, repentance and baptism are essential to it in every case. Now, it is clear that Mr. Campbell must renounce, either his argument, or the salvation of infants. As infants can neither believe, repent, nor properly be baptized, and if these are essential to salvation, they cannot possibly be saved. Clearly, he should relinquish his reasoning. To affirm that because faith, repentance and baptism are essential to the salvation of an intelligent, moral agent, to whom the Gospel is preached, it is essential to the salvation of unconscious infants, is new sophistry—but sophistry of precisely the kind by which the reviewer opposes infant regeneration.

Mr. Campbell maintains that God does nothing without means; and concludes, therefore, that he does not regenerate dying infants. In Campbellism Examined, I stated incidentally that *God can work with means or without them.* This is a favorite text with the reviewer, and he expatiates on it, frequently, largely, and eloquently. I quote from pp. 132, 133. "I will charge myself and credit Mr. Jeter for a proof, even one proof, of the proposition, that '*God works without means,*' in creation, providence or redemption! Moses forgot to name any of those things which God created without means!! But my friend, Mr. Jeter, is the man to set him right, or at least, to fill up that chasm in the account of creation. Paul says that 'by faith we understand that the worlds were framed by *the word of God.*' This statement is fatal to Eld. Jeter's speculation. If God *did not,* for reasons good and valid, create anything *without his word,* or without means, what shall we say of the wisdom or the presumption of the affirmation, that '*God who made man* without means, can renew him without means!'

"I knew that creatures, even the mightiest, could do nothing without means; but I had supposed, in my simplicity, or, perhaps, in my "*presumption,*" that God, greater than creatures, can, and sometimes, does work without means. I had never doubted but that he created the world—that he inspired holy men to write the scriptures—that Christ wrought miracles—that God will raise the dead, without means; and, if I had been convinced that all these things have been done, or will be done, by means, I should still have thought, that he formed by mere power the means, or instrument, whatever it may be, by which he did, or will accomplish these things. But it appears that I was entirely mistaken. " Paul says that by faith we understand that the worlds were framed by *the word* of God." And this statement, it seems, is fatal to my speculation. I am surprised that Mr. Campbell should so bewilder himself on this subject. I do not charge him with quibbling, but it is not easy to see how quibbling could be more futile than his reasoning. I can easily comprehend that words may be a means of good or evil, when there are ears to hear, and hearts to understand them. The scriptures are called the word of God, not because they are words which he uttered, but human words employed by the Spirit of inspiration for the instruction of mankind. They are appropriately called the *means* of conversion. They are adapted to enlighten, awaken, and purify the hearts of men. Words are, literally, significant sounds, formed by the human voice. It is obvious that words are ascribed to God only in a figurative sense. As words are indicative of man's will or purpose ; God is said to do that by his *word*, which he does by his will, or the direct exercise of his power. So the language is understood, as far as I have seen, by all commentators and critics, except Mr. Campbell ; and this interpretation is in harmony with God's incorporeal nature. But suppose, for the sake of the argument, that the infinite Spirit did, before language was formed, without organs of speech, and without air to modulate, utter words in empty space ; to call them the *means of creation* is to ignore the import of the word. *Means* signifies an instrument fitted to accomplish an end. What fitness was there in words to effect the creation of the world? There were no ears to listen to them, no hearts to be impresed by them, and on inert matter, had it existed, they were not suited to act. But suppose, for the sake of the argument, that God did utter, in no matter what language, in the infinitude of space, words as a means of creation. I would inquire, Were these words uttered by means, or without them? Man utters words by *means* of his *vocal organs*. But has the infinite Spirit vocal organs? If he spake, it must have been by the mere force of his will—without organs of speech, or any means whatever. Mr. Campbell's exposition of the language of Paul is as abhorrent to sound philosophy, as it is to just principles of philology. The *word* of God, employed in creation, can mean nothing more than his fiat, or almighty power, as Mr. Campbell, fated to contradict himself on every important point, plainly affirms. "We know," he says, "that God is spirit and not matter—yet he created matter, and moulded and animated portions of it, by mere volition"—yes, "*by mere volition*"—and, consequently, not by instrumentality.—p. 123.

After all, when the mist is dispersed from the subject, the reviewer will be found to agree with me. I cheerfully admit that infants dying in infancy, are regenerated by the word of God—not the written word, nor any word spoken by the human voice—but the very word by which the worlds were framed—the almighty fiat—the word of God's power. Heb. I : 3.

But says Mr. Campbell, "How spirit acts on spirit, or mind upon mind, otherwise than by arguments, reasons, or motives, we have never met with the man or book that could explain or demonstrate by any species of argument, analogy, or proof." p. 123. This may be true. I do not understand, much less can I explain, how God "created matter, and moulded and animated portions of it, by *mere volition*." That he should act on mind, "by mere volition," is certainly as plain and philosophical as that he should thus act on matter. I cannot abandon the truth because of Mr. Campbell's inability to comprehend it; nor will I insinuate as he does, in another case, with reference to myself, that because "there are not a few things in science, in learning and in religion," which he cannot understand, that his inability indicates a peculiar defect in his "head or heart."

I freely admit that the regeneration of an infant, at death, does not imply all that is comprehended in the regeneration of an adult. The enlightenment of the mind, repentance, and faith in Christ are of necessity excluded from infantile regeneration ; but in this change a new, holy nature is imparted, by which the infant soul is fitted for the heavenly felicity. The salvation of an infant and of an adult, though differing in some respects, is substantially the same. Redeemed by the same blood, sanctified by the same spirit, and made partakers of the same inheritance, they will unite their voices in the same doxology, "Unto him that hath loved us, and washed us from our sins in his own blood, and made us kings and priests unto God and his Father ; to him be glory and dominion for ever and ever. Amen."

I close this part of the discussion with a reasonable request—that Mr. Campbell, in his forth-coming book, will distinctly inform his readers that I believe and maintain that *the regeneration of sinners is ordinarily effected by the Spirit through the Word, and that the only exceptions for which I contend are dying infants, and persons in a similar moral condition, and that they are regenerated not before, but in "the article of death."* I make this request, because I am quite sure that the review is calculated to mislead as to my opinions on these points those of his readers who have not examined my book.

MR. CAMPBELL'S NEW PLAN OF INFANT SALVATION.

The Reformer, having repudiated the popular doctrine, that dying infants are, by a direct influence of the Holy Spirit, renewed, and fitted for heaven, found it necessary to adopt another method of explaining the process of their salvation. This process is more fully developed in the Debate with Dr. Rice than anywhere else. I will permit Mr. Campbell to furnish, in his own language, a full statement of it :

" What then, let me ask, is the philosophy of regeneration according to Mr. Rice ? It is a change of heart. There we agree again. What sort of change ?—not of the flesh, but of the spirit—a *change of the affections*, of the feelings *and sympathies of the soul.* Agreed !—a change so great that we love our former hates, and hate our former loves. We love God and our Saviour supremely, and our brethren fervently. We hate Satan, falsehood, and sin. Hence comes the annihilation of his hypothesis—can an infant love or hate, without previous knowledge, faith or apprehension of things amiable and hateful ! ! No, says every man ; where there is no light, no understanding, no intelligence, there can be no disposition at all, no moral feeling, no change of affections, no change of heart ; consequently no infant moral or spiritual regeneration. It is impossible—it is inconceivable ! No man can demonstrate, illustrate, or prove it."---p. 654.

"If moral disposition be a part of regeneration, and if moral disposition be to love God and hate Satan; to love righteousness and hate iniquity—Query—Can an infant then be regenerated? Can it love or hate a being or a thing, concerning which it knows nothing more than a rock? Mr. R. cannot explain this difficulty, and it is fatal to his theory. If a child be regenerate, it must love holiness and hate iniquity; but this cannot be without knowledge—because in religion, as in everything else, intellect pioneers the way, while the affections and the heart follow. We must see beauty before we can love it. We must see deformity before we can hate it. And, therefore, 'the love of holiness and the hatred of sin' are impossible to an infant."—p. 668.

"But now with regard to our physical regeneration of infants, my faith is in the Lamb of God, who hath taken away the sin of the world. The atonement of the Messiah has made it compatible with God, with the honor of his throne and government, to save all those infants who die in Adam. He has made an ample provision for extending salvation from all the consequences of Adam's sin tc whomsoever he will. Ever blessed be his adorable name! THE LAMB OF GOD HAS BORNE AWAY THE SIN OF THE WORLD. Infants then need that same kind of regeneration that Paul, and Peter, and James, and John, and all saints need—the entire destruction of this body of sin and death. The most perfect Christian that I have ever seen, needs a regeneration to fit him for the immediate presence of God. The infant that falls asleep in its mother's bosom, and after a few short days breathes out its spirit gently there, needs no more change to fit it for Abraham's bosom, than that which the Spirit of God will effect in the resurrection of the dead, or in the transformation of the living saints at the time of his coming. Philosophy, reason, and faith, are alike silent on the subject of any infant regeneration before death. It is all theory—idle, empty, suicidal theory. Experience lifts her ten thousand voices against it. Whoever saw a child regenerated growing up from birth a pure and exemplary Christian! Persons have been sanctified, that is, set apart to the Lord from their birth; but that any one was, in our sense of regeneration, changed in heart from birth, reason, revelation, experience, observation depose not; on this subject they are all as silent as death. While, then, I believe in the physical regeneration of infants after death, I repudiate their spiritual or moral regeneration in life, because unscriptural, irrational, and absurd."---p. 655.

"Man, with me, when contemplated in his whole person is a plural unit. He is one man, having a *body*, a *soul*, and a *spirit*. So both my philosophy and my Bible teach. Paul prayed for the Thessalonians that God would sanctify them wholly (*holo-*

teleis) their *body*, *soul*, and *spirit*. Their *pneuma*, *psuche*, *soma*. Not only have the Greeks these three names, but the Latins also. They had their *animus*, their *anima*, and their *corpus*. So had the Hebrews. So have the moderns, as we have—*body*, *soul*, *spirit*. The body is a mere organized material machine—the soul is the seat of all the passions and instincts of our nature, and is intimately connected with the blood. It is the animal life. The spirit is a purely intellectual principle, as intimately connected with the soul, as the soul with the blood, and the vital principle. Now the spirit, or intellectual principle in man, is not the seat of corruption, or of depravity abstractly, any more than the mere materials of human flesh. The understanding or intellect is indeed weakened, and sometimes perverted by the passions, the animal instincts and impulses. But the soul is the great seat of all those corrupting and debasing propensities and affections that involve the whole man in sin and misery. Man was not condemned for reasoning illogically; nor was he condemned because he was either hungry or thirsty, or had these appetites, but because captivated by his passions, he was led into actual rebellion. This is still the depravity of man. His spirit is enslaved to his passions and appetites. Its approvings and disapprovings are all more or less contaminated, biassed, and tinged by these rebellious elements, this 'law of sin which is in his members,' warring against the law of his mind, reason and conscience. Now these not being developed in infancy, any more than reason or conscience, places them under quite a different dispensation and destiny. Dying in that undeveloped state, they are not the subjects of condemnation eternal, never having disobeyed God, nor refused the Gospel. They need not those operations of the Spirit of which the theory of Mr. Rice so often speaks, and with which it is so replete, all of which originated too in the brain of one Saint Augustine.

"Hours might be consumed in the development of these principles; and without a full development, perhaps they ought not to be introduced. I have, indeed, spoken thus far, merely to show, that we have reason to repudiate the notion of the abstract, undefinable metaphysical regeneration of an infant, as essential to its salvation. It only needs, as before observed, a physical regeneration; a destruction of that body in which those seeds of passion and sinful appetites are so thickly sown, in consequence of the animal and sensitive having triumphed over the intellectual and moral man, and so entailing upon our race this natural proneness to evil. Hence the necessity of physical regeneration. The adult saint needs it as much as the infant. 'That law (or power) of sin,' in the members, of which Paul complained—that 'body of sin and death,' under which he groaned, and which made him, in his own esteem, a 'wretched man,' must be *destroyed.* While 'the inward man delighted in the law of God, he saw another law in his members, warring against that law of his mind, and bringing him into captivity to the law of sin, which was in his members.' This will be destroyed in the saint before admission into heaven—and that is what I mean by physical regeneration; and this is destroyed before development in the dying infant, and, therefore, through the Lord Messiah; the RESURRECTION and the LIFE; the sin-atoning *Lamb of God;*—the SECOND ADAM—it slumbers in the bosom of its Father and God, till the great regeneration of heaven and earth."—pp. 675, 676.

The above extracts contain a pretty full statement of Mr. Campbell's views on the subject of *infant salvation;* and they are entitled to careful examination. The subject is abstruce, and, in the absence of direct revelation to guide me, I shall aim to write with becoming modesty.

The first point that strikes my attention in Mr. Campbell's scheme of infant salvation is, that it is a *mere assumption.* He speciously objects to the doctrine of infant regeneration, that it is not taught in the Scriptures. Its advocates admit that the Scripture proof of it is not direct but inferential. They deem it, however, clear and decisive. He rejects their doctrine, as a vain speculation, and sets up in opposition to it a plan of infant salvation, for which the word of God furnishes neither direct nor inferential evidence; and which, so far as I can perceive, has nothing to recommend it but novelty. Let us, however, examine it in detail.

I have already remarked that the denial of the regeneration of dying infants tends to *Pelagianism, or a rejection of the doctrine of inherent depravity.* That tendency is, if I mistake not, clearly involved in the above quotations. I do not charge Mr. Campbell with holding the doctrine of Pelagius. In passages already cited from the Christian System, he distinctly and fully endorses the popular doctrine of man's innate moral corruption. I exculpate him, therefore, from the charge of teaching Pelagianism; but shall be able, nevertheless, to show that the seeds of this pernicious system are wrapped up in his scheme. He may not, I presume, he does not perceive the consequences of his positions; but still they are of Pelagian tendency; and it may be well to point out this tendency that he may have an opportunity of counteracting it in his promised book.

In the foregoing extracts, Mr. Campbell, if I understand him, teaches that man has a *body, a soul* and a *spirit*—that the body is a mere organized material machine—that the soul is the seat of the passions and instincts of our nature, and is intimately connected with the blood—that the spirit is a purely intellectual principle—that depravity exists primarily in the soul, and not in the spirit, any more than in the mere materials of human flesh—that the spirit, or higher nature of man, can be defiled only through the passions and appetites of the soul—that these, not being developed in infancy, the spirit escapes conception—and that the infant, dying before the contamination of the spirit, is placed under "quite a different destiny"—needs no moral renovation---but will be saved "a physical regeneration," or the resurrection from the dead, just as the saints will be saved. "The *spirit—is not the seat of corruption or depravity abstractly*, any more than the mere materials of human flesh." "But the *soul is the great seat of all those corrupting and debasing propensities and affections* which involve the whole man in sin and misery." It would seem then that the spirit is not corrupt abstractly, or by itself, but only through the impure affections of the soul; and these "not being developed in infancy, any more than reason or conscience, places them," (infants, I presume, though the pronoun has no antecedent,) "under quite a different dispensation and destiny." "*Dying in that undeveloped state—they need not the operations of the Spirit.*"

An inspired apostle distinguishes between "*spirit*, and *soul*, and *body*;" but the precise distinction between πνεῦμα, spirit, and ψυχή, soul, which he intended, it is not easy to perceive. The terms seem to be used frequently in the New Testament, as their corresponding terms are among us, in the same sense. We cannot, perhaps, better define them than by saying that *spirit* denotes the *intellectual*, and *soul* the *emotional* nature of man: but these are not separate, or separable parts. but the same part contemplated under different aspects. Be this as it may, the spirit of man is, undoubtedly, his highest nature. *Spirit* is placed by the apostle Paul before *soul* and *body*. Thess. 5 : 23. It is the inward eye of man. "For what man knoweth the things of a man, save the spirit of man which is in him?" Mr. Campbell assigns to the spirit a pre-eminence over the soul and the body. The spirit is the responsible, and controlling agent—the seat of the understanding, memory, will and conscience. It does not act independently of the soul, nor of the body, while it is incarnate, but is appointed to govern them. If there is depravity in man, it is in his spirit. We are taught that bodiless spirits may be corrupt. We read of "seducing spirits," "a foul spirit," and "lying spirits." Satan is a depraved spirit. I can see no reason why embodied spirits may not be corrupt. The Bible informs us that there is a *filthiness of the spirit*, as well as of the flesh. 2 Cor. 7 : 1. Into some sins man is seduced by the solicitations of the flesh---the animal nature—but others have their origin in the spirit. Pride, ambition, envy, malice, and such things, are the filthiness of the spirit. Satan infuses his evil dispositions into the spirit of men. "Ye are of your father, the devil," said Jesus, to the wicked Jews, "and the lusts of your father ye will do." What I maintain is, that man's spirit—his highest nature—the indestructible inner man—is, at birth, and undoubtedly to the development of the "passions and appetites" depraved. By what authority, of revelation or of reason, Mr. C. maintains that the spirit is free from sin until it is perverted by the propensities of the soul, he has not informed us. He will, perhaps, do so in his expected volume. It may be well for him to consider the import of the Saviour's words, "*That which is born of the flesh is flesh.*" Is not the whole man body, soul and spirit, born of the flesh? and are not all involved in a common corruption and ruin?

I have not yet disposed of this matter—Mr. Campbell assumes a principle which, if carried to its legitimate result, is utterly subversive of the doctrine of infant depravity. "Where there is no light," he says, "no understanding, no intelligence, there can be no disposition at all, no moral feeling, no change of affections, no change of heart; consequently no infant moral or spiritual regeneration." Again, he writes, "We must see beauty before we can love it. We must see deformity before we can hate it. And, therefore, 'the love of holiness and the hatred of sin' are impossible to an infant." According to this theory, knowledge must precede all dispositions, good or bad, all moral bias, right or wrong. "In religion, as in every thing else, intellect pioneers the way, while the affections and the heart follow." These statements are incompatible with the doctrine of inherent corruption. What is depravity but an evil disposition or tendency of the heart? Some moral quality of the inner man—of the soul and spirit—which inclines it to do evil? In the infant the moral quality, or disposition, is latent, undeveloped, but real and innate, depending not on knowledge, education, or circumstances. Just as certainly as the young mind is developed, it will, impelled by this evil disposition, hate holiness and love sin. We find in the history of the primeval father of mankind the illustration and proof of this position. God created man in his own image, and that image consisted in "righteousness and true holiness." Or, as Mr. Campbell expresses it, "Man, then, in his natural state, was not merely an animal, but an intellectual, moral, pure, and holy being."—Christian System, p. 26. If man was created *holy*, then it follows that knowledge is not indispensable to the existence of holiness. Adam was holy in the very moment of his creation. His moral constitution was sound. His dispositions were all turned in the right direction. When light dawned on his mind, he rejoiced in truth, loved what was lovely, chose what was good, and did what was right. It is true, that the conscious, joyous exercise of the affections was consequent on the acquisition of knowledge ; but it was the readiness, or tendency of the affections to flow in the right direction that constituted his holiness. Now, it is the opposite disposition—the readiness of the affections to pursue the wrong direction—that constitutes depravity ; and this disposition, dormant in infants, is certain, if their faculties are unfolded, to be aroused into active exercise. Now, I readily grant that by Mr. Campbell's theory, he fairly precludes the necessity, and, indeed, the possibility of "infant moral or spiritual regeneration ;" but in evading this necessity, he aims a serious blow at the foundation of Christianity. This reasoning when fairly carried out, runs thus—Where there is no knowledge, there is no disposition, or moral character—where there is no disposition, there is no depravity—where there is no depravity, there is no need of spiritual regeneration—and, what is equally clear, no need of an atonement. Infants have no knowledge, consequently no disposition—no depravity—no need of regeneration—or of an atonement. Where then, so far as infants are concerned, is the necessity of Christianity ? I know Mr. Campbell will repudiate these consequences, but they are bound to his principles by hooks of steel.

It is now time that we should examine more closely Mr. Campbell's theory of infant salvation—

a theory that seems to have been adopted, from no reverence for the teaching of revelation, but merely to evade the necessity of admitting the regeneration of dying infants.

Having shown, as he supposes, that the *soul*, which is "intimately connected with the blood," is primarily the seat of depravity, and that the *Spirit*, "a purely intellectual principle," is free from sin, until the "corrupting and debasing propensities and affections" of the soul are developed, which development cannot occur in infancy—he thus unfolds his scheme of infant salvation. "We have reason to repudiate the notion of the abstract, undefinable, metaphysical regeneration, of an infant as essential to its salvation. *It only needs a physical regeneration;* a destruction of that body in which those seeds of passion and sinful appetites are so thickly sown.—The adult saint needs it as much as the infant." "Infants then need that same kind of regeneration that Paul, and Peter, and James, and John, and all saints need—the entire destruction of this body of sin and death." What Mr. Campbell means by "physical regeneration"—a phrase which I am surprised to see used by one whose avowed mission is the restoration of a pure speech—he explains in the following language.—"The infant that falls asleep in its mother's bosom, and after a few short days breathes out its spirit gently there, needs no more change to fit it for Abraham's bosom than that which the Spirit of God will effect in the resurrection of the dead, or in the transformation of the living saints at the time of His coming"—Christ's coming, I suppose he means, though the "Spirit of God" is the grammatical antecedent of the pronoun.

For this scheme of infant salvation, the reader hardly needs to be informed, Mr. Campbell is indebted solely to human invention. It is as much a work of imagination as any tale of fiction. From the Scriptures it receives no support, either direct or inferential. It has no basis in sound philosophy. The doctrine that man is at birth depraved in his spiritual nature, and that he needs a spiritual renovation, is the dictate of philosophy as well as of revelation. Mr. Campbell does, indeed, furnish a comparison, but a most unfortunate one, in support of his scheme. "Infants need the same kind of regeneration that Paul, and Peter, and James, and John, &c., need." The Scriptures teach that the saints at death, freed from bodily appetites and passions, will enter into Paradise. For them "to be absent from the body (is) to be present with the Lord." There is, however, an essential and most important difference between dying saints and dying infants. The saints have in them a principle of life—of spiritual, divine, eternal life. "Whosoever," says Jesus, "drinketh of the water that I shall give him shall never thirst; but the water that I shall give him shall be in him a well of water springing up into everlasting life." When the saints die they find, in heaven, society, occupation, and enjoyments for which they have been fitted by regeneration, and a course of moral discipline.—Freed from the encumbrance of their bodies, and the temptations arising from their connexion with them, their spiritual life is fully developed and matured. But what agreement is there between the condition of dying, regenerated men, and dying, unregenerated infants. Surely, the dying infant needs a regeneration different from that of the dying saint—not merely of physical, or bodily, but a moral, or spiritual regeneration. The infant has, as Mr. Campbell teaches, in one place, a *sinful* nature, and it cannot, without a moral renovation, be otherwise than corrupt, either before or after death.

To one of two conclusions, Mr. Campbell is, by his theory, fairly driven.

First—Infants are not sinful, in their higher, immortal nature, previous to the development of the corrupt propensities of their inferior, mortal nature; and consequently, they need, in the evangelical sense, no salvation. This conclusion is irresistible. Where there is no sin, there can be salvation. Christ came to save sinners, and only sinners. If infants are not sinners, they may, indeed, be, as Mr. Campbell calls it, physically regenerated, but they cannot be saved by the blood of Christ.

Secondly—If sinful infants are, in any case, fitted for heaven by physical regeneration, sinful adults may be prepared for it by the same process. If the resurrection of the dead can cure the spiritual maladies of an infant, why may not the spiritual maladies of an adult be cured by the same process? If this reasoning is false, Mr. Campbell cannot object to it. I will refresh his memory by recalling his own method of reasoning. "*Whatever is essential to regeneration in any case, is essential in all cases.* * * * If it be a new heart given, a new life communicated, it is accomplished in all cases, as generation is, by the same agency and instrumentality." Now, according to the theory under discussion, sinful infants, dying in infancy, are fitted for "Abraham's bosom," by a *physical regeneration;* and as whatever is necessary to produce this fitness, in any case, is necessary in every case; it follows, with logical certainty, that all who are fitted for "Abraham's bosom," are fitted for it, as dying infants are, by a *physical regeneration.* Mr. Campbell is welcome to either horn of the dilemma. Take which he may, he will find himself involved in serious difficulties; from which, however, he is well fitted to extricate himself.

THE IDENTITY OF BAPTISM, REGENERATION AND CONVERSION.

In his various works, Mr. Campbell has earnestly, and unequivocally insisted that, in Scriptural use, the above words have precisely the same import. In Campbellism Examined, pp. 191–216, I endeavored, after acquitting him of the charge of holding, in its popular sense, the doctrine of baptismal regeneration, to prove "that neither the term *regeneration*, nor *conversion*, nor *any equivalent term*, nor the *Greek* words which they properly represent, nor any of their *cognates*, are ever used in the Scriptures to denote baptism."---p. 199. I have the most unwavering conviction that this position was sustained by incontrovertible arguments. On this point, at least, I did sincerely hope that Mr. Campbell would confess his error, and return to the Scriptural use of terms; but I was disappointed. Having taken his position, he is exceedingly reluctant to abandon it. Well, what has he done? He has not so much as made an attempt to answer the arguments by which I sustained my position, and showed that his use of these terms is incorrect. Let us hear what he says. "We will proceed to notice his (Mr. Jeter's) declarations on Christian Baptism. We say his *declarations*, for on this subject he has not adduced the Christian doctrine"—certainly, not the doctrine of the *Christian System*—"but his own conceptions of it, and speculations upon it.

Prior to any analysis of his dogmata, we must claim the right to complain of his garbled quotations, from 'Christianity Restored,' and his calling my quotations 'unintelligible jargon.' That is, to be sure, quite complimentary to me, and quite as much so to the diction of the Holy Spirit, whose language we have employed."—*Mill. Har.*, p. 438.

There are three counts in this indictment—

First—That I made "garbled quotations from Christianity Restored." Mr. Campbell furnishes an extract of two pages from that work as "an exposition alike of his (my) taste, and of his (my) understanding." He might with equal propriety have printed a dozen pages for the purpose. Let the intelligent reader compare the quotations in my book, p. 203, with the context given in the review, and satisfy himself of the correctness of my "taste," and the soundness of my "understanding," in making my selections. I ask nothing more. Will Mr. Campbell pretend that the passages as in my book do not bear precisely the same meaning which they bear in his? Having disposed of the charge of garbling in another place, I will not dwell on it here.

Secondly—That I called Mr. Campbell's language "*unintelligble jargon.*" To this count I must plead *Guilty*. I ought, perhaps, in view of his age, learning and reputation, to apologize for the use of such an epithet. But "great men are not always wise."

If the terms, however, are libelous, I may be permitted to plead their truthfulness in abatement of damages. Let us re-examine the passages pronounced to be "unintelligible jargon." "Persons are begotten by the Spirit of God, impregnated with the Word, and born of water." It is admitted that physiologically there is a distinction between *begotten* and *born;* but Mr. Campbell, and every tryo in Greek, know that these terms in the New Testament represent precisely the same word.—Whether believers are said to be "begotten of God," or "born of God," depends merely on the taste of the translators. Whosoever, in Scripture phraseology, is "begotten of God," is "born of God." When a person, according to Mr. Campbell's theory, is "begotten," or, which is precisely the same thing, *born* of God, he is next impregnated by the Word. Conformably to physiological laws the mother and not the fœtus is impregnated. But Mr. Campbell inverts the order of nature, and insists that "persons begotten of God (are) impregnated by the Word;" and they are begotten, and become pregnant, before they are "born of water." "Now, as soon as, and not before," he affirms, "a disciple, who has been begotten," that is, *born* of God, "is born of water"—immersed—"he is born of God, or of the Spirit." Who has ever noted a greater confusion of metaphors, or a greater obscurity of conception. If this is not jargon, I have misconceived the meaning of the term, and how the extended context, quoted by Mr. Campbell, mends the matter, I do not perceive. I am constrained to admit that it is to me "yet *unintelligible jargon.*"---p. 438.

Thirdly--That I was quite complimentary, in an ironical sense, "to the diction of the Holy Spirit." To this count I plead, *Not guilty*. For the "diction of the Holy Spirit," I would cherish the most profound reverence. If Mr. Campbell will only point to the chapter and verse in which the language is recorded, I will promptly retract all that I have written on the subject. It is bad for him to use unintelligible language himself, but to make the Holy Spirit responsible for it is far worse.

Mr. Campbell having made a quotation "from the Book of Common prayer of the Church of England, showing," as he conceived, "unequivocally that the learned Doctors of that church used the words *regeneration* and *baptism* as synonymous," adds—"This 'unintelligible jargon' belongs to the Church of England, the Protestant Episcopal Church of the United States, and to the Presbyterian formulas, confessions of faith, and catechisms." The extract from the Book of Common Prayer, seems to me to teach the doctrine of baptismal regeneration--of a spiritual renovation through the influence of baptism—which I understand Mr. Campbell to repudiate; but, certainly, not the identity of baptism and regeneration, much less that a disciple who *is* begotten, or born of God, *is not* born of God, until he is baptized; and if it is taught in any "formulas, confessions of faith, or catechisms of the Presbyterian," or any other church, orthodox, or hetorodox, Latin, Greek, or Protestant, I have not seen it.

"These extracts," says Mr. Campbell, referring to the quotations by which I showed that he taught the identity of baptism, regeneration, and conversion, "are true and faithful; and in their contextual import I do not, I would not, change one word. And yet they are made to do me the greatest injustice—just as much as if, while maintaining that the Scriptures teach that 'a man is justified by faith,' some envious, querulous, discontent, to say nothing of his pride of opinion, or vanity of mind, should quote, 'was not Abraham our father justified by works'"!! Yes, the Father of all believers *was justified by works!!* James 11 : 3. Again: Paul says, '*the doers of the law* shall be justified. Rom. 11 : 3. Again: Paul says, 'Being now justified by his blood, we shall be saved.' Rom. 7 : 9. Once more, we are said to be '*justified freely* by his grace.' Tit. 3 : 7. What can we think—what could we think of the man that would quote any of these passages as conflicting with justification by faith? And need we add, what can we think, or what need we say, of Mr. Jeter and his New York encomiasts?"—p. 455.

The above is a favorite line of defence with Mr. Campbell—he frequently resorts to it. It amounts to this—In the Scriptures, and in my writings, there are seeming contradictions, but they may all be reconciled. It is conceded that the Scriptures, written by different penmen, at different times, under different circumstances, and for different purposes, contain some statements which are apparently inconsistent, but which are easily harmonized by sound principles of interpretation. They have been satisfactorily reconciled by the labors of the learned. But it does not follow that because the contradictions of the Scriptures are seeming, those of Mr. Campbell are not real. For my own part, I have far greater confidence in the intelligence, discrimination and stability of the inspired writers than I have in those of the Bethany reviewer. Besides, the cases are not parallel. The different statements of the apostles concerning justification are apparently, but not really contradictory—they have been reconciled--butthe contradictions in Mr. Campbell's books are real, not imaginary—in no contextual light, and by no just laws of interpretation, can human ingenuity harmonize them, either with themselves, or the teaching of Revelation. Had Paul, in the same epistle, affirmed, in one place, that we *are* justified by faith, and, in another place, that we are *not* justified by faith---a supposition wholly incompatible with his plenary inspiration---the contradiction would have been of the kind with which Mr. Campbell's writings abound. Take a proof of this remark from the review under consideration. He writes, p. 185, "Regeneration is found but twice in the whole Bible---Old Testament and New. Once it indicates the resurrection epoch, or the announcement of the reign of Christ, and once Christian baptism." Reader, mark this—"*Regeneration indicates* once *Christian baptism.*" He refers to Titus 3 : 5. Now turn over to p. 308, and read —"Baptism is once called in the epistles, not *regeneration*, but 'the *washing* of the new birth,' or of regeneration. It was not by Paul presented as the new birth, but only the washing of those already born by the Spirit." "*Regeneration indicates Christian baptism*," says Mr. Campbell : "*baptism is not regeneration*," says Mr. Campbell. I may, surely, be excused from any farther examination of this subject.

PROGRESSIVE SANCTIFICATION.

"I am really sorry," says Mr. Campbell, "to have to expose a second radical error in his (Mr. Jeter's) second proof, more serious, though less palpable, than the first. His words are : 'My second proof is derived from the *nature of sanctification*. It is progressive holiness. * * * Elder Jeter needs to pray save me from my friends ! ! Sanctification, progressive holiness ! ! ! Why, my dear doctor, did you not consult your Greek Concordance! We have the word *sanctification* but *five* times in the New Testament, and the word holiness also but *five* times, and one and the same word, *hagiasmos*, represents them both. * * * No *state* in the universe---paternal, maternal, filial, conjugal, political, ecclesiastic---changes. They terminate. A child of one day and of one hundred years, are equally children. *There is no progression in relations.* * * * Sanctification is, therefore, no more than justification, a work of progression. Whenever a believer is baptized, he is—sanctified."

The intelligent reader, by turning back to pp. 260, 261, will find that the above extract is almost a verbatim repetition of the note recorded there. It would seem from this repetition of his remarks and the batallions of exclamatory notes with which they are escorted, that Mr. Campbell deems them exceedingly important. Well, I acknowledge myself indebted to him for the information that the Greek word *hagiasmos* is rendered sometimes *holiness*, and sometimes *sanctification*. Overlooking this obvious truth, I adopted a slightly inaccurate definition of the term *sanctification*. I stated that sanctification is progressive holiness. It is, indeed, progressive, and is, of course, progressive holiness, but the last word is redundant. It is sufficient to say that *sanctification is progressive.* So much in deference to the criticism of the reviewer. Now, let us examine his theology. He teaches that sanctification denotes a *state*, by which he means a *relation*. "*There is no progression in relations*." I may not clearly understand what he means by state or relation; but it is, I think, clear that *hagiasmos*, and its cognates, have reference, not to any legal state or relation, but to moral qualities. The word signifies "separated, consecrated." The believer is separated, consecrated to God. This consecration involves moral purity. The Saviour says, "Blessed are the pure in heart, for they shall see God;" and Paul does but repeat this truth when he writes, "Follow holiness—without which no man shall see the Lord." Consecration to God may be partial or entire—and, consequently, may progress from one measure to another. This has certainly been the prevailing, almost universal, doctrine of theologians. But, says the reviewer, "*Sanctification is, no more than justification, a work of progression*." It always affords me sincere pleasure to be able to adduce in support of my teaching the authority of some renowned Biblicist, whose name will secure for him an influence to which I can lay no claim. That pleasure I now enjoy. I quote the words of Mr. Alexander Campbell, the Bethany Reformer, in opposition to the position of the reviewer. "Sanctification in one point of view, is unquestionably a progressive work. To sanctify is to set apart; this may be done in a moment, and so far as *state* or *relation* is concerned, it is as instantaneous as baptism. But there is the formation of a holy *character* as well as a holy *state*. The formation of such a character is the work of means ; Holy Father," said Jesus, " sanctify them, (my disciples,) through the truth ; thy word is truth." Of the *sanctification of state*, I know nothing, and believe nothing. It was of that sanctification which consists in moral purity—the proper ordering of the affections and conduct towards God—the only sanctification, so far as I can perceive, revealed in the Bible—that I affirmed progression ; and on this point Mr. Campbell fully concurs with me. This being established, my argument in the premises remains, intact. See Camp. Examined, p. 171.

MISCELLANIES.

It would be easy to pass over all the Nos. of the review, and point out mistakes, and sophistries, which abound on almost every page, but the labor would be bootless. I will, however, notice very briefly a few more of them.

A false quotation.—Mr. Campbell maintained that the church of Christ, described Eph. 4 : 6, is a body—not a mass, but an organized, beautiful and visible body—that he has but one body—and that this body is not the Romish, Episcopalian, Presbyterian, Methodist, or Baptist body—but, he would have us to infer that it is the body embracing the "ancient Gospel," or the "Disciples." In the examination of this high claim, I inquired, "If the party adopting the peculiar views of Mr. C., is really the body of Christ, where was his body before the light shone from Bethany?"---Camp. Ex. p. 41. The question was important and respectful. Believing, as I did, that the body of Christ is spiritual and invisible, I was under no necessity of attempting the solution of the question. But Mr. Campbell maintaining that the body is organized and visible, was under pressing obligation to show that Christ, the Head, was not without a body, foı centuries before the "light shone from Bethany." In the absence of information on this point, the intelligent reader would be apt to conclude that the Reformer had misconceived the meaning of the text in the epistle to the Ephesians. *Where was Christ's body before the light shone from Bethany?* That was the question, and no man could answer it better than he from whom that light emanated. Let us read his reply.---p. 72.

"There is another argument against our position, and with the notice of it we shall conclude our present article in review of 'Campbellism Examined,' by Elder Jeter. 'Where was Christianity before the light shone from Bethany?'" These questions are, by means, identical; but Mr. Campbell, quoting, I presume, from memory, unintentionally substituted "Christianity," which could always be found in the Scriptures, for the "body of Christ," which, according to his definition of it, could be found nowhere. But let us hear his reply to this isolated and perverted question, which he terms my "grand argument" against his position. Here it follows—"It is only necessary to put a 'fool's cap' on any head, however wise, to create a fool's grin. So Mr. Jeter might ask a question about the man in the moon, which no astronomer, star-gazer, or moon-gazer, could at all answer to Mr. Jeter's satisfaction. But what of that? If, as Solomon has said, 'that which is wanting cannot be numbered,' where good sense, or genius, or even common sense is wanting, there is no one can give it or create it. There are not a few things in science, in learning, and in religion, which Mr. Jeter will not understand until he get another head or heart." I acknowledge myself fairly confounded, but not convinced. "I will lay mine hand upon my mouth. Once have I spoken; but I will not answer: yea, twice; but I will proceed no further."

A slight mistake.—Mr. Campbell says, p. 372, "Being refused line for line in the Religious Herald, we tender to Elder Jeremiah B. Jeter page for page with us in the Harbinger, with this motto, 'He that doeth truth comes to the light, that his deeds may be made manifest that they are wrought in God.'" The truth is that the Editor of the Religious Herald expressed a willingness that the controversy should be published in his paper, and that fact had been printed in the preceding No. of the Harbinger, p. 339 ; but having chosen my method of bringing my views of Mr. Campbell's system before the public, I did not deem it expedient to change it, for his convenience.

An insinuation.—Speaking of my book, the reviewer says, " It is, indeed, mechanically viewed, a merchantable duodecimo of 369 leaded pica pages ; the whole of which we could, in quite a legible type, print in two numbers of the Harbinger. But it was made to sell for one dollar ; and being endorsed by anti-revisionist Baptists, will have quite a broad circulation. But this, by the way, only proves that there is, even yet, some policy in ecclesiastic war." —p. 549. The insinuation seems to be that the book was published from a mercenary motive. It comes, however, with ill grace from one who has spent his life in writing books, and publishing them under the protection of copy-rights. It is a pity that Mr. C. should have resorted to such an insinuation for the support of his cause ; but necessity has no law, and taste cannot be opposed by argument.

My reformation ---We read on page 144 of the review, as follows—" But has not Mr. Jeter himself become a reformer, in the fair import of the term ?" It is a great reproach to me, if I have made no progress in knowledge and piety, within the last thirty years ; but I certainly have not become a reformer in the Bethany sense of the term,

—" Does he now baptize *upon* or *into* an experience ?"—I have already confessed my ignorance of what Mr. Campbell means by *baptizing into an experience.*—" Does he require every candidate to relate his Christian experience before he will dispense to him the ordinance ?"—Certainly—I either require a connected relation of the Christian experience of the applicant, or propound to him such questions as will elicit the best evidence the case will admit of, that he is acquainted with the fundamental principles of the Gospel, and is a true penitent.—"Does he bring him before the Church, and take a vote upon his experience before he baptizes him ?"—By all means--"Does he immerse him into a faith, or into an experience ?"---Mr. Campbell must explain his terminology before I can answer.---I fear by this time, he will be ready to conclude that I am not quite so much reformed as he had hoped I was, and to repeat the inquiry, printed p. 550, "Is Dr. Jeter yet standing where I first saw him, at the Dover Association, in 1825, gazing at some spasmodic negroes, displaying experimental religion by muscular twitches and embraces ! Is he *yet* an advocate for such fearful delusions !" I proceed with the first extract---" Does he immerse *into the name*, or '*in the name* of the Father ?' &c."---This is an important point, in speculation, with Mr. C. He dwells on it frequently, learnedly, and earnestly. In the use of the formula in baptism, I am not reformed. His criticism on this subject is probably correct. I am unwilling, however, to change my practice on my own imperfect knowledge of the Greek ; and the learned have not yet spoken on this point with such distinctness and harmony as to dissipate all my doubts. And I have no respect for the authority of a critic who asserts, as Mr. Campbell does, that regeneration, conversion and baptism, all mean, in Scripture usage, the same act---that active participles, in Greek, when united with a command, *invariably* express the *meaning* of the command, or the *manner* of obeying it ; and who supports the criticism by a long string of English sentences, coined by himself in harmony with the rule---and who bases an important doctrine on the distinction between "begotten of God," and "born of God," though both phrases represent the same terms of the original ; and persists in sending forth these stereotyped criticisms, without correction or retraction, in spite of unanswered and unanswerable refutations of them spread before his own eyes, and the eyes of the world. And especially does all the learned ado about substituting "*into* the name," for, "*in* the name," in the formula of Christian baptism, seem unimportant, when the critic himself, baptized, as I doubt not he was, "*in* the name," &c. does not repeat the ordinance. He must, following the example of his quondam co-adjutor, Dr. Thomas, be re-immersed, before I can be convinced that even he attaches any serious importance to his labored criticisms on this point.

THE ANNOTATED PARAGRAPH BIBLE

According to the authorized Versions, arranged in Paragraphs and Parallelisms, with Explanatory Notes, Prefaces to the several Books, and an entirely new selection of References to parallel and illustrative passages: an issue of the London Religious Tract Society, republished.

THE OLD TESTAMENT

is now ready in one large octavo volume of 1050 pages. Price, in Muslin, $3. Library sheep, $3 50. Morocco, full gilt, $5.

BLIND BARTIMEUS;

Or, The Story of a Sightless Sinner and his Great Physician.

By Rev. WILLIAM J. HOGE, Professor in the Union Theological Seminary, Prince Edwards, Virginia.

1 vol. large 18mo. 257 pages. 75 cents.

"A most excellent book, full of sound instruction and the very spirit of the Gospel."—*Boston Recorder.*

"We wish it could be placed, this winter, in the hands of thousands of sightless sinners."—*Cincinnati Christian Herald.*

DAILY THOUGHTS FOR A CHILD.

By Mrs. THOMAS GELDART, author of "Truth is Every Thing," "Emilie the Peacemaker," etc., etc.

1 vol. 18mo. Price 50 cents.

"In exquisite simplicity of style, beauty of illustration and religious power, this book has few superiors in juvenile literature."—*Era, Boston.*

TRUTH IS EVERY THING.

By Mrs. THOMAS GELDART.

1 vol. 18mo. Price 50 cents.

THE BAPTIST CHURCH DIRECTORY:

A Guide to the Doctrines, Discipline, Officers, Ordinances, and Customs of Baptist Churches, embracing the questions of Baptism and Communion.

By EDWARD T. HISCOX, D.D.

1 vol. 18mo. Red edges. 60 cents, plain 50 cents.

SERMONS TO THE CHURCHES.

By FRANCIS WAYLAND, D. D. 1 vol. 12mo. Price 85 cents.

CONTENTS.

From the Christian Intelligencer.

"Dr. Wayland is a clear thinker, and a strong and elegant writer. His Sermons are models worthy of study."

MEMOIR OF DAVID TAPPAN STODDARD,

Missionary to the Nestorians.

BY JOSEPH P. THOMPSON, D.D.,

Pastor of the Broadway Tabernacle Church, New York.

Illustrated with a beautiful Steel Portrait of Mr. Stoddard, a View of his Birthplace, and several Scenes in and around Oroomiah.

1 vol. 12mo. Price $1.

Dr. Thompson was a classmate and intimate friend of Mr. Stoddard. The Memoir is framed almost entirely from material furnished by Mr. Stoddard's correspondence, in which his rare excellence as a Christian was always conspicuous.

THE "PRECIOUS STONES OF THE HEAVENLY FOUNDATIONS."

By AUGUSTA BROWN GARRETT, author of "Hamilton, the Young Artist," etc., etc. 1 vol. 12mo. Price $1.

This volume is entirely novel, both in conception and execution. It treats of the beatitudes, the glories and the beauties of the Heavenly Home, as figured forth in the Inspired Volume. The Gems are classed under separate heads, beginning with the Great Corner Stone. Each head embraces—the most characteristic phrase recorded of the Apostle to whom the Gem appertains, taken as a motto—some account of the Gem itself; occasional allusion to the tribe which was represented by the corresponding stone on Aaron's Priestly Breastplate, and an application of the subject.

THE LOSING AND TAKING OF MANSOUL;

Or, Lectures on the Holy War.

By Rev. A. S. PATTON, A.M.

1 vol. 12mo. Illustrated with eight spirited engravings. Price $1.

"Bold, striking, and original in its handling of the subject, it is a book that can not fail to arrest the attention and make a deep impression on the reader. It brings out the great work of salvation by the various steps of trial, suffering and joy, so that a whole body of practical theology is here discussed, and important truth presented, so as to instruct while it deeply interests the religious mind. It is a book for saint and sinner—for all who have souls to be lost or saved."—*New York Observer*

THE NEW YORK PULPIT,

IN THE REVIVAL OF 1858,

SERMONS PREACHED IN NEW YORK AND BROOKLYN,

By the following Clergymen:

Rev. Dr. ALEXANDER.	Rev. Dr. HAGUE.	Rev. Dr. PARKER
" ADAMS.	" HATFIELD.	" PECK.
" BETHUNE.	" HISCOX.	" POTTS.
" BUDINGTON.	" HITCHCOCK.	" SMITH.
" BURCHARD.	" HUTTON.	" STORRS.
" CLARK.	" KENNADY.	" THOMPSON.
" CUTLER.	" KREBS.	" VERMILYE.
" CUYLER.	" LATHROP.	" WILLIAMS.
	" M'CLINTOCK.	

1 vol., 12mo. Price $1.

The publishers believe this volume will have an immediate and permanent interest and a large sale throughout the land.

SELECT DISCOURSES.

Translated from the French and German.

Embracing some Twenty-five of the choicest Discourses of Adolphe Monod, Krummacher, Tholuck, and Julius Müller.

With Dr. Monod's celebrated Lecture on the Delivery of Sermons, and a fine Steel Portrait of the Author.

By Rev. H. C. FISH, and D. W. POOR, D. D.

1 vol., 12mo, about 400 pages. Price $1.

THE LIFE AND MISSION OF WOMEN.

By ADOLPHE MONOD, D.D.

Translated from the French. In one handsome volume, 12mo, 82 pages. With a Portrait from Steel. Price 50 cents.

We are here presented with the ablest and most practical discussion of this great subject which it has ever received. It is a book for the times, and should be in the hands of every mother and daughter.

GLIMPSES OF JESUS, EXALTED IN THE AFFECTIONS OF HIS PEOPLE.

By Rev. W. P. BALFERN, of England.

18mo. 267 pages. Price 60 cents.

This will be an excellent book for young converts and inquiring minds.

THE LIVING EPISTLE;

Or, The Moral Power of a Religious Life.

By Rev. CORNELIUS TYREE, of Powhatan, N. C. With an Introduction, by Rev. Dr. FULLER, of Baltimore.

1 vol. 18mo. 185 pages, 60 cents.

THE PASTOR'S HANDBOOK.

Comprising Selections of Scripture, arranged for various occasions of Official Duty; Select Formulas for the Marriage Ceremony, etc.; Rules of Order for Churches, Ecclesiastical and other Deliberate Assemblies, and Tables for Statistical Record.

By W. W. EVARTS, D. D.

Price 50 cents.

THE BIBLE MANUAL.

Comprising Selections of Scriptures, arranged for various occasions of Private and Public Worship, both Special and Ordinary, together with Scripture Expressions of Prayer, from MATTHEW HENRY.

With an Appendix, consisting of a copious Classification of Scripture Texts, presenting a Systematic View of the Doctrines and Duties of Revelation.

By W. W. EVARTS, D. D.

12mo. Price $1 50.

"It is hardly possible to conceive of an arrangement under which can be shown the teachings of Scripture on a greater number of subjects."—*New England Puritan.*

THE SCRIPTURE TEXT-BOOK AND TREASURY.

Forming a complete Index to the Doctrines, Duties, and Instructions of the Sacred Volume.

By W. W. EVARTS, D.D.

12mo. Price 75 cents.

MANHOOD:

Its Duties and Responsibilities. By Rev. W. W. EVERTS, D.D.

1 vol. 12mo., with Steel Portrait of Author.

Price $1.

"He wields a graceful pen, and throws about his allegorical style so much real truth as to carry conviction to the minds of his readers."—*Milwaukie Paper.*

DOMESTIC SLAVERY CONSIDERED AS A SCRIPTURAL INSTITUTION.

In a Correspondence between the Rev. RICHARD FULLER, D. D., of Beaufort, S. C., and the Rev. FRANCIS WAYLAND, D. D., of Providence, R. I.

18mo. 40 cents.

"In this book meet two great minds, each tried long, known well, clear, calm, and strong. It cheers the heart, when there is so much strife, and so free a use of harsh words, to see men like those whose names are at the head of this piece, write in a tone so kind, and so apt to turn the edge of strife. But, though its tone be kind and calm, its style is not the less strong. Each brings to bear all that a clear head and a sound mind can call forth. When two so strong minds meet, there is no room for weak words. Each word tells—each line bears with weight on the main point—each small page has in it more of thought than weak men crowd into a large book."—*Correspondent of National Intelligencer.*

THE LIFE AND TIMES OF CAREY, MARSHMAN AND WARD.

Including the History of the Serampore Mission.

By JOHN CLARK MARSHMAN. 2 vols. 8vo. Price $5.

HOME LIFE.

Twelve brilliant Lectures on the Duties and Relations of the Family Circle.

By Rev. WM. HAGUE, D. D. 1 vol., 12mo. $1; Gilt, $1 25.

THE LIFE OF THOMAS COLE, N.A.

With Selections from his Letters and Miscellaneous Writings

By Rev. LOUIS L. NOBLE.

415 pages. 12mo. Price $1 00.

MEMOIR OF THE REV. THOMAS SPENCER.

By THOS. RAFFLES, D. D., LL. D., his Successor in the Pastoral Office.

With an Introduction and a Steel Portrait.

1 vol., 12mo. Cloth, 63 cents.

THE MEMOIR OF MRS. HELEN M. MASON,

Seventeen Years a Missionary in Burmah.

By her Husband, Rev. FRANCIS MASON.

16mo. With a Portrait and several beautiful Engravings. Price 60 cents.

MEMOIR OF SARAH B. JUDSON.

By Mrs. E. C. JUDSON.

Forty Thousand sold. 1 vol., 18mo. 300 pages. Cloth, 60 cents; Cloth, gilt edge, $1 00.

"Rarely have we read a more beautiful sketch of female loveliness, devoted piety, missionary zeal, fortitude, sacrifice, and success, than is here drawn by a pen that is well known to the reading world. We trust its wide perusal will awaken the mission spirit in the hearts of thousands."—*New York Observer.*

THE JUDSON OFFERING.

Intended as a Token of Christian Sympathy with the Living, and a Memento of Christian Affection for the Dead.

By Rev. JOHN DOWLING, D. D., Author of "History of Romanism," etc.

Twentieth edition. 18mo. 60 cents.

LIFE OF SPENCER H. CONE, D.D.

With a fine Steel Plate Portrait.

1 vol., 12mo. Price $1 25.

"America has produced but few so popular preachers; his personal interest was unbounded; he was indeed a man of talent, of large attainment in the school of Christ, a brilliant preacher, a noble-hearted, zealous Christian philanthropist."—*Christian Chronicle Philadelphia.*

www.ingramcontent.com/pod-product-compliance
Lightning Source LLC
LaVergne TN
LVHW020936110826
845150LV00004B/877

* 9 7 8 1 4 2 5 5 5 2 5 3 4 *